CW01084037

David Henry Sterry, best-selling author of *Master of Ceremonies: a True Story of Sex, Drugs, Rollerblades, and Chipendales* and *Chicken: Self-portrait of a Young Man for Rent,* and who has been translated into ten languages, says...

"*The Devil in Miss Jones* was not only a revolutionary movie, it was a great movie. I do believe the reason it transcended into the Pantheon was the magic of Georgina Spelvin. Imagine my delight when I found her writing to be as deep, exciting, spellbinding, passionate, playful, and yes, I must say it, S*E*X*Y as her acting was."

Annie M. Sprinkle PhD: artist, sexologist, author, "Post-Porn-Modernist," noted Feminist, and pioneering film producer/director and performer was consulted and quoated by best-selling author Mary Roach in her latest book, *Bonk: The Curious Coupling of Science and Sex.* Annie said of Georgina's book...

"It's like *Siddhartha* meets *Boogie Nights* meets *A Chorus Line* meets *The Devil in Miss Jones.* This juicy memoir truly captures the spirit and creativity of the era."

Cap'n Pegleg Flix: video editor/graphic artist says...

"Hey, I'm no critic, just an old, busted up, retired motorcycle dude who happens to be a friend of Georgie's. I reckon she wants a few words from me about her book 'cause she knows I'm an honest man. I gotta tell ya, I was damned surprised what a great story this turned out to be."

The Devil Made Me Do It

By
Georgina Spelvin

Cover photo by A. Ginsberg, 1981

Published by
Little Red Hen Books
Los Angeles, California

ISBN 978-0-6151-9907-8
First Edition: April 2008

Acknowledgements:

Thank you...
Cindi Loftus, writer and publicist (cindisnakedtruth.com)
who made me do it.
David Henry Sterry, book doctor (davidhenrysterry.com)
who showed me how.
Wendy Cohen, editor and all-round-great-gal, (wendycohen.com)
who made me do it right.
Sandee Curry, copy editor, (www.tinkerbettie.com)
who made sure it was.
Wyatt Doyle, media maven and fellow author, (NewTexture.com)
who launched me into Cyberspace
at
GeorginasWorld.com

Dedicated to
my far better half, John,
who needs a new kitchen.

Caveat

In 1972, a sexually explicit film called *Deep Throat* erupted over the cinematic landscape sending shockwaves of horror and titillation down the fault lines of society. It redefined pornography. It also made a lot of money.

Once a Broadway gypsy, I'd grown up to be a respected producer of multi-media business meetings. But when the Flower Children marched by, their songs resonated in my ultra-liberal head and I fell into step beside them. The music was our Internet. It told us what was going down and when and where and what to wear: flowers in our hair.

Then things got really ugly. Bam! Bam! Bam! Two Kennedys and a King shot dead before our hopeful eyes. We were told to go kill people we didn't even know in some place we'd hardly heard of called Viet Nam, and we really, really didn't want to do that. So we marched and shouted and sang and got busted and generally made pains-in-the-ass of ourselves. One particular collection of anti-war filmmakers became my family.

The rent was due on our film commune, The Pickle Factory. About that same time the folks who brought you *Deep Throat* decided to make another pornographic film: *The Devil in Miss Jones*. I played the title role of Miss Jones and paid the rent.

I write here of real people doing surreal things in bizarre situations, but if you're looking for the ordeals of a victim, this ain't your book. And it most definitely is not a reference work. I've written what I can remember of these folks and events as they altered the course of my life. For facts, go to Google.

The pseudonym Georgina Spelvin (an obvious homage to the "Theatah," where George Spelvin is synonymous with John Doe) though not assumed until the release of *The Devil in Miss Jones*, is used throughout this narative for clarity. Most of the player's names herein are fictitious – for obvious reasons. Moreover, conversations are hardly exact. I mean, come on, it's been thirty years.

That said, welcome to my head.

Georgina Spelvin

New York City – 1972

You Want Me to What? 11

Marc "Mr. Ten-and-a-Half" Stevens 22

So You Wanna Be in Fuckfilms 31

Eyes Wide Open 38

Acid Bath 47

Into the Woods 52

Ready For My Closeup, Mr. D 61

Not Just Another Pretty Cock 70

Water Sports 79

Sartre and Sandwiches 83

Movie Magic 93

Bergman with Bugs 98

A Fruitful Venture 108

New York to California – 1974

Playing Dress Up 117

Porn Chic and Publicity 122

Out of the Pickle Factory and Into the Fire 128

Busted 136

The Journey of the Dorabelladonna 143

The Swallows 151

Atlantic City to Texas – 1976

The Intervention 161

Opening Night of a Closing Act 165

The Morning After 173

Stage Mothers 180

Nudity and The Latin Quarter 187

Wedding Bells 195

Binge 202

Ribs and Revelations 211

Cashiered 221

Time Out in Texas 228

Swan Song 233

California to Texas – 1983

Dancing Lessons From God 243

Higher Education 252

Hollywood – 1983

A Hollywood Ending 261

Hollywood – 2004

An Offer I Couldn't Refuse 271

Life in the Fast Lane 283

A Living Legend of Erotica 290

New York City – 1972

You Want Me to What?

IT'S A PENIS. OK? It's not the first time
you've seen one. You can do this. You've
done it before. OK. Maybe just four
times, but you survived, right?

Concentrate.

Looking past the trembling member I can see the A camera, and standing just behind it, the director Beau Buchanan. I can sense the B camera behind me, presumably focused tightly on the neatly circumcised organ I am to stick down my throat. The grips are still messing with the lights.

Yeah, the first time was pretty awful.
What was that guy's name? No matter. I
couldn't pronounce it anyway. I still can't
believe you fell for that "I have many
friends in high places" shit.

Was getting in a ballet company
important enough to let this guy lead
you down the proverbial garden path to
the dark deserted pool area and put his
dick in your mouth?

Well yes, it was. Besides, I was drunk.

Well, yes. You usually were at parties.
Cute, blaming the booze when you threw
up after the damn thing exploded in your
mouth.

"Mom…"

That's Beau, the director. He's talking to me. I'm playing The Mother. She's the High Priestess in this movie I'm in. It's called *High Priestess of Sexual Witchcraft*.

"…from here on you're on your own. Any dialog you want to use is fine. Just try not to drop out of character."

I'm insulted! Has he seen me drop out of
character yet? OK. It's only the second
day of the shoot, but I haven't muffed a
line and all the ad lib dialogue he's
needed has been delivered in character
thus far.

Like that last shot yesterday. I was dragging my crawling milquetoast of a hubby around on a leash, berating and demeaning him with every foul epithet ever devised. The three lines of dialogue in the script didn't go very far so I spouted a lot of words I didn't even know I knew. All the actor playing my husband had to do was to scream in agony while I thrashed his bare bony flanks with a cat-o-nine-tails. The prop department gave it to me. It was very soft. I thought the guy was one hell of an actor. Then I saw what the bare wood floor did to his knees.

"Remember. You're her son, for crisesakes," whispers the director intensely. "You don't really want to do this, but you can't help yourself."

"Mother," back to me, "you really have to force him to do this, you know?"

> I know. I know. What kind of idiot does he
> think I am? I read the script.

The writing was quite clear about how (if not why) the mother first punishes, then consoles, and finally sexually abuses her young adult son. Classic Et-a-puss stuff, thought I in reading it. This might be a no-budget Sombrero Productions film, but I was giving it my Uta-Hagen- drama-class best, by gosh. The only thing the script hadn't made clear was that the sex scenes would be explicit.

I was still adjusting to the situation.

"Hold his hands behind his hips and make him hold still while you blow him. OK? And be sure to leave enough air for the camera to see the strokes."

> Yeah, yeah. Where the hell is my key
> light? Got it. Remember. Don't tuck your
> chin. Oh god. He's bigger than I thought
> he'd be.

"OK. Let's roll," says the director.

"Speed," calls the sound man.

"Don't let her get you too near to the money shot, OK?" admonishes Beau. "Keep pulling away from her but really pull back if you feel like you're gonna shoot. OK? You have to control it."

The attractive young man vigorously nods his understanding.

"And… action!"

> Yawn. If you yawn you won't gag. It's not
> really THAT big. Concentrate. Remember
> the second time? The night you and CB
> slept in your old room at your parents'
> house? You didn't want to get pecker
> tracks on the sheets, so you took the
> initiative — and the cock of your adorable
> husband of eight days into your yap —
> much to his surprised delight. Think
> about how you relaxed and yawned.
> Remember that thrill of power? How it
> turned you on? Feeling like you were

> doing him instead of him doing you? Get
> that manic mamma in here now.

There it is: the click. The character, in this case the High Priestess, takes over. She grabs the firm, flexing butt of the kid before her and pulls him forcefully into her yawing gullet.

They shot the beginning of the scene earlier this morning. Rick Livermore, the actor playing my son, turned out to be a hunk and a damn fine actor. The scene was packed with emotional goodies: accusations, recriminations, plenty of juicy angst. We rehearsed while the crew was setting up. Beau got all of our dialog in two masters and several closeups. The script then simply said, "Mom seduces her son..." and here's what happened.

"OK, now Mom, hop up on the bed. We'll pick up where you stretch out beside him," says Beau.

"Bert," he continues, speaking to the cameraman hunkered on the floor, "stay close on his crotch while she's fondling him."

> FONDLING HIM? There was no fondling
> him in the script!

"You guys stay wide until he's up on his knees. OK?"

"Got it," answers the director of photography. He is manning the A camera on the side of the bed toward the door.

"Right," echoes Bert, the Assistant DP. He's seated on the floor on the other side of the action balancing a hand-held camera on his knees.

"Rick, soon as you're hard..."

> Hard? HARD? They expect him to
> actually get an actual erection?

"...get up on your knees and face camera A. Try to push her away."

"Mom." His eyes bore into mine. "Don't let him."

> Don't let him... Don't let...Ye freakin'
> gads. You idiot!
>
> You're in a.......FUCK FILM!

"When he gets up on his knees, cheat out a bit. Be careful not to block the camera's view of his business, you know?"

Yeah, I know… Business. How archaic.

Let me here state, I was not a total stranger to fuck film footage. I'd synched dailies of it at editing shops where I worked on occasion. I knew what was expected of me at this point. Could I have revealed my naiveté and split? Of course I could. But… Troupers don't walk off sets. And, yes, I still considered myself one of that sacred fraternity.

Good grief. It wasn't like I was a virgin or something. Hell, at thirty-six years of age I was twice divorced and now a free-wheeling free-loving hippy, for pitysake. My hymen hadn't been intact since I was fifteen anyway, if then. I was an adventurous child.

Did any possible ramifications cross my mind? Not for an instant. Films of this genre weren't seen by anyone I knew, and certainly not by anyone to whom I was related. Nor by anyone who might be related to anyone I'd ever been married to. I doubted they even knew such things existed. No one would ever know.

Besides, it was for the cause. What cause? Keeping the Pickle Factory afloat. How could we bring about world peace if we couldn't pay the rent?

And lastly, but certainly not leastly, Rick, my cinematic son, was, well, a lovely young man. Under other circumstances I would hardly have kicked him out of bed. Hell, I wasn't that much older than he was.

I just bet you know what happened next.

"Come to Mama," I croon as I spoon my nearly nude body around the cute bare butt beside me on the bed. I reach over him and gently place my hand around his penis.

"No, Momma, don't. Please don't," he pleads as he puffs up like a blowfish.

He's up, and up on his knees before you could say "eat my pussy" (the hip phrase amongst this crowd I had just come to know), and his stiff cock is now ready to try and reach my tonsils.

Guided more by the racy banter heard through the years from my many gay dancer buddies than by much actual experience, I give it my all.

I tease the hole with the tip of my tongue. I caress the head with my lips as it slides in and out of my mouth. I open my throat, as my many singing teachers through the years vainly admonished me to do, and plunge as far down upon the shaft as I can. I must be doing something right. The young man pulls away from me and pushes me down onto the mattress.

He takes control like one possessed, throwing me onto my stomach and forcefully lifting my buttocks into the air. With no teasing or preliminary moistening – amenities to which I am accustomed – he plows into my vagina like he's drilling for oil.

After the initial shock, I respond with enthusiasm – AND in character, thank you very much.

"Roll over on your back," our director, now crouched at the head of the bed whispers near my ear. The hand-held camera operator is by his side.

I flip over and pull the sweating actor down on top of me, wrapping my legs around him.

"No, no," hisses the director. "We can't see anything with you on top like that. Eat her out for a while."

Shit. I was just beginning to really get into it. Now I gotta lie back and let the kid take stage? Oh well. That's show biz.

The director orders up a sixty-nine. Yes, I know what he means. A flip and flop and we're in position. I take the now flaccid penis into my mouth again. The resting member soon snaps to attention.

"Reloading," whispers the A cameraman.

"Noted," says Beau. "Bert," turning to the B cameraman, "get in closer on the cock-sucking. You can relax for a minute."

He's speaking to my son, I assume. He can't mean me. I'm the one sucking the cock.

I try to think of what else I can do with this protein Popsicle. I run my tongue along the sides. I swirl it around the head like a Dairy Queen cone. I tickle the tip with my tongue. I try to suck the skin right off the damn thing. It quivers and shimmers in the lights. My mascara has made a clown face of my own. Now it starts to drip down and make a peculiar pattern on the slippery dome waving before my nose. It looks like a cantaloupe sno-cone with chocolate sauce dribbled over it.

My eyes were on fire from the mascara. But just as it's common for dancers to break a bone during a performance and not realize it until the dust settles, I didn't notice the pain until I heard "cut." That didn't happen until we missionaried for a while, did a bit more doggie, and then arranged ourselves so the money shot could land properly all over my face – a time-honored tradition of porn, it seems.

Beau seemed happy with the scene. Rick graciously suggested he and I get together without benefit of cameras some time. I took that as a compliment. The wardrobe lady collected the now sodden black negligee hanging limply from my shoulders and dropped it into a plastic laundry bag with the bed linens. The crew started setting up the next shot totally unaware that I was shaking like a leaf: my heart pounding like a jack-hammer. There was more adrenalin rushing through my body than it had experienced in years. I tingled all over. It felt good.

Later in the shower it hit me. What the hell was I going to tell my roomies at the Pickle Factory about my day at the office? One thing about our happy, hippy family: we shared everything. We could be totally honest with each other. No one ever judged anyone else. No wonder we got in so much trouble.

Claire, my sidekick-pal-lover, Corey, her former college chum and now another Pickle Factory resident, plus two more of the male auxiliary were lined up to participate in the big Sabbat Orgy scene scheduled to be shot the next day.

Granted, our bunch was all for freedom – especially the sexual kind that had recently blossomed from the tight little pod of the Fifties' code of conduct. Every possible coupling of our assembled ménage had been tried at one time or another, up to and including some rather bizarre group gropes. At one such, Corey, ever the wag, admonished me to stop seeing to it that everyone had someone or something to play with. He called me the Perle Mesta of the orgy set. (Well, someone had to empty the ashtrays.) These romps were always among friends, however. Participate in a porn film with a lot of strangers? I wasn't sure any of the bunch had ever even seen a porn film. I'd seen only one: a poorly hand-held testimonial to the oral skills of Candy Barr. (I do believe it was the film that landed her in Huntsville prison where she excelled in barrel races.) This had been shown on a sheet hung for the occasion on a wall of the scenic shop where I was working as an apprentice. This particular shop had built a spider web set for Miss Barr's strip act. The film was given in payment for that effort.

The current situation definitely needed to be clarified.

17

"Ahem, can I bother you for a minute?" I catch Beau on the fly.

"Sure. What's up?"

"The big orgy scene tomorrow... Are the extras supposed to – well – get it on for real?"

"If they feel like getting into it, we'll shoot it, but I just need lots of bodies squirming around, you know? Why? Is there a problem? Your pals know this is hard core, don't they?"

"I don't think it's been discussed," I equivocate.

"Will they back out? Because I gotta have bodies. I'll have to scrounge up some more if your guys don't show."

"No. No. I'm sure they'll be fine with it. With it being hard core, I mean. But I don't know if they'll want to – well – fully participate. Like I say, we haven't discussed it."

"Well, I would never have anyone do anything they didn't want to, you know that."

(I did.)

"Why don't you give me a call tonight after you talk to them? Then, if I need to find more actors, I'll call a few more of the regulars. Tell your guys they just have to get naked and look like they're having fun. Who knows, maybe they'll get into the spirit of the thing. Or not. It really doesn't matter."

"Thanks. I'll get back to you this evening."

"Hey, nice scene," he says as he turns back to his clipboard.

That's all I needed to hear. Pat me on the head and I'll follow you anywhere. Did he know the un-simulated sex was a surprise to me? He never mentioned it. I wonder if he knew all along that I wasn't completely hip to the program? No. I doubt a fuckfilm producer would risk hiring someone that stupid.

How in the world did I get into this situation?

Less than a year ago, I was working nine-to-five and living in all-but-marital bliss with Ian, the man for whom I'd left my second husband ten years before.

Ian (director/writer extraordinaire who would one day see his plays produced on Broadway) had two beautiful sons. They lived with their mom a few blocks from us, and referred to me (at my suggestion) as their wicked stepmother. Their mom and I referred to each other as wives-in-law. It was a model extended family in our brave new world.

Then I went to a peace march and gave a couple of waifs a lift back to the city. One of them was Claire: a Jane Fonda type in both looks and intensity who asked to be taken to the airline transportation depot. She had it in her twenty-two-year-old head that she was dropping out of college and flying to Alaska with about a hundred fifty dollars, a knapsack, and a heavy plaid flannel shirt. Granted, I had come to New York in 1954 with about two hundred dollars, a round-trip ticket and several pairs of toe shoes, but that had been a far gentler age.

I insisted she spend the night at our house and reassess her options in the cold light of day. Three weeks later I began searching for someplace, any place, to park her. The boys referred to her as "the couch lady."

A gorgeous long-haired well-muscled biker-type cameraman who shot some of the films I produced in my day job had a motorcycle repair shop in Greenwich Village. It was called Iron Co. He was called Iron Mike. Nearby were some industrial lofts. One on Little West 12th Street was for rent.

Mike and his brother, Charley, a master carpenter, helped us turn it into a studio. It solved the problem of where to house my waif. It also scratched my itchy dissatisfaction with my life in Korporate Amerika. I was tired of making commercials like "The Perils of Polly Ester" – a film extolling the virtues of the JC Penney line of polyester fabrics. I burned with the desire to make meaningful films. I was probably burning with a lot of other desires, too, but I was reluctant to acknowledge them at the time.

The front of the loft building opened onto the street. That area would house the editing room. Charley built a sleeping loft above it. The kitchen and bath went under another loft in the rear third of the space. Off-duty cops put in some top-of-the-line copper plumbing for us. Wiring was done by a local character named Chuck Dynamite. How did he come by his nickname? We didn't ask. Our lights, however, were the only ones functioning during a blackout that befell lower Manhattan a few months later. (This wasn't the BIG blackout of '65 – just a small local glitch.)

Until we could afford to buy the editing equipment we needed, we loaned out the front area to one of Mike's customers: a biker artist named Jimbo. He needed a space where he could spray-paint amazing images on hogs (large motorcycles). The same equipment was used to paint amazing images on the torsos of his and his customers' mammas in the course of the parties that materialized there on a fairly regular basis.

The forty-by-eighteen foot space with its twenty-foot high ceiling had once been a pickle factory. The name seemed to fit a rag-tag bunch of underground filmmakers who were prone to getting themselves into difficult situations. This was our plan. Piggy-backed on commercials and industrial films, we would make scathing indictments of the so-called police action in Viet Nam. Then we were gonna run Tricky Dick out of office, win a lot of awards, and end world hunger while we were at it.

One month when the rent was due, I picked up the showbiz trade papers looking for production work. There was nothing but ads for actresses willing to show their tits. I picked one at random and called.

"I'm probably not what you're looking for in an actress, but I can operate a Nagra (sound recorder), load magazines (film containers), handle a boom mike, run cable, scout locations, shop wardrobe, make coffee – need any help?"

They needed a boat in a marina. I knew someone who had one. They were looking for young studs to play sailors. Work for our biker buddies! They were also in the market for a mature actress to play a madam. Hello! I'm mature and the three major performers' unions (Equity, SAG, and AFTRA) list actress as my primary qualification for membership. We were in business.

The biker buddies were delighted to make some small change pushing around young naked women. The guy who owned the boat was delighted to collect a few bucks for its use – as long as he was allowed to watch the action and chat up the young naked women. I had a ball playing a cold-hearted boss of some white slave trafficking operation or whatever-the-hell it was. It was a nice day and evening on the water, even though the boat never left the marina, and it more than paid the rent.

When the final scene was in the can, Beau Buchanan, who had been setting lights all day, approached me and handed me a script. *High Priestess of Sexual Witchcraft* was neatly typed on the cover.

"Would you read this and see if you would like to play the role of the High Priestess?" he asked. "She seduces her son," he continued in a cautionary tone that went right over my head.

Wow! One day on a tits-and-ass quickie and here I was being offered a lead role in a film that actually had a script! It was just like in the movies.

Thoughts of an acting career had been jettisoned with my practice clothes years before – on the day I heard that Carol Haney had died.

Carol was the great kooky dancer who originated the role of Gladys in *The Pajama Game*, that wonderful musical from 1954: the role I was lucky enough to play for the last six months of the New York run. Yeah, right on Broadway.

I was due at an audition, and doing my usual futile vocalizing. No amount of practice or lessons with the best coaches in the business would ever give me enough voice to make it as a musical comedy performer, but at this juncture I was still deluding myself and pushing my poor psyche into the torture of futile auditions. The cold announcement that Carol had succumbed to her diabetes hit me right between the eyes. I just sat down on the floor and bawled. I was crying for Carol, yes, but in truth, I was crying for my own unrealistic ambitions now lying in shards about me. As painful as it was to admit it to myself, it was time to hang up my toe shoes and find another line of work.

Production work on industrial shows introduced me to a job at the JC Penney Co. The operative word here is work. Many shows, many all-nighters, many three-martini lunches with visiting VIPs, and many many many interminable meetings later, I jumped from the corporate rat-maze right into the flaming heat of the Pickle Factory, still with no thought of ever performing again.

Now, someone was handing me a script, offering me a job and not even asking me to audition. I was going to play the lead role in a film!

Marc "Mr. Ten-and-a-Half" Stevens

THE "STEERING COMMITTEE" of the Pickle Factory sprawls comfortably on a nest of large cushions that surround a wired-together quartet of milk crates. This is the living/dining/conference room area of our film emporium. I continue to fill them in on Beau's film: the production that will bail us out of our latest financial crises.

"...so there may be people actually fucking all over the place, but you don't have to. You just have to sort of look like you are and wriggle around naked."

"I'm not shaving."

"We know that." Corey darts an arch glance at Claire. She ignores him and continues speaking to the group at large.

"And I'm sure as hell not fucking anybody. Will you be?" She glares at me inquisitively.

"Any pizza left from last night?" Jimbo's muffled growl comes from inside the refrigerator.

"In the back," directs Corey.

"Not according to the script," I answer Claire.

"Lurch'll fuck anything, but I'm pretty picky, you know?" A large pizza slice disappears into the maw of our artist-in-residence. He seats himself astride one of the folding chairs.

Lurch is named for the TV Addams Family's butler to whom he bears a striking resemblance – except our Lurch has long blonde hair. He may also have acquired the nickname because his day job is morgue attendant at St. Vincent's Hospital where he answers his phone, "Parts department." He's one of Jimbo's best customers and sometimes works as a grip for us.

"So, can I let Beau know he's got four extras?" I ask.

"Fifty bucks to sit around naked all afternoon? I'm in," declares Corey.

"Do we still get the fifty if we get laid?" asks Jimbo around the pizza.

"Of course," I assure him.

"I'll tell Lurch." He swallows the last of the pizza as he dismounts from the metal chair and thrusts his tattooed arms through the frayed holes of his colors (sleeveless denim jacket with Harley insignia among others).

"See you guys at the crack of fuckin' dawn." He swings his slightly bowed legs along in that peculiar rolling gate of life-long bikers. They are often thought to be swaggering. They aren't. It's the scooter butter caked in the crotch of their jeans that makes them walk that way.

Up a dusty flight of magnificent mahogany stairs in a formidable lower Manhattan mansion march a file of grips like ants, each burdened with the maximum possible load. The boys, Claire and I follow. At the top we find the green room (waiting space on a set) and meet the rest of the cast. Beau leads me to my personal makeup artist who is eager to make me beautiful – as he had the day before.

"Marc's already out on the set. Have you met him?" asks my new friend as he wraps me in the reassuring folds of the makeup cape.

I shake my head no and take a sip of coffee while I can.

"You're gonna love him. He's an absolute riot…" he chats on as he makes me look exactly as I did yesterday. Well, like I did when we started at least.

I begin to dress.

"Do you need any help getting into that shroud?"

"Don't make fun of my costume. I was up all night building this thing."

"There must be twenty yards of chiffon on your ass, Sweetie. I'll bet there hasn't been that much material covering a fuckfilm star in history."

Ignoring the epithet, I sweep royally from the room, tripping on my regalia, of course.

Marc Stevens, known as Mr. Ten-and-a-half (not his hat size), sits regally on an elevated throne at the far end of a forty-foot long ballroom. A huge furry headdress with great curled ram's horns almost obscures his droll features. A foot-long dildo suspended from a tasteful gold chain rests on his hairless chest. This is the sum total of his costume.

I take my seat on the throne next to his.

"I should have refused to wear this damn thing," he groans, waggling the rubbery replica in my direction. "What're these idiots trying to do? Intimidate every poor guy in the audience? Look at the size of this dopey thing. It's a drag queen's wet dream."

Having never seen one before, I have no idea what size they're supposed to be, but I nod in sympathetic understanding.

We engage in get-acquainted chit-chat until Beau calls for quiet and filming gets under way.

A few minutes later Marc leans toward me and strokes my knee. I tense instinctively.

"I'm not getting fresh," he whispers, "I just wanted to get close enough to ask you something, and this way, if the camera catches us, we'll be in character."

He is quite serious about staying in character.

I lean my head close to his and whisper, "What?"

"Would you like to meet Jerry Damiano?" he asks.

"Who?"

"Gerard Damiano."

He lowers his voice to imitate an announcer, "The famous director of the greatest fuckfilm of all time, *Deep Throat*."

"Deep who?"

"*Deep Throat*? You don't know *Deep Throat*?" he asks in mock horror. (Well, maybe it wasn't all that mock.)

"I've never heard of it. What's it about? A giraffe?"

That puts Marc on the floor.

"Cut!" screams the director from midway across the room. "We're making a movie over here, you guys."

We signal our contrite assurance that we will behave properly. The actors on the floor resume their erotic pas de trois. I look but I can't spot any of the Pickle Factory four. There are dozens of bodies sprawled about. They could be tucked in anywhere.

"So, do you want to meet him?" continues Marc from the side of his mouth. "He's shooting a film next week. I'm pretty sure it's cast, but he might have some production work for you."

"Sure. I'm always looking for work."

Was there ever a time when I wasn't looking for work? Well, not while I was gainfully employed as a media producer for Penney's. I had a title on the door if no Bigelow on the floor. That is, I was considered management, but saw few perks.

The wife of my co-producer was an ardent Peacenik. I joined her for one of the marches – if memory serves, in support of the Chicago Eight. There I met Claire. She asked for a lift to the Westside Air Terminal in Manhattan.

"Why in the world do you want to go to Alaska?" I shake my head in bewilderment. "You're leaving college just six months short of a degree?"

"My folks lost a lot of their money. They say I have to come back and live with them in Scottsdale, Arizona and finish college there. They want me to get a job! I've never been trained to do anything except maybe host a dinner party for forty. I can't see selling cosmetics in a department store."

Dinner party for forty? How broke could her family be if they still live in Scottsdale?

I offer motherly advice. "I think you need to think this over. Why don't you stay at our house tonight and see how you feel after a good breakfast."

That's how it started. Over the next three weeks the two of us became joined at the hip, though not yet by any other parts of our anatomy. The filmmakers that I worked with welcomed her to the fold. Her unfettered enthusiasm for the revolution was infectious. Why *couldn't* we change the fuckin' world?

Work on the Pickle Factory occupied the hours that work at Penney's didn't. One day I was headed out the door of our apartment with a change of clothes when Ian asked, "Are we – you know – still living together?"

That hit me in the gut like a ton of bricks. It hadn't even crossed my selfish mind to wonder how my best friend and lover might be feeling about my latest endeavor – much less the waif I seemed to have acquired. We hadn't talked a whole lot in the last few years. He worked all the time: writing and directing industrial shows mostly. I was no longer a performer, so our paths just didn't cross much during the day any more.

"Why do you ask?" I ask.

"Well," he says, "if we aren't, there's someone I'd like to start seeing."

The ton of bricks dropped to the floor – taking my guts with it.

"Oh. I see." I fish in my purse for my keys. "Here." I hand them to him. "I'll come up next Sunday and clear out the rest of my stuff."

It was all I could do to keep my voice light; I fought back the tears that threatened to blow my cover.

"Sure. Anytime."

"I'll call first," I add simultaneously. We laugh at the overlap.

In this insanely civilized manner we dissolved a relationship begun in a fever of passion so intense – for me, at least – that it was responsible for a severe rash, two suicide attempts, and a year in therapy. A Mexican divorce cleared up the rash.

Six rings. Finally someone picks up and mumbles unintelligibly.

"Is this Harry?" I inquire.

"You got him."

"Marc Stevens suggested I call you regarding possible work on a film that you're shooting with Jerome Damiano."

"Gerard," says the gruff voice.

"I beg your pardon?"

"Gerard." Harry clears his throat. "Gerard Damiano. What kind of work?"

"Oh. Excuse me. Gerard. Right. Well, I've worked just about every job on a film set and in post. Marc thought there might be something I could do for you on your upcoming shoot." I tried very hard to keep the quavering need out of my voice.

"Can you come over here to my place?" he asks, and gives me the address.

"I'm about ten minutes away," I reply. "Is now good?"

"Sure. I'll put on the coffee." I could hear a yawn.

"I'm sorry. Did I wake you?"

"S'OK. I had to get up to answer the phone, anyway."

I knock confidently on the door at the top of four narrow flights of stairs. It opens mid-knock and I almost land a knock on a hairy chest.

"Hi," says the actor known as Harry Reams: a tall well-built young man sporting a huge Groucho-esque mustache. It almost eclipses the tanned face, but not the twinkling eyes. With his prominent nose, all that's needed to complete the traditional disguise of a porn actor is a pair of thick black-rimmed glasses. And, oh yes, black socks. His feet were bare.

"You found the place," he smiles buttoning a colorful Hawaiian shirt.

"No problem. Did you know your downstairs door is wide open?"

"Yeah, it sticks if you close it all the way."

"Aren't you afraid you'll be robbed?"

"Of what?" he looks around the small room, tastefully furnished in early Salvation Army. "Have a seat. Want some coffee? I just made it."

"Sure. Thanks."

"You're carving a Jack-o-lantern!" I notice as I sit down at a wee table in the kitchen area. "Can I help?"

"Sure. Here." He hands me a large spoon. "Knock yourself out."

I scoop out pungent pulp. Harry pours a mug of the worst coffee I ever tasted in my life. We carve and chat and discover several mutual friends in show biz – the non-porn kind. Harry had a strong theater background, but, like most of us, he couldn't make a living at it. I don't know how he ended up in *Deep Throat*, but his performance in it assured his future as a sex star, that's for sure.

"Hey, Jerry?" Harry speaks briskly into the phone. "There's a nice lady here, just worked with Marc on a shoot. She's looking for production work. Got anything?"

To me: "Can you cook?"

"Well, yeah. But I hardly know you," I quip in my best Mae West.

"Not for me. For the shoot."

"How many, and what's the budget?" I inquire – all business.

"She's OK with it. Wanna meet?" Harry asks into the phone.

To me: "Can you drop by the office tomorrow morning?"

"What time?"

Into the phone: "What time?"

To me: "Is ten too early?"

I shake my head no.

Hell, I was up by 4 AM every morning anyway. That's when the meat trucks arrive at our neighbor's loading dock. Swinging sides of beef emerge from the refrigerated processing plant on an overhead metal trolley. Wrung, wrung, wrung, wrung, bump. splat. thunk. Each gory carcass is caught on meat hooks by the blood-spattered crew, then transferred to a rail inside the truck. Slam, SLAM. The doors close and the idling engine guns into action, moving the truck out of the way so the next one can pull in – vroom, screech, bump.

These trucks, parked as they are on the deserted area under the Westside Highway during the night, are favorite trysting nests for the gay crowd. The Stonewall Café, famous as the location of the first Gay Rights rebellion of that age, is conveniently located at the end of our block near the Hudson River.

The Pickle Factory sat between Brookdale Butter and Eggs, and Asia Meat. Stracce Produce was directly across the cobblestone street known as Little West 12th. Not only did we enjoy wholesale prices on butter, eggs, and meat, but our good neighbors across the street often gave us crates of produce too shopworn to sell. It was the perfect spot to live if you were gonna do craft services for a movie.

"You're all set." Harry replaces the handset of the phone that hangs on the wall beside his sink.

"May I use your phone to call Marc?" I ask. "He wanted me to let him know how it went."

"Help yourself." He waves toward the phone.

Marc answers on the first ring.

"It's your dime."

"Hey, Marc. It's Georgie. I'm over at Harry's. I got a job."

"Doing what?"

"Cooking."

"Great. Why don't you stop by while you're in the neighborhood?"

I check the address in my book. It was, indeed, only a few blocks away.

"OK. Sure. See you in a few."

"You going by Marc's?" asks Harry.

"Yeah."

"Would you mind taking these books to him?" He hands me a couple of paperback westerns.

"Glad to."

"If I'm in the office tomorrow, I'll see ya," he continues as he walks me to the door. "If not, I'll see you on the set."

"Cool," I reply, nonchalantly, even though my heart is a-twitter.

"Thanks for the help with the jack-o-lantern." He leans forward and busses me lightly on the cheek. He was so sweet! Part of me wanted to bake him brownies. Another was ready to jump his bones.

Marc's apartment is only three flights up – one less than Harry's. I knock on his slightly ajar door. Don't these guys believe in locks?

"Come on in. Welcome to the jungle. Watch your head."

The room is filled with huge plants. Some could be called trees. An old-fashioned dentist's chair dominates the space near a bay windows that overlook the street. There are two huge aquariums on the divider that separates the eat-in kitchen from that area. One is filled with some silvery fish about the size of your hand. The other holds jillions of teeny bright goldfish.

"Wow," I exclaim, admiring the tanks. "What are those?" I point to the larger fish.

"Piranha," he says, matter-of-factly.

"You're kidding."

"No. They really are. Yeah, they're illegal. Most of my life is."

"And these?" I nod toward the tank of small, orange guys.

"Piranha kibbles. Want to feed some to the big guys?"

"Uh... no thanks."

"Glass of wine?"

"Got a beer?"

"Sorry."

"Wine's fine."

He pours me a tumbler of something from a large jug.

Yup, it's wine – sort of. Yup, it's way before noon.

"Here." I hand him the books. "Harry asked me to give you these."

"Oh. Thanks. Come meet Herman."

I follow him into a small bedroom that scarcely manages to contain a king-sized bed and a huge aquarium wherein a beautiful Brazilian boa drapes elegantly over an attractive array of branches.

"Hey, guy." Marc greets the reptile in a friendly voice and the snake's head lifts in response.

"Want to hold him?"

"Sure. I'm an equal-opportunity pet lover."

Marc rests the four-foot long Brazilian Boa across my shoulders. The slithery creature coils around my arms and slides down over my bosom. A charge of almost sexual excitement shoots through me.

"You're a good snake handler. Ever seen one of these boys before?

"I've handled small snakes. Hell, I grew up in Texas. But I've never been this intimate with anything this big before."

Marc laughs at my practiced Mae West double entendre delivery. Yeah, I used to do that a lot.

I run back across the Village to the Pickle Factory. I couldn't wait to tell everyone about Harry, Marc, and Herman – and my upcoming appointment with a real film director the very next day.

OK. A real fuckfilm director. Hey, a job's a job.

So You Wanna Be in Fuckfilms

MY APPOINTMENT AT MR. DAMIANO'S OFFICE is for 10 a.m. At 9:57 I stride into the modest rooms in mid-town Manhattan clad in a slinky burgundy colored silk velvet calf-length thigh-hugging skirt and knee-high lace-up boots. My near see-through blouse opens in a V down to a spot between my small perky breasts. These are alternately revealed and concealed by a spangled gypsy vest.

For my first visit to a porn production office I wanted to dress appropriately. All is borrowed. I dumped most of my clothes when I moved into the Pickle Factory having no plans to ever again wear pantyhose in this life.

Jerry is expecting me. We discuss how to feed 17 people for three days on $500. Then he gives me a slim script to read.

An actor arrives to audition for the part of Abaca – sort of a front office man for the Devil. Jerry asks if I would mind reading the part of Miss Jones with him since I'm just sitting there.

31

Mr. Clemons (probably not his real name) is a bona fide actor. We tear into the script and happily chew up gobs of imaginary scenery. Jerry signs him on the spot.

As the actor makes his way out the door, a dapper little guy in a pinstriped suit, dark hair brushed meticulously straight back from a high forehead, almost runs him over. The incoming gent's name is Jimmy. He skids to a halt beside Jerry's desk. Before he can articulate whatever urgent message has brought him into the office, Mr. Damiano, who has been gazing intently into my eyes, speaks.

"How would you like to play the role of Justine Jones?"

My mouth falls open. So does Jimmy's.

"But, Jerry. She's gotta be at least thirty!" gasps the dapper gent, not quite under his breath.

He then quickly turns to me and says, "No offense. Really. I could hear you guys from the next office. You really can act."

"Yeah," says Jerry, "what's a nice girl like you doing in a porn shop like this?" That ice-melting grin of his makes me throw caution – not my strong suit to begin with – to the winds.

"Besides," Jimmy rants on, turning to me again, "no offense, but..." back to Jerry in a horrified squeak, "she's flat-chested!" He bounces up and down on his tiny, shiny, pointy-toed black shoes in agitation. "What are you gonna do about the tits?"

"I'll shoot around them," says Jerry.

Again I feel like I'm in a scene right out of a Judy Garland movie. Now I was to STAR in a film. OK, I had to cook, too, but that just meant another twenty-five dollars a day. Jerry said they would pay me a hundred a day to play Miss Jones! I was happily signing a contract when a striking young woman in stylish attire breezed into the office.

"Sue," Jerry waves in my general direction, "meet our new Miss Jones."

We exchange hellos. Jerry fishes a huge wad out of his pocket and peels off bills which he hands to the new arrival.

"Here's the wardrobe budget. Why don't you two kids run down to the Pleasure Chest and pick out some nifty outfits?"

Sue counts out the twenties and looks at Jerry. "You want four outfits for two hundred bucks?" She smiles at me. "Guess you won't be wearing much."

"Just get all the usual S&M crap and a bunch of bondage gear," says Herr Director blandly.

> S&M? Sado-masochism?! Bondage?!!!
>
> There wasn't anything about any of that shit in the script!

"You know," he continues, "think 'Barbarella in Hell.'"

> Barbarella? Chains? Whips? Good grief!
>
> Oh, come on. Jerry is just too damn nice. He'd never have you do anything that actually HURT. Would he? It's only a movie. Right?

Forth we go, Sue and I, deep into the bowels of the West Village. We ferret out the infamous Pleasure Chest: emporium to the weird and twisted. I'd never heard of it.

The small display window beside the door is draped with black sateen. Leather accessories in all shapes and sizes (liberally studded with bright metal pointy bumps) are strewn about in an artistic array. It looks like the tack shed of a Nazi riding school.

Undaunted, we enter.

From behind the counter, a person of indeterminate sex approaches with a welcoming, "Yeah?"

I'd never before seen anyone who pierced anything other than an ear lobe or two. There is more hardware dangling from various parts of the face before me than you'd find in the average angler's tackle box.

"We'd like to rent some costumes for a film," Sue explains in a reasonable voice.

"We don't rent," the androgynous one states in a neutral voice.

"Well, of course you don't," I acknowledge. "What were we thinking?"

I note the price ($69.95!) on an elaborate, three-speed dildo gracefully displayed in the glass-topped case. Our paltry two hundred bucks isn't gonna get us much coverage here. I grab Sue's hand.

"C'mon. We're going to Brooks Van Horne. It's OK. They know me there."

(And, indeed they do. I spent many hours being fitted for costumes at that famous Manhattan landmark – in my former life.)

"I need a dressing gown for when I meet The Teacher. Do you have that covered?" I ask Sue as we depart the little shop of horrors.

"I think I can come up with something. Jerry didn't say anything about that, but I've got a lot of stuff at my place."

Jerry didn't say anything about it because I just thought of it. He may be thinking Jane Fonda. I'm thinking Gloria Swanson. Sue's place is another walkup – just two flights this time.

"How 'bout this?" she asks, holding up a sheer peignoir with way too much marabou sewn on at every opportunity. Just looking at it makes me want to sneeze.

"Have you got anything more – understated?"

She finally comes up with a floor-length slinky ecru silk number that's perfect. At least for my vision of Miss Jones' vision of herself as a hot number, ready to dive into the inferno of our favorite deadly sin.

On to Brooks Costumes.

"Good Lord," shrieks my old pal Bruce. "Where in tarnation have you been, girl?"

"Hold on to your garters, Mary," I announce in my very deepest, most conspiratorial voice. "Yours truly is about to star in a fuckfilm."

"Noooo! Chaz! Chaz! Get over here. You won't believe this!" Another pal from the past joins us.

"I need a corset, silk hose, anything that looks like it belongs on a World War I French postcard," I explain.

"That's not what Jerry has in mind, I don't think," says Sue without much conviction or concern.

"I'm screwing in it. I'm picking it out."

From whence this sudden burst of assertiveness? Well, I'm always more at home in my skin around gay folk. They are portraits in courage.

I'm beginning to "see" Justine Jones now. Fuckfilm or no, I'm creating a character here. What a seductive nectar that can be.

We plunge into the working guts of this, the biggest costume house on the East Coast. Three hours later, we stagger out with a classic Merry Widow, several pair of shimmery silk hose, and a silk kimono to die for. No heart-shaped cut-out crotches or stiff net ruffles on our Miss Jones.

The entire bill for the weekend rental came to $180 and change.

Jerry barely winced when he saw the new look for his lead character. True to his good nature (and infallible instincts), he was happy to go with whatever worked for me. He could see I was getting really jazzed about the whole thing, I think.

"Now, about the craft services..." I begin, tentatively.

"Don't tell me I'm gonna have to find another cook at this late hour," he wails, eyes rolling to the ceiling.

"No. No. Not exactly. But, just to make sure everything goes smoothly – and nobody goes hungry if I'm, you know, busy – how about hiring my roommate Claire as my assistant for just another twenty-five a day?"

"Are you and your roommate a couple?" asks Jerry, with a gleam in his eye.

"I think one might say that," I respond with my usual decorum, confirming for the first time to myself that this was undoubtedly the case.

"Would you two do a scene for the movie?" (He wasn't exactly drooling, but his grin could have been used for a key light.)

"I'll ask her," I promise, knowing full well she will jump at the chance to jump my bones – especially in a situation where she knows I will feel obliged to respond enthusiastically, something I'm not always inclined to do in real life. (I'm conflicted. OK?)

"We'll pay her a hundred for the scene," purrs Jerry.

"Plus the twenty-five a day to help cook?"

"Plus twenty-five dollars a day to help you in the kitchen. You're busting my budget, you know," he smiles.

"So they'll actually pay me a hundred dollars to eat you out?" Claire grins shamelessly.

"Plus twenty-five a day to help cook and clean up," I nod.

"Can't you get me in a scene?" demands Corey with mock indignation.

35

"Doing what, exactly? I haven't seen you expressing much interest in fucking girls since I've known you," I kid good-naturedly.

"What? Girl-girl scenes are OK, but no gay guys? That is blatant discrimination. Are they homophobic or something?"

"Yes," I reply. "My guess would be that they are decidedly homophobic, and I strongly suggest you keep your patrician nose out of it."

"I won't shave," says Claire needlessly.

"Don't bring it up," I instruct. "So shall I let him know it's OK?"

"Sure. Do you want me to fix lunch on the set tomorrow?"

My character's suicide scene is scheduled to shoot the very next day. Fortunately there's no dialog to learn.

"No," I respond. "Jerry says no cooking on that set. They'll send out for something."

"Do you need me for makeup, wardrobe? I do windows."

Like hell. Claire will happily spend a day up to her elbows in gasoline cleaning a carburetor, but put her hands in sudsy water? Fahgeddaboudit.

"It's gonna be a pretty tight set."

Like I have any idea what the set will be like.

"They probably don't want any more bodies on hand than absolutely necessary."

"OK. Sure. I can run you uptown on the bike," she persists. Claire is the proud owner of a new used Honda 350 motorcycle – complete with helmet, tool kit and a fine set of leathers.

"Thanks, I better take a cab. I've got a shitload of stuff to schlep."

"I can help you carry... OK. I'll help Corey shop."

"Good. He has the list and the money. Also, would you check with Lilly? She said she found a great antique black velvet dress for the first scene.

Lilly is our neighbor in the apartment above us. She is a budding designer who works in an antique clothing store. It was her slinky burgundy velvet skirt I borrowed to wear to Jerry's office.

"You're not going to wear something from that flea-infested junk store?" screams Corey.

"Geez. One little case of scabies and the poor girl's reputation is ruined forever?"

"It only takes one time, you know," pontificates Corey. "Don't worry. We'll find you something suitably macabre, bug-free, and sexy."

"I'm not doing Vampira, you nut. I should look like your Aunt Ida from Idaho. It's gotta look like something Miss Jones would be buried in."

"It should be something you can wear that beautiful old lace collar with," says Claire.

"You mean my great grandmother's lace collar?" I had a small box of family treasures still on board.

"What could be more Victorian? That's what you're going for, isn't it?"

Claire could be quite insightful at times. She was being not only cooperative but downright supportive. She helped me check and double check my makeup kit. Then we hit the sack in our cozy loft above the kitchen.

Her arm and leg flopped across me as she curled into our usual position of repose. In that buzzy place just this side of sleep I felt her hand move ever so casually down across my stomach and come to rest gently on the mound of my crotch.

If I don't move, she'll think I'm asleep.

I move. I can't help it.

Much as the first time she made the leap from daughter-like affection to unabashed seduction, the warm fingers brush gently over the top of my clit. The sleeping dragon stirs, uncoils and stretches. Soon the fire spreads through my groin. My innocent little waif lodges one finger firmly inside my snatch and fixes her eager little mouth on my left tit. An irrepressible moan escapes my lips and that's all she needs to send her on her way to lunch at the Y. Her hands grip my butt and she does her best to send me over the falls. Not gonna happen, but my cooperation is appreciated. She finally gives up and I hold her as she finds her own climax against my thigh.

She rolls off and lies panting beside me on her back. I run my hand gently over the fine peach fuzz on her stomach. It feels like a rose petal. Her soft snore flutters against my hair. "Black Magic Woman" pulses from beneath the loft, palpable through the thin mattress that is our bed. She has cast her spell on me, baby, that's for sure. Is she trying to make a devil out of me? Has she?

Eyes Wide Open

"GEORGINA?" calls a young man, obviously one of the crew. Why movie crew people are so easily identified as such, I'm not sure. Maybe it's the bandanas. Whatever it is, I've always had a soft spot in my heart for 'em. (Still do. My favorite bumper sticker reads "Get a Grip on Yourself.")

"Here, let me take that for you."

He grabs my tacklebox makeup kit and the small duffle that I pull from the back seat of the taxi.

"We're up on the second floor. It's the only door at the top of the stairs." He nods toward the sedate, five-story modern apartment building behind him.

"No. I'll get that," he insists as I start to pay the cab driver.

I'm becoming more impressed with this outfit every minute. Up the steps to the front door I stride with an air of self-confidence donned especially for the occasion.

What am I getting myself into? What
made me think I could pull this scene off
with any believability whatsoever? Act?
I'm gonna make a complete ass of
myself.

Oh, calm down. It's just a fuckfilm, for
crying out loud. Nobody will ever see it.

"Hey – Georgie Girl. How ya doin'? There's coffee and Danish over there."
My director points to a kitchen table covered with hot drink containers and
open boxes of pastries.

"Where do you want me to park?" I ask, holding up the care-
fully-ironed kimono on its hanger.

"Over here in the bedroom, Sweetie," pipes a thin fruity voice. A
bearded face peers out around the corner of a door at the far end of a very
long hall.

"Oh my gawd. What are we going to do about your hair?" the fuzzy
face screeches. "You didn't set it or anything? Oh, Jerry. I'm gonna need
WAAAAY more time with this one," insists the wiry little guy whom I take
to be the makeup artist.

"No you don't," responds the director in a reasoning tone. "She's not
supposed to be glamorous (under his breath he adds) you twit. She's about
to cut her wrists. She should look like she just got out of bed."

"Well, she's achieved that with no help from me," declares Mr. Makeup
Man emphatically.

"Sit," he commands, flipping open a folded smock pulled from his
huge makeup kit.

I set down my little foot-long dented green fishingtackle box. It's been
with me since my first teenage ballet performances – a gift from my dad. It
saw me through about a jillion industrial and summer stock shows. It even
sat proudly upon my dressing table in a couple of Broadway theaters. It
looked rather puny next to the amazing arrangement of levered trays and
cubby holes opened beside the makeup table.

I sit.

"OK. Natural look," muses Mr. Makeup Man. "Let's use these brown
lashes." He selects the fringe of choice from an extensive collection.

"Let's not," I parry. "No false eyelashes. No eye shadow. No blush. No kidding. Just slap on some base the same color as me. You'll get to paint me pale for the last shot. OK?" I was getting my sea legs.

"Well, mercy me. What the fuck did they call me in at eight fucking A fucking M in the fucking morning for anyway?" spits out Mr. Makeup Man, throwing his array of brushes and pencils back into his folding closet of a makeup kit in rhythmic percussive accompaniment to his complaint.

"To make me look like a woman so ugly she slits her wrists," I explain with a chuckle in an effort at lightening the mood. "And don't you dare say, I can do that on my own."

"Georgie," calls Jerry from the hall. "Can you come in here for a minute? You can finish your face while we're lighting."

Happy to escape, I call out "Yes sir," and slip hurriedly from the tall canvas chair.

Jerry is standing by a window, looking back over his shoulder at the cameraman.

Oooooo, that cameraman. A Brazilian. So sexy it hurt to look at him. Eye to the lens of the huge 35mm machine set up in the middle of the room, legs in tight jeans slightly splayed, he oozed sensuality. His name is credited in the film as Harry Flex, which is as phony as Georgina Spelvin, of course. I just can't think of him as a Harry, though. Herein, he shall be known as Joaquin.

"Stand over here by this window and look sad." Jerry motions me over to him.

"What do you know," says Joaquin, the hunk, "you two guys are the same height."

"We won't be when I take off my shoes," cracks Jerry.

"Look out the window," he then instructs me. "How much face are you getting?" he asks Joaquin.

"Not enough. Can you cheat toward me a bit, Georgie?"

The soft "g" and intimate tone makes it sound like a proposition.

> Sure. Anything you want. Anything.
> You've but to ask.

I nod and turn my face more toward the camera.

"Yessss. That's good. Are we ready to shoot?"

"I am," says Jerry. "How 'bout you, George?"

> What? They want to start shooting now?
>
> I haven't even talked about the scene
> with Jerry yet. I haven't the vaguest idea
> why this woman has decided to slit her
> wrists. Oh sure, the script says she's
> never gotten any, but is that reason
> enough to slit your wrists? She's not
> deformed or anything. Maybe it's a
> religious thing. I haven't begun to find
> this woman.

"I just have to slip into my kimono," I respond confidently.

"Can't I even put a little mascara on her?" squeals Mr. Makeup Man, bordering on hysteria.

"No," I squeal just as hysterically. "It will run and burn my eyes. Do I have to?" I whine to my director.

"Hell, no. You can do whatever you want. It's your scene, Kiddo."

"OK. Fine. I'll be in here if anybody needs me for anything." Mr. Makeup Man's flouncing exit leaves the sexy cameraman's shoulders shaking with repressed laughter. They are very broad shoulders.

> My scene! He said it was my scene. This
> is the first time anyone's ever said that
> to me. Oh, I'm gonna make this movie
> work for this wonderful man no matter
> what I have to do.

I rush to the back bedroom, peeling off my sweatshirt as I go.

I'm out of my jeans and skivvies in a single jump.

I check the mirror and make an even bigger mess of my hair. Mr. Makeup Man can't help himself. He attacks me with one of those fluffy brushes that looks like an old-fashioned barbershop lather thingy on a really long handle.

I submit.

It's a truce.

41

He helps me on with the kimono and carefully smoothes it over my shoulders.

I head down the hall tying the sash as I go.

"Shoes," cries Mr. Makeup Man.

I kick off my sneakers. He grabs them and I continue my brisk, businesslike walk through the empty, echoing, unfurnished apartment.

Jerry takes my arm, looks me over front and back, and guides me gently into position by the window. He and the cameraman speak in tongues of lenses and zooms. Little do they know I understand every word. And I love what I hear. I give the director my undivided attention. Not easy with the Brazilian six feet away.

"OK. George. I want you to look out the window. Just keep staring. Cheat around a little more toward camera. Good."

He pats me on the shoulder and joins Joaquin behind the camera.

"Now, close the blinds," Jerry continues in a low, intense voice. "Slooooowly. Good. Now walk over and look in the mirror."

"A little slower, George, and not quite so close to me, OK?" purrs Joaquin's soft, baritone.

I move back to the first position and make the cross again.

"Start to take off your wrapper," instructs Mr. D. "Good. Now look at your tits. That's it. Now touch them."

> Ah HAH! My motivation for committing suicide: little tits! And Jerry's off the hook for his departure from the norm in hiring me.

I look at my small, perky mammary mounds with feigned disdain and disappointment.

"Hmmm. That's not very sexy," laments my director.

Not what he had in mind! What? Was I supposed to get myself aroused before I cut my wrists?

"But it'll work!"

That's a definite "Eureka." Maybe I AM on the right track...

"OK. Now go ahead and take off your robe and head on into the bathroom. How's that look?" he asks Joaquin.

"She's a Rolex. I'm ready to shoot," says the director of photography.

Does that mean he thinks I'm reliable?
Maybe I'll ask him if he wants to check
out my mainspring after work.

Pay attention.

"How 'bout you, Georgie?" queries the director. "You ready for this?"

"You bet," I reply. And I am. A little approval was all I needed to chase away the self-doubt demon.

Gazing out the window I think about the hurt and humiliation I felt when I lost my cherry. The hurt was real physical pain. The humiliation was not at losing my cherry but because there was nary a trace of red, and the horny trombone player probably thought I was a slut. The pain of the deflowering was nothing compared to the pain of watching my insistent Romeo give his band jacket to a blonde majorette with huge tits two days later.

Oooh, good. Tears trying to well.

Still half a scene to go though.

Use the second time – the second deflowering... sort of.

New town. (We moved frequently.) Clean slate. The gorgeous boy with eyelashes out to here was known to his posse as BD. (Short for Big Dick and not because his name was Richard and he was tall.) The oversized member that inspired his nickname brought a bit of the blood that was missing the first time around. The pain was equivalently huge. He at least thought I was a virgin. Even so, dates with him were a quick burger and an even quicker hump in the back seat of his dad's Buick. Never was I taken to the movies or escorted to a formal by my well-endowed Lothario. Poor, poor me.

That did it. I am soooooo ready to slit my wrists.

"Cut. That was GREAT. Marty! Are the burgers here?" Jerry calls into the kitchen area.

"Flyin' in," comes the answer along with several sacks reeking of yummy grease.

Jerry turns back to me. "Go relax. Have some lunch. We'll start on the bathtub stuff as soon as we get set up. OK?" Mr. D squeezes my cheeks with his big hands and plants a kiss on my forehead.

"Just holler when you're ready," I reply cheerfully and head for the makeup area.

It was a great relief to smile after wallowing in the depths of dreary emotions all morning. I was even looking forward to chatting up crabby Mr. Makeup Man.

"So, in the next scene you're dead, right?" says the artiste as he sponges a layer of almost white pancake on my upturned kisser.

"Yeah, Jerry wants to get the long dolly shot next. Oh. That's good. I really look awful!" I enthuse.

"Gee. Thanks." Makeup Man borders on cheerful.

I slip on my grubby makeup wrapper. The beautiful borrowed kimono has been hung carefully on its hanger on one of the work lights set up near the makeup table. Mr. Makeup Man was worming his way into my heart.

I'll be naked from here on. I check my middle for jeans marks. All clear. I'm ready for my close up, Mr. De - amiano!

"Now George, we're gonna put you in the tub and pan from your bleeding wrists to your face. When I say go, you die and drop your head to the right. Don't move after that. We're gonna pull back very slowly to the end of the hall. Think you can look dead for, oh, about two minutes?" asks Jerry.

"Piece of cake," I assure him and climb into the steaming water.

I had no idea how difficult it would be. I've always been a bit of a blinker, possibly the result of swimming under water with my eyes open all my life. Through sheer force of will, I lay with my face utterly slack and did not blink for the entire – interminable – shot. If I thought I was a blinker before, after that eye-drying experience I was never able to do a lengthy closeup without looking like I was sending semaphore.

Jerry was very happy with the shot. I relaxed, gratefully accepting the soothing eye drops Mr. Crabby Makeup Man handed me. Soon my own tears began to flow easily and the burning let up.

"That was perfect. Just terrific. You were great." Jerry spews forth all the right things. I glow with pride and satisfaction as I wipe away tears and blow my nose.

"Ready to shoot the safety?" he calls to the Brazilian Bombshell who is crouched beside the camera, reloading.

The WHAT?

"I want to reset a couple of lights," replies Joaquin over his shoulder.

"OK. Let me know when you're ready," says Jerry.

"Now George," he turns to me, "just do everything exactly the same."

> He's kidding, right? Wrong. He's gonna
> shoot the whole thing AGAIN!

"Makeup!" he shouts.

"Right here," squeaks the gnome, waving a sponge with pale pancake over his head.

With frantic strokes he mops my tear-smudged face, which has now started to sweat as well.

"Can you get her face back exactly as it was?" Jerry inquires of the makeup maven.

"Not a challenge," replies a definitely more cheerful Mr. Grumpy.

> Well, I'm facing a challenge. I barely made
> it through the first take. How the hell
> am I going to do it again?

How I did it, I don't know, but I did. In the next few days, I learned I could do a lot of things I might not have thought I could.

"So, how'd it go?" asks Corey from his regal repose on the makeshift couch.

I drop my gear by the stairs to the loft and head for the little refrigerator to grab a cold beer.

"I was fabulous," I concede, modestly. "Where is everybody?"

"Some bash at the bike shop. Somebody's birthday, I think."

That would be the Iron Company where Mike spends his days tuning spokes on motorcycle wheels. Precision delights him.

"You didn't go?" I plop down beside him on the cushions that serve as our couch.

"Beer and blasting rock music in tight quarters surrounded by sweat-stained leather is not really my idea of a good time," he avows in his elegant manner.

"Unless it's at the Stonewall," I suggest, slugging back a hefty gulp of my beer.

"That's different," he assures me.

I'll say.

"So, really. How'd it go?" he persists. "Did you nail it?"

"I surprised myself," I confess.

"Good. Want to listen to some Manon?"

A really good recording of Puccini's opera, *Manon Lescaut,* was one of the many refinements Corey brought to our abode. He arrived at the Pickle Factory late one night a few months after we moved in with a couple of other former classmates of Claire's. Along with the extensive record collection, Corey came with a taste for haute cuisine, fine wine, and cashmere sweaters. Long before any Queer Eyes appeared on television to upgrade the slobs of the world, Corey brought style and refinement to the PF and its scruffy crew.

"How did you know that's what's been running through my head all day?" I demand.

"What else for a suicide?"

Corey sweeps over to the phonograph, colorful caftan swirling about his lithe frame. While he adjusts the sound, I mix us a couple of Salty Dogs from his private stash of gin and we settle comfortably into the cushions. The lush sounds wash over and around us. Curled in the comfort of Corey's benign embrace, I fall into contented sleep well before the end of the first act.

Acid Bath

FRYING BACON! The smell yanks me out of my sweet, very sound sleep.

Half a cold burger and a few mushy fries was all I had to eat yesterday. My stomach rumbles louder than the ever-present trucks out front. Eyes still burning from my spectacular death scene, I slowly focus on the big brine pipes running along the ceiling 20 feet above.

> Guess I didn't make it up to bed.
> Somebody covered me with the quilt.
> How nice. Bacon. Yeah!

I stretch and note the burr of a slight hangover. A quick beer will fix that. I look toward the rear section of our tree-fort of a film factory.

Stella stands at the gas range in the teeny kitchen that's tucked in under the rear sleeping loft. She tosses a magnificent mane of curly, light brown hair out of her view and sizes up my condition.

"Boy, you must have been beat. You never made it up to bed, eh?"

Stella came into my life courtesy of Iron Mike. I had a huge editing job to do for an upcoming business conference. He was a regular member of the Penney film crew by then, usually working as a sound technician but sometimes manning one of the cameras as well. When he said he could also cut film, I called him in on the compilation job – jillions of commercials to be culled for highlights. He asked for an assistant. That was Stella. It didn't take long to figure out who was actually doing the cutting and splicing. As long as it got done, I cared not. Besides, he was so gorgeous, in a biker sort of long-haired way, it brightened my life just to have him around. The truth is, wanting to stay within his sphere had a lot to do with the whole Pickle Factory endeavor.

Stella was seventeen going on forty and had more film editing experience at her tender age than the rest of us in the PF put together. She also had more sense, but nobody paid much attention to that at the time. Though not a full-time resident – she lived with her parents in New Jersey – much of her time away from school was spent with our motley crew. She was to become my best friend for life.

Stirring the pan with practiced skill, she inquires, "Want some scrambled eggs and bacon?"

"In a sandwich, please," I mumble as I stumble into the bathroom which is squeezed in behind the kitchen.

This tiny accommodation is a monument to Charley the carpenter's skills. Charley, Iron Mike's younger brother, is as cheerful and upbeat as Mike is dour. The two are inseparable, even though they argue most of the time. Charley's luxuriant hand-crafted woodwork makes our bathroom look like something out of a 1920's Art Deco cruise-ship movie.

The toilet behind the enclosed tub/shower had been the only amenity present when we moved in. Well, that and a pipe topped by a faucet that rose from the floor beside it. A sturdy galvanized bucket and parts for the non-functioning old pull-chain toilet were the first of many purchases we made at the nearby hardware store where the friendly proprietors were foolish enough to open a charge account for us.

Along with the elegant woodwork, our tub enclosure sports a phantasmagorical landscape painted by Chip, another of Claire's college chums. Once a model for the Campbell's Soup ads of the '50s, Chip's cute kisser hadn't changed a bit. Alas, he was a resident for but a short time soon subletting Bette Midler's Village apartment. She mentioned him by name in a TV interview once saying he'd left her place a mess. Chip was artistic, not neat. Bathing in his creation is like being immersed in a psychedelic poster. It's especially effective on acid.

"What time did you get in?" yells Stell from the kitchen.

"It wasn't real late. I don't know. Did you go to the party?"

"You kidding? School night. I ditched after Chapel this morning. I've got a bunch of dailies to sync. You guys're gonna be gone all weekend, right?"

Hmmmmm. Bet she's hookin' up with
that tall sexy editor she's been working
with. Well, I hope she does! He's a hoot.

"Yeah. Looks that way," I respond.

"On camera today?" she continues.

I know she knows what kind of film it is I'm doing. Not her cup of tea, but as I said, we're a nonjudgmental lot.

"Don't think so. Far as I know we're just driving to the location. You gonna be working here?"

"Nope. Uptown at Franyo's."

Franyo is a filmmaker from what was once Yugoslavia. Tired of his family's estate being occupied by first the Nazis then the Commies, he built himself an airplane from a kit and flew across the Alps. He crashed it into a farmer's field in Germany, walked to the nearest coast, signed on as crew of a freighter, and worked his way across the pond to America. By the time I met him he owned a single-engine Apache airplane and a small but thriving film company. We hired him for most of the Penney projects. The formidable Iron Mike worked for him frequently. He also hired me as an assistant editor when I threw off the corporate traces. His support was about all that kept us afloat much of the time.

"When you getting back?" continued Stell.

Yep. Hookin' up. I can tell by her voice.
Good.

"Sunday night. Don't know how late."

I emerge from the bathroom and take the sandwich from Stella's out-stretched hand.

"Want some coffee?" she asks.

"I do," says a voice from above. Looking up, I see the pixie face of Claire poke out over the edge of the loft.

"Where's Corey?" I ask around my mouthful of scrambled eggs, bacon and sourdough toast. Butter drips down my chin and forearm. I reach into the little fridge for a beer, pop it open and wash down the succulent combination with a long satisfying pull. The little refrigerator is for the beer. The full-size box beside it is for everything else.

"Out picking up stuff for the shoot. He was goin' out as I came in," says Stella starting up another skillet of bacon.

Right on cue the front door slams open and Corey bangs his way through the hall bearing a large crate of fruit: apples, oranges, pears, plums, even a couple of pints of strawberries – this near the end of October!

"Geez, Louise. Abbondanza! What'd you have to pay for that?" I gasp.

"Nada. They just gave me a crate and said to pick out what I wanted from the reject boxes. I picked up three flats of eggs and four pounds of bacon from next door. Here. There's five dollars and eighty cents left over."

"Jerry will faint. I can't wait to hand him change. I don't think he really believed we could feed everyone for under five hundred bucks!"

"And without resorting to brown rice," chimes in Claire as she pounds down the stairs. Brown rice sustained us more frequently than we might have liked.

"Good morning," she says in Corey's direction in a decidedly cool tone.

What gives? She hasn't spoken to me at all.

"Anybody home?" rings out a melodic soprano from the still open front door.

It was Lilly, our Vampira look-alike from the second floor. Bounding across the studio, she holds aloft a freshly cleaned and pressed, decidedly shabby black velvet dress.

"Ta da! Funeral garb for the soon-to-be-departed," she tootles.

"Already departed," I correct. "We shot the suicide scene yesterday."

"Ooooo. Right. How'd it go?"

"She dazzled 'em with her footwork" says Corey, taking the dress from her and folding it neatly into the open suitcase waiting on the worktable.

"Now, don't forget to invite me to the premiere."

"Of course not. As soon as I find out which garage it's gonna be in I'll let you know."

"Should we invite the orange guy?" she snickers.

The only other resident of this strange building is a corpulent man who lives on the third floor. He has a crate of fresh carrots delivered to his door every day. The guys at Stracce Produce across the street told us about his standing order. They also informed us that carrots were good for more than your eyesight. It seems they are reputed to prolong an erection. The man was undeniably orange. Hair, skin, eyeballs – all bright orange.

"By all means. Maybe we can find out if his diet is working for him," I quip sardonically.

"Everything's packed." Corey announces as he hands me a detailed inventory. The contents of each box are neatly listed, and each box is carefully labeled. His loft over the editing room is a mare's nest, but his personal appearance and organizational skills are paragons of detailed elegance.

"The salads are in the fridge, and there are three bags of ice in the freezer. The turkey's iced down in the red cooler. We'll fill the other coolers just before you go. When is your ride due?" He finally takes a breath.

"Jerry said between 12:30 and 1," I reply, putting the lists carefully into my backpack. "I'm gonna go have a nice leisurely soak while I can," I announce to the room at large. "Who knows when I'll get another chance?"

I grab another beer and head for our acid-trip bathroom, sans the benefits of any psychotropic enhancements, of course. I'm on duty. (Beer doesn't count.)

Into the Woods

HARRY REAMS (of the twinkling eyes) and Marty (the friendly grip), cram the boxes of food, utensils, etc. into the spacious trunk of a sedate old Town Car. Our backpacks and my makeup kit fit on the floor of the back seat. I climb in and sit in the middle of the seat. A slight dark-haired girl reeking of a heavy floral scent sits scrunched behind very dark glasses on the right. Claire climbs in on the left. Harry skillfully maneuvers the ample car into the ever-present truck traffic. Corey stands waving from the door of our factory. I wave back. Claire does not.

"So what's up with you and Corey?" I ask.

"What do you mean?"

Claire didn't try to hide the fact that she was thoroughly pissed off.

"Why are you mad at him?" I press.

A long silence ensues.

Finally she turns to me and blurts, "OK. Not once since he came up here – I thought to see me – has he so much as kissed me on the cheek.

Much less curl up and listen to opera and fall asleep in my arms. For that matter, when have you ever curled up and listened to opera with me? You guys looked like you'd gotten it on, you know."

"Whew. Wow. What do I say? Are you jealous of him or me?"

"Both, damn it."

"I didn't even know you liked opera."

"I don't."

"Sweetie. I promise. The next time we listen to Manon, you will be in the middle. But we have to start with the last act. I always fall asleep before the end, and I would like to know how the damn thing comes out."

Claire can't quite keep a straight face. We're soon giggling. Marty leans over the seat and demands, "Come on, you guys. Share."

"S-s-s-s-sorry," I sputter apologetically, "you really had to be there."

We roar up the Westside Highway, a country-western station blaring. Not my first choice of music but at the moment it's the perfect up-beat accompaniment for this insane adventure. Fortified by my usual morning beer, I slump into a comfortable, semi-snooze.

"Da dee da da G eat a lot of peaches..." penetrates my groggy consciousness. The boys are having a great time singing along with the radio. Marty breaks off his harmony and leans over the seat. Head cocked, he addresses the quiet passenger to my right.

"So, how come you backed out of doing the Miss Jones part?"

Ah HAH! The mysterious lady on my right is the one originally cast as the heroine of this film. The story Jerry gave me was that she was having trouble with a wisdom tooth and only wanted to work one scene.

She wants to be my partner in the double fellatio number with Marc Stevens? A heavy-duty cock-sucking gig is the last thing I'd want to do with an impacted wisdom tooth, but what do I know?

"Waddaya, crazy?" she responds. "You think I want to end up like Linda Lovelace?"

"What? You mean, like, FAMOUS?" bellows Harry from the driver's seat. "*Deep Throat* made her a STAR!"

"Yeah — a fuckfilm star. You think I want that screwing up my career? I'm a serious actress, you know."

"Oh," says Marty. He and Harry resume their duet.

Late in the afternoon we pull up before a looming nineteenth-century barn-like structure. It stands in majestic isolation on a slight knoll. The last quarter of our trip had been through towering trees sporting vivid fall colors. The only sign of civilization seen for a half-hour or more, a small roadhouse tucked in amongst the abundant foliage. Now before us an expansive field of long amber grass stretches to thick woods on three sides. The place is a freakin' Norman Rockwell painting!

Crew members offload cable, crates, light stands, and all manner of mysterious bundles from the equipment truck and hump it all through gaping double doors to the dusky interior of this old cider mill.

There is nothing that thrills me more than watching grips handle their equipment. A scene in the Peter O'Toole film, *Stuntman*, comes to mind. A mustachioed grip with hair in a single braid down to his fanny pulls open the doors of a mammoth lighting truck with a muscle-rippling thwump. Now that's erotic.

The huge barn of a building was in the early stages of a remodel meant to turn it into a residence. The owners had run low on funds, and the work had halted a bit short of habitability. A single line of electricity powered a huge refrigerator in a partitioned-off corner. An extension cord ran from the lone outlet to a bulb dangling above a long table near a modern range. The only other resident light was a fixture over the basin in the small bathroom on the opposite side of the huge room. In it there was also a tub and toilet. (Whew!) That was about it for modern conveniences.

Jerry stands in the strip of light that streaks from the open doors across the concrete of the mill's expansive ground floor.

"Jo!" He shouts up a stairwell that leads to a large dark loft space above the rear half of the building. "Can you rig some lights so we can see what the hell we're doing?"

"We're getting the generator going now," comes the accented reply of Joaquin, the Brazilian bombshell. Not from the loft above, but from outside the rear of the building. "You'll have lights in ten minutes."

Peering around the corner of the giant barn, I see the Director of Photography (Lighting Designer, Cameraman, and second-in-command to our-director in his spare time) busy pouring gasoline into a huge generator the crew has just muscled into place on the far side of the building – the side you can't see from the road.

Entering the huge building, I spot Claire helping the boys load our gear into the kitchen area. I hurry over to help. Setting my duffel on the counter by the sink, I hold my breath and turn on the faucets.

"The water works!" I shout gratefully.

It's cold and sputters rust, but it's running. The propane stove, too, seems to be functioning, and there are several spare tanks of gas at the ready.

"Hallelujah!" I explode. "There is a God. I found a hot water heater! Anyone know how to light this thing?"

The work lights blink on. The sparse lamps poke only a small distance into the yawning dark that's fast filling up with the mysterious trappings of a film set.

"Get everything stowed and we'll go back down to that roadhouse for burgers. My treat," Jerry calls into the echoing vault.

No cooking tonight! Yay. More time to learn lines.

"Georgie," he turns to me, "you and Claire take the bedroom at the top of the stairs. The rest of you guys," he says to the crew, "grab space on the sets wherever you can find it."

"Where am I supposed to sleep?" demands the serious actress named Brandee-with-two-ee's. (That name doesn't appear in any of the film credits, but I swear that's what she told me.)

"There's a charming little single behind the kitchen for you, Madam. I have deposited your bags there for you." Harry simpers in imitation of an English butler as he brushes by with an armload of light stands.

"Here," says Marty, handing Brandee a large flashlight. "You'll need this."

"Where are Herman and I going to bunk?" asks Marc, holding up a carrying case not unlike that used for a cat. He has brought his pet boa!

"There's a bed up here just to the left at the top of the stairs," calls Harry back over his shoulder. "Stake your claim."

"You brought your snake." I plant a kiss on Marc's cheek and give Herman a scratch through the mesh of his case.

"I didn't want to leave him alone for a whole weekend. He's just a baby," explains Marc as he sets the case on the edge of one of two large double beds pushed against the far wall. He opens it and lifts the snake up into his arms.

55

I'm happy to see the writhing reptile again. He seems happy to see me, too. Marc hands him to me and I lie back beside the case and let Herman the boa wind his curious way about my various limbs.

"Be still my aging heart," exclaims Jerry, skidding to a halt beside us, hand clutching his chest. "You're a snake wrangler! Would you do a scene with it?"

"Herman?"

"That its name? Yeah."

"Depends on what you want us to do," I reply gingerly.

"Whatever you two kids feel like doing."

"Well, sure. I guess so, if it's cool with Marc. I don't know what he'll do, you know."

"Just what you're doing looks hot."

Herman's having a good time exploring the warmer areas of my anatomy.

"Except you might want to wear something a little sexier."

I give Jerry a withering do-you-think-I'm-stupid-or-something look then realize he's seriously joshing me.

"He gets the same as me," interjects Marc, forcefully: "one hundred a day and meals."

"I didn't pack any mice," I giggle. Not at my own wit. Herman was tickling.

"No problem," Marc says to me in a stage whisper. "He ate two days ago. I'm just yankin' Jerry's chain."

"Harry," calls Jerry to the figure disappearing up the stairs, "tell Joaquin we're going to shoot another scene in the brass bed set."

He turns back to Marc. "When's a good time to handle snakes?"

"Anytime. They mostly sleep unless they get too hot or too cold. Or hungry...grrrrrr," he growls mockingly.

"Tell him we'll shoot it right after the Teacher scene," Jerry shouts.

"Right," Harry calls back as he reaches the top of the stairs.

"Can you make your corset look different for another scene?" Jerry asks me.

"What if I wear just the black stockings?" I suggest.

"I love it."

"Where will it come in the final cut?" I ask.

"I don't know. Somewhere around the middle."

"OK. I'll go to a darker purple-pink nail polish and mauve shadow, or maybe the greens?" I muse, more or less to myself.

"Whatever," Jerry shrugs. "Come on guys. Let's go eat. I'm starving."

I wolf burger and fries, washing it down with iced tea, as I watch the action at the pool table. Claire's kicking ass. Jerry sits down next to me.

"Ready to head back?"

"How could you tell?" I ask from the side of my mouth.

"Your leg was still bouncing when the jukebox stopped."

The jukebox had not suffered from neglect throughout the evening. It was very loud.

"Well, I don't shoot pool and I don't want to drink tonight – that kind of puts me outside the wave, you know?"

"Yeah, I know how that is. Me too," says my director, placing his half-empty beer bottle on the table and grinning that mischievous grin that conveys, "OK, I'm busted. But how can you get mad at anyone as cute as this?"

"Harry's gonna make a run back to the set. Wanna go?"

I did. Claire didn't. Marc, Mr. Makeup Man, and a couple of the grips did. In the front seat, Harry and the grips reprised "...eat a lot of peaches" a capella. What it lacked in musical accuracy was well-compensated for by enthusiasm. Marc and Makeup Man got into a bitch-battle over real or imagined slights. I wasn't really paying attention. I dozed and went over the coming day's dialog in my head.

Propped up in the big double bed studying lines by flashlight, I hear an argument escalating below. Flashlight in hand, I make my way to the top of the stairs. Mr. Makeup and two grips are in a heated debate.

The crew's hard at work, setting up light stands and laying cable. Claire is in the kitchen stowing supplies.

Suddenly, Makeup Man slams his huge leather purse (there's no other way to describe it) down on the long sturdy table where some of the crew are loading film magazines.

"That's it. I quit." His squeal pierces the air like fingernails on a blackboard.

Heels clicking a fierce staccato on the concrete floor he swarms furiously the length of the large room. Skidding to a halt by a pay phone that hangs on the wall by the entrance, he feeds coins into it and shouts into the handset.

"Hello? Hel-LO? Operator? Get me a taxi."

We are in the middle of a freakin' forest, you understand. Everyone in earshot cracks up.

"I don't KNOW where I am," the irate artiste squeals into the phone. "It's some sort of old mill or something. It's near that awful honky tonk..."

To the room at large, "What's the name of that place?"

No one can stop laughing long enough to tell him – if anyone knows. I don't.

From my perch on the stairs I see Harry stride from the area beneath the loft. He is not laughing. He carries a big leather satchel, reminiscent of Gucci saddlebags, and the familiar gigantic makeup case. Without breaking stride, he picks up the odd-shaped black leather pouch, throws it over his shoulder and slams out the door beside the phone. Mr. Makeup Man goes screaming after him, leaving the handset dangling.

> Good thing I brought my old makeup kit along.
>
> Looks like I'm gonna be pretty much on my own. Suits me.

I head down the stairs. The overhead light in the kitchen makes the area an amber oasis. Claire is busy making room in the refrigerator for the perishables.

"That's everything we need to worry about tonight," she states. "You hungry?"

"Not really. I'd love a plum, though." She hands me one from the bowl in the refrigerator then closes the door. The plum is cold and sweet.

"It's freezing up there," says Marc as he rounds the corner into the kitchen area. "Is there anything I can put some hot water in for Herman?"

"Here." I pick up a jumbo-sized jar. "I'll put these pickles in a plastic bag and we can fill this up."

Claire fires up the propane stove and puts a kettle of water on to heat.

The kitchen, though primitive, is well-appointed. There are plenty of pots and pans and a good supply of flatware. Mismatched but attractive dishes are neatly stacked in the many open shelves that ring the work area.

As soon as Herman's hot water bottle is handed off to Marc, we say our goodnights and head up the stairs. Dousing the kerosene lamp, we throw off our clothes and hop into bed. This is somewhat like diving into a snow bank. Snuggling and shaking, we eventually get warm enough to fall asleep.

Sometime later a gentle nudge between my legs wakes me.

"Oh, Honey. Please. No. I don't want to get into anything tonight," I mumble, turning my back to Claire's side of the bed.

"Huh?" says Claire. "I'm not touching you."

Then who is?

I grab the flashlight and lift the covers. A small gray and brown beaded head with soft shiny eyes rests happily on top of my bush.

Evidently when the hot water bottle cooled off, Herman decided to find a warmer spot. I scoop him up and carry him back to his case beside Marc's bed. Marc doesn't stir. I slip the complacent serpent into his quarters and snap the pressure catch on the front firmly into place.

The big, saggy, double bed is still warm and sleep quickly returns.

How much later, I don't know, but again, a gentle nudge wakes me – this time in my right armpit – the one away from Claire. I don't even bother with the flashlight.

"OK, kid. Have it your way," I murmur, wiggling into a more comfortable position.

"Humph?" says Claire.

"He's back," I explain.

"Who?"

"Herman."

"The damn snake?" she squeals.

"Well, what the hell," I say. "We're gonna do a sex scene together tomorrow; might as well get acquainted."

Claire throws back the covers, gets up, and stalks off, presumably to sleep elsewhere.

Oh Geez.

Now she's jealous of the damn snake.

That thought slithered its way through my head, but it didn't keep me awake for very long.

Ready For My Closeup, Mr. D

"OK, BIG GUY, back to your own bed."

The snake snoozing contentedly between my legs barely stirs when I gather him up in my arms and head for Marc's bed. This time I push down all four pressure latches on his carrying case.

The floor is freezing and it's still pitch-black night, but every rooster in the neighborhood is summoning the dawn. I pad hurriedly back to the bedroom. My watch on the night table says it's just coming up to five. I throw on my jeans and every shirt, sweater and pair of socks I can find. The bobbing beam of the flashlight guides me down the stairs and into the kitchen area.

Some clever soul has fashioned a conical shade out of foil for the bulb dangling overhead. A nice bright puddle of light hits the big work table when I pull the cord. Faint stirrings begin to rustle through the quiet of the cavernous hall.

It takes a while for the water to run from rusty brown to clear and pure. When it does, I fill the 40-cup coffee maker, add the grounds and plug 'er in. A friendly light winks a red hello. Merry bloops and a gripping aroma fill the area with a sense of warmth that is not entirely justified.

The propane stove fires right up. Soon, strips of bacon are sizzling on the grill. Little pig-link sausages begin to brown in two big iron skillets. I'm vigorously beating hell out of about a dozen eggs in a big crockery bowl when Claire comes around the corner wrapped in a blanket. All she needs is a headband and a feather.

"I'm goin' upstairs and get into more clothes," she shivers, scooping up the big flashlight from the table. "I'll be right back."

"Don't trip over anything," I call to her retreating form. There's equipment stacked all over the place.

"Good morning." A polite baritone rumbles from the gloom beyond my private fishbowl. I can't quite place the voice but it's familiar.

"Is that coffee up for grabs?" The owner moves into the light. It's the actor that was in Jerry's office. The one I read the scene with.

"Hey. Good morning. You bet. There're some mugs up in that cabinet above the sink. Would you mind bringing a few over to the table?"

"Sure. Where are the spoons? Never mind. I found 'em."

"Didn't see you at the bar last night."

"I didn't get in until after you guys left. I helped myself to some of your beer," he says apologetically.

"That's what it's there for," I assure him. "You drove up alone?"

"Yeah. Took me a while to find the place."

"How'd you get in?"

"The door was unlocked. I'm glad you left the light on in the kitchen. I couldn't find any others."

"There aren't any. Except in the bathroom."

I finish beating up the eggs and start in on the pancake mix.

"You're gonna wear yourself out. Let me give you a hand with that." He takes the big bowl out of my hands.

"I understand you're doing the Miss Jones part?"

"Yeah. Ain't that a hoot? And it's all your fault you know." I start putting slices of bread on a cookie sheet. No toaster.

"My fault?"

"Yeah. After you left the office, Jerry asked me to do the part. I guess because of the reading we did. But, that's OK. I forgive you."

Claire bounds back into the work area and pulls open the refrigerator door.

"Shall I set the juices out on the table?"

"Please."

The work lights come on with an audible shock. The guys file in and out of the one-and-only bathroom and parade by the coffee pot in a steady stream of soft mumbles.

Mr. Clemons pitches right in and the three of us feed the troops in brisk precision. About halfway through the cleanup, Mr. D arrives and helps himself to coffee. Claire continues the cleanup as Mr. Clemons and I join our director at the big table.

"We'll shoot your scenes in the office set first," he says. "Got your lines down?"

"Pretty much so," I lie. "Shall we run them? My script's upstairs…" I start to rise from the bench.

"No. That's OK. Finish your breakfast. We'll see how it goes when we block."

Jerry seems a bit under the weather.

"Soon as you're ready, go get in makeup. Joaquin says we'll be ready to shoot in about a half hour."

"Shall I head for the set, or would I just be in the way at this point?" asks Mr. Clemons.

"Go on in. But be careful. You might end up hauling cable. Do you want any makeup?"

"Not unless you insist on it."

"You look fine to me."

"Good."

The crew bustles about lighting the brass bed set in the far end of the big loft area. The small bedroom that Claire and I share is at the front end near the stairs. All my costumes and makeup are stashed there. I enter and assess the situation.

There's not much light and no place to lay out any makeup. The bathroom downstairs has only that very small bulb over the sink, and no work surface to speak of either. Hmmmm.

Tacklebox makeup kit in hand, I tuck a mirror that is propped against the wall on top of the chest of drawers under my arm and huff my way to the set. I prop the mirror against some boxes and ask the guys to put some lights around it. They rig a very respectable makeup room in a trice.

There's no pancake in my kit the exact shade of the stuff I wore for the suicide scene. Yes, I took notes. Good thing, since Mr. Makeup Man seems to be out of the picture. An undercoat of good old clown white adjusts my Max Factor Ivory enough to get by. Hair goes back in a priggish bun. Black stockings, sensible shoes, white lace collar slapped in place around the neckline of the funky black dress, and I'm ready for prime time.

When I reach the set, I can see Mr. Clemons (Abaca) is already in place seated regally behind a mammoth desk. Light floods the floor-to-ceiling windows behind him creating an aura around his almost obscured features. The effect is chilling.

"Now light the match and stare into the flame a while before you light the cigarette," murmurs Jerry to the ominous Mr. Abaca. "That's it. A bit longer. Good. Get that Jo?"

"Yeah. Let's do it one more time. I want to start in tight on the flame and pull back."

> They're already shooting! We haven't even read through the scene, much less blocked or rehearsed ANYTHING.
>
> Relax. They're just getting cutaways.

"Ah, Georgie. Let's see you." Jerry takes my hand and leads me toward the chair in front of the massive desk. He scrutinizes my dress and makeup, makes a slight adjustment to the lace collar and says, "Well, you certainly do look like a spinster."

"Thanks."

> That WAS the idea.
>
> Why else would I slick my scanty locks back into this hideous bun?

"We want you to walk into the scene from behind camera and sit here."
He indicates the chair. "What's her first line?" he asks Harry, who hovers
beside the camera, script in hand.

"Abaca says, 'Please be seated.' Then she says 'Thank you' and sits,"
reads Harry.

"OK. Let's just walk it through and see how it goes," says Jerry. "When
he gets to the line... lemme see the script." He reaches back to Harry who
puts the stapled pages in his hand. "...when he says '...through that door...'
Mr. Abaca, you point to that area behind her. OK? No, more that way.
Good. Georgie, you look back over your shoulder and hold it till I say cut.
OK?"

I nod and move behind camera to wait for Jerry's cue.

"Action."

We zip through the entire scene non-stop. Mr. Clemons is totally pre-
pared. I'm fighting for almost every freakin' line!

> Don't worry about it. You'll have it down
> by the time they shoot.

Jerry calls cut and I start to get up.

"No. Stay there," he says. "We're gonna get the closeups, now. Let's do
Abaca first from about here," he moves into the set and stands near where I
hover half out of the chair.

> Did they just shoot that? I thought
> Joaquin was just checking lights. The
> freakin' camera was rolling? This is
> terrible. I was terrible.

> Take it easy. Breathe. It's a fuckfilm, for
> pity sake. No one you know will ever see
> it. Press on.

And press on we did. It takes about a half hour to shoot all of Abaca's lines
from my POV (point of view), and another to reverse and get mine, and
that's fucking it! At least I had my lines down for the closeups.

"Do you want to do anything to your makeup for the next scene?"
Jerry asks.

In the second scene in Abaca's office, this dispatcher to Hell tells Justine her time is up and sends her to her destiny. It's after her sojourn through every lustful possibility of the mortal coil.

Of course I need to redo my makeup! Not only that, I need time to lock the lines and remember where her head is and... oh, to hell with it.

"Can you gimme a half hour?" I ask.

"Sure. Want me to send you up some coffee or anything?" asks my director solicitously.

"I'll take some up to her," offers Mr. Abaca.

Good thinking, Abaca. We can run lines.

The makeup for the second office scene must match the film's last scene wherein Miss Jones encounters a mysterious denizen of the lower depths (played by Mr. Damiano himself). Now, that's a scene I'm looking forward to shooting. I keep careful notes. Strangely, there's no continuity person working the shoot. No Polaroid pictures to reference when it comes time to repeat the look. It's a fairly simple one, though. Just your basic debauched whore. Piece of cake, as we say in the film trade.

The scene goes well. With the lines down, I can wallow in Miss Jones' fear. Delicious. Master, closeups, sweeping cutaway of the set: badda bing!

"Cut. That was perfect." Jerry hurries over from his post behind the camera.

"How long do you need for your meet-the-teacher makeup?" he asks checking his watch.

The crew is already breaking down the lights and moving them and the camera to the set upstairs.

"Can I have an hour for this one?" I plead.

I've got to scrub down to a clean palette, set my hair, change nails: the works. This will be Miss Jones' transformation from frump to floozy.

"Sure," answers Mr. D "You're wearing the corset with that slinky satin robe thing over it, right? Can you do something with your hair? Fluff it up or something?"

"Trust me."

Harry sprawls in a throne-like chair wearing an elegant silk dressing gown that casually exposes most of his magnificent manhood. He could not have looked more at ease. I walk toward him with my best Harlow slink. He looks me up and down with an expression somewhere between disdain and hunger. I hit my mark and deliver my first line with all the aplomb of a high-school senior auditioning for the school play. We zip through the sparse dialog without a glitch. I know the drill now. One take and unless something falls over, it's on to the next shot – one I've been dreading. The Teacher (Harry) is to insert a dimpled rubber butt plug in my anus.

I steel myself to deal with it, no matter how much it hurts.

(Surprisingly, it didn't hurt at all. In fact, after the initial unfamiliar sensation, I barely felt it. I might have forgotten it was there if Jerry had not called it into play later in the scene. We'll get to that.)

Next shot: Harry rises from his throne, crosses to the big brass bed, throws off his silk dressing gown, and sprawls regally upon the elaborate pillows. He gestures imperiously for me to join him, which I do – carefully holding butt plug in place as I cross. I sure as hell didn't want the silly thing to pop out.

My next assignment, Jerry explains, is to fall in love with Harry's cock and inspire its rise to glory. I'm doing my best when Jerry halts the action and leans his head in close to mine.

"I can't photograph your thoughts. I need dialogue. Talk to him about his cock. Better yet, talk to the cock. Call it every name you can think of and make it sound like you just found heaven. Can you do that for me?"

Oh. OK.

I nod.

Lavishing every name for the male appendage I've ever heard upon the member in question, I then make up a few new ones. Once said member is ready for its close-up, Jerry asks me to straddle Harry and make the insertion myself – facing the camera. This suits me just fine. I can play right into the lens (and right into Joaquin's eyeball).

Miss Jones rides the beast with joy and abandon. I could feel Joaquin's eye on me and that's all it took to keep me wet and wild. OK. That and the camera.

"That's great." Jerry hisses. "Now, tell him to take that thing out of your ass."

"Take that thing out of my ass," I breathlessly command, in my best Garbo.

"Tell him to give it to you."

"Give it to me," I continue in a frenzy of passion. I reach behind me as I feel Harry pull the little plug out of my butt. He places its outer rim carefully in my outstretched fingers. I bring it around to the front of my still pumping torso.

"Now suck on it."

WHOA!

I hold out the nasty little bugger by its edge. "Either I can get up and go wash it or hold position while someone else does."

"Don't we have a backup of this thing?" calls Jerry to the crew at large.

"Flyin' in," comes the predictable reply.

"Can you go back to where you tell him to take it out..." begins Joaquin.

"Yeah. Yeah. Here." I hand the fresh replacement for the little rubber thingy to Harry. "I'll reach back for it on cue. OK? And don't you dare spit on it."

He knows I'm joking and laughs. It breaks the tension. It feels kind of good, too. I'm still impaled on his magnificent manhood remember.

After the dimpled nipple sucking is played to the hilt (literally) Jerry says, "OK. That's enough of that. Let's get to the anal stuff. You got any particular position you like for that?"

The solicitous inquiry is directed at me!

Now, about anal sex...I was a dancer. Most of my best friends were gay. I never actually probed for information, but I was all ears when their banter got specific about their sexual encounters. I confess, the idea of anal sex had always titillated my libido. This, however, would be my first actual go at it.

The big camera is repositioned to catch the action from the reverse angle. The hand-held that covered the butt plug extraction is still in place for extra coverage.

"Lie on your side and put your leg up a bit," Harry whispers to me quietly. He keeps his erection at its peak with slow practiced strokes. I quickly comply.

"I won't put it in until I'm real close. You won't have to put up with it for too long," he whispers. "You OK?"

"I'm fine. Go for it." I whisper back

He puts his hand on the small of my back. I feel his fingers slip around my hipbone. His touch is gentle and reassuring. I can't see it, but from the feel of his cock against my cheeks, I bet you could bounce a ping pong ball off of it. I can also feel that it is well lubricated. He holds it right against that dark secret ring and presses slowly, slowly, but firmly. Ta da! It's in.

I stiffen at the sharp pain that flashes through me like a white hot light. Harry immediately holds absolutely still. I will myself to relax. When I do, the pain melts away.

It crosses my mind that taking it up the ass is much more erotic as a fantasy than when actually doing it. Miss Jones, however, gets into it.

Harry carefully resumes the business at hand. True to his word, he's in, out, and off — ejaculating thick hot semen all over my ample backside — before I have time to think very much about it.

Miss Jones, however, is left furiously aroused and rather unfulfilled. The slut's so wet she could fuck a donkey.

Jerry calls, "Cut." I fall forward into the rumpled bedding and collapse in shuddering spasms. I hold my hands against my clit and will it to calm down.

"Save the lights," calls the AD from somewhere beyond the camera

"You OK?" Harry speaks softly into my ear as he gently pats my fanny.

"Fine," I squeak, regaining my composure and rising to my knees.

"You're a fuckin' natural," declares Mr. D taking my head between his hands and kissing me right on the very lips that had so recently been around Harry's cock. (That thought never crossed his mind, I'm sure. If there was one thing Gerard was not, it was bi.)

"Now get out of that corset and go fix us some lunch." He slaps me playfully on my bare butt as I bounce off the bed and pick up my peignoir.

"Marty," continues Jerry, "I want to get the cocksucking scene with Marc next. Nice scene, Harry. When you get dressed, go wake up Brandee and tell her we'll need her right after lunch."

Not Just Another Pretty Cock

BY THE TIME I GET TO THE KITCHEN Claire has everything set up for lunch. The crew straggles in ATP (as time permits). Some sit at the long table, some fix plates and disappear back to their chores.

"What do you want me in for the next scene?" I ask my director as he sits down to his sandwich.

"Doesn't really matter," he mumbles around a mouthful. "We won't see anything but your face. You can wear that."

He nods at the comfy wrapper I threw on after my quick shower in our one-and-only bathroom. There was one of those old-fashioned hoses with a showerhead on the end attached to the faucet in the tub. The guys had rigged a hook out of coat hangers nailed to the wall so you could get yourself under it in installments.

"Shall I wear the apron?"

"Only if you take off the wrapper," he replies with a twinkle in his eye. Jerry almost always had a twinkle in his eye.

"What do you want me in?" asks Brandee as she joins us at the table.

"Nothing," says Jerry. "I want to immortalize these fabulous tits in all their natural glory." He playfully buries his face in her ample bosom.

She pushes him away, not so playfully. "Then don't bruise 'em," she says. "I'd like some scrambled eggs and bacon." She tosses the order over her shoulder at Claire who is busy at the sink.

I catch Claire's arch look. She, however, says not word one but pulls eggs and bacon from the fridge and efficiently completes the task. She doesn't even bang the plate down.

I look at the script. I can't remember just where in the sequence of scenes this upcoming double fellatio feat takes place. Ah. It's the third adventure to follow The Teacher's introduction of Miss Jones to the joys of lust. OK. Aqua shadow, medium lashes, dark red nails.

"You OK with the cleanup by yourself?" I ask Claire.

"Sure. Go immortalize your tits." It isn't said sarcastically. Claire is actually in a very good mood. She seems to have gotten with the program.

"Is Joaquin gonna get some lunch?" I ask Jerry.

"Fix him a ham sandwich and put some of that potato salad on a plate. I'll take it up to him," he replies.

"That's OK. I'll take it up." And I do.

While Joaquin has his lunch, I get into my makeup and nails. Marc sidles over to where I sit cross-legged on the floor before my makeshift makeup table. We gossip and giggle like schoolgirls. Jerry soon arrives with the buxom Brandee and summons us to the set.

Marc is instructed to just lie back and enjoy himself. Miss Brandee and I are asked to sit on either side of his hip area. Marc is already beginning to tumesce as we take our places.

"Save it for the camera, Big Guy," suggests Joaquin, jocularly.

"You worry about my key light. I'll take care of my hard-on." They chuckle amiably. Marc and Joaquin seem to have a strong and friendly bond.

"Want me to fluff?" asks Brandee.

"No, thanks," says Marc, even though the question was directed at Jerry. "I can control it better myself."

I'm in absolute awe of the off-hand manner of these pros.

"Now girls," begins our director, "we'll start shooting when Marc is good and hard. I want you two to be like a couple of two-year-olds sharing an ice-cream cone. Yank it away from each other. Fight for it. Compete for who gets the money shot. OK?"

"Will there be a prize?" asks Brandee.

> My gawd. The girl has a sense of humor —
> I think.

"You all set?" Jerry calls back to Joaquin, who is enthusiastically finishing up his lunch.

"This is the best potato salad I ever ate! Did you make this?" he asks in my direction.

"It's Southern style," I explain. "Eggs, pickles, pimiento, lots of onion, mustard and a dash of Tabasco sauce. That's the secret ingredient."

"I love it. Is there more?"

> Oh my stars and garters. As if I weren't
> smitten enough, he likes my freakin'
> potato salad!

"There was when I came upstairs. Send word down to Claire to save you some," I suggest.

"I'm about ready, you guys," calls Marc from his sultanic repose.

"Flyin' in," says Joaquin. He positions himself behind the camera. "Rolling."

"Speed," sings out the soundman.

"Oooooo-kay — and — action," says the director — just like Otto Preminger. "Lot's of noise. OK girls?"

We give it our all. Occasionally Jerry leans in with a suggestion, but mostly he leaves us on our own to marvel at the phenomenon that wobbles before us. We stroke it, nibble at it, suck it like it's a caramel Sugar Daddy. The kind you used to get at the movies that got longer and longer the longer you sucked it.

"Jerry," calls Marc, in a tense whisper.

"Yeah," answers the director, moving up to where Marc's head is cushioned against the brass headboard.

"I'm close enough to go anytime. Don't you want to get any cutaways — like of my face?!"

"We can pick that up later. Let 'er rip."

"OK. About 15 seconds," says Marc.

(I didn't have a stopwatch handy, but I'll bet he was within two seconds of his estimate.)

"That's it, girls. Lap that stuff up. Brandee – drip some onto Georgie's tongue. Good. Now, George, try to get some more out of it. Suck hard. Let it dribble out of your mouth so we see it. Good. Now girls, you two kiss like you really mean it, OK?"

"Aaaaaaand cut. Set up for the snake thing as quick as you can."

"Save the lights," calls Marty. They pop off all around us, leaving us in chilly semi-darkness.

"Hey," says Marc, sitting bolt upright, "don't I get a closeup?"

"We were as tight on that thing of yours as we could get," says Joaquin quite seriously.

"Well, excuse me. I thought a reaction shot of my face might lend a bit of authenticity, you know. That could have been a mechanized dildo for all anyone could tell. To you, I'm just another pretty cock, is that it?"

Jerry, seeing no coin in continuing the conversation, I suppose, moves off into a tight conference with Joaquin and Marty behind the camera.

Marc grabs his towel and heads toward the stairs. I'm close behind.

He turns back to me and asks, "You want to get in the bathroom first?"

"You go ahead. I'll brush my teeth in the kitchen."

"Thanks. I want to let Herman have a little swim in the tub before his big scene. Those lights get damned hot."

Claire has the kitchen all cleaned up from the lunch rush and is setting out afternoon snacks – chips, cookies, fruit, cheese 'n' crackers, olives, pickles, candy and stuff   I head for the sink, toothbrush and mouthwash in hand.

"Is anybody going to make a run for ice anytime soon?" she asks.

"Ask one of the guys," I suggest. She departs to do so.

The turkey is already in the oven. The stuffing that wouldn't fit inside it stands by in a large baking dish. It will join the bird for the last half-hour before dinnertime. There's not much else to do at this point.

I finish a vigorous mouth rinsing and head for the stairs. A shriek from the bathroom halts me in my tracks.

Brandee comes stumbling out of the bathroom door with her pants around her knees.

"That damn snake is in the TUB!" she screams. "I'm sitting there and this monster's head comes right up over the edge of the tub. This close to me." She indicates the short distance with her hands, which frees her pants to continue their downward plunge. She grabs for them.

"This close!" She feels compeled to repeat. Unable to do so without demonstrating the close proximity with her hands, the pants again head for the border. She makes a final grab for them. "I have never, ever," she shrieks, "been on a shoot as – as – PRIMITIVE as this."

She exits though the gaggle of grips gathered in the center of the room – still hauling futilely at her pants. No one makes a sound.

"Do you want him wet or dry?" Marc dangles a dripping Herman over a towel in his lap.

"Wet's sexy," muses Jerry.

"Well. It will keep him cooler under the lights," says Marc.

"Maybe we should put Vaseline all over him," suggests the director.

"I don't think so," I reply emphatically.

"Why not?"

"Would you want someone to put Vaseline all over you?" I ask.

"It would depend on the circumstances," replies the facile Gerard with seeming sincerity.

"Trust me. No Vaseline."

"It's your scene, Baby," he smiles. "Just make me wanna grab my python."

Gawd, the man had a way with words.

When we're set to roll, Marc places Herman on my bare tummy. I grasp him gently just behind his head. He flicks me a happy "hello" with his tongue, then stretches out and slides his tail down into my crotch. It flicks lightly back and forth across my clit.

I swear, I am not making this up.

That scene was the hottest of the film for my twisted libido. Really. I almost came. OK. Here it comes. The big confession. At this point in my life I had rarely experienced the full-throttle vaginal climax of literary repute. Oh, I have had lots of clitoral climaxes and am genuinely aroused and wet when I fuck – on or off camera. But for all the sexual exploration throughout my life, that plunge over the falls had eluded me except when flying solo

– without interruption – or observation. I'd about resigned myself to being a clinical nymphomaniac like Miss Jones: doomed to experience everything but the Big O. One never loses hope, though, and the light tickling of Herman's length slithering over my stomach and down into my crotch was maddeningly erotic.

With no dialogue to record, Jerry and Joaquin are free to direct and suggest action as we shoot. Making the Brazilian moan was my goal in life. But, other than trading tongue flicks and gently persuading the boa to stick his head in my mouth, there isn't much we can do. Joaquin signales to Jerry that he's got it covered and Jerry just nods. He doesn't even say "cut."

I hand Herman to Marc. Jerry walks solemnly over and sits down on the bed beside me.

"Now, this next scene," he begins in a tone that says he is about to explain the meaning of the whole damn film – if not life itself, "is the scene where Claire gives you an oil massage and then fucks your brains out."

I check my script. Right. The scene with Claire follows the deflowering by The Teacher. Perhaps the oil rub is to soothe away the aches left by the hard lessons just learned?

I strip back down to the "no makeup" look and add a bit of dark mauve shadow and natural nail polish. Oh yes, and a little mascara. No mention of costume had been made. It seemed logical to me that I should be nude. Who gets dressed for a massage? I pull off my black stockings, brush hell out of my snarled hair, slip into my slippers, wrap my wrapper about the bod, and head back down to the set.

Claire is busy basting the turkey. She has put on makeup for our scene and looks gorgeous. The crew is busy spreading a huge, clear plastic drop cloth over the tops of the two big beds that have been pushed together in the copious space of the main floor.

"Jerry, I can't shoot them on top of that. It's like a mirror," complains Joaquin from behind his lens.

"Well, we can't drip oil all over these beds," states Harry.

"Marty, see what happens if you scrunch it up," suggests Joaquin. The Assistant DP crawls up onto the middle area of the expanse and begins to do as asked. "This might work. Jerry, come take a look."

Jerry climbs up onto the elevated camera rig and peers through the lens. Marty begins posing in outrageous imitation of a horny fornacatrix. It cracks everyone up.

"Yeah, that looks great," announces the director. "Everybody. On the bed and scrunch." All able bodies comply. Much levity ensues.

"Where do you want me?" asks Harry, poised halfway down the stairs in the silk dressing gown and slippers he had worn in our first scene.

"Stand by right there until Joaquin cues you to get into the action," says Jerry.

"Standing by," replies the veteran sex actor.

"You ladies ready?" continues our director with a decided leer. He walks over to where Claire and I stand by the beds. "Here's what I need you to do. Georgie you'll already be on the bed, looking used up and exhausted. You can do used up and exhausted, right?" he asks me.

"After the day I've had?" I respond with exaggerated gravitas.

"Claire, you come down the stairs. That slinky satin thing looks good on you." He playfully turns her this way and that. Clearly, she's delighted by the attention.

"Carry this little bowl of oil in your hands like a sacrifice or something. Climb up on the bed where Georgie will be doing used up and exhausted. Dip your hands in the oil and let it drip back in the bowl so we can see that it's oil. Then drip a bit on George and start rubbing it in."

"Where?" asks Claire.

"Start with the tits. Give us about three or four minutes of erotic massage then get personal. You know?"

"She knows," I answer. Jerry chuckles.

"Ready Jo?" he calls back over his shoulder to the cameraman.

"Gimme ten," responds Joaquin. He continues directing the crew as to where to set lights, reflectors, gobos (cutout sheets that cast patterns), masks, and so forth.

"We're not shooting sound, so don't say anything unless you have to, OK?" Jerry instructs us.

Fine with me. I was fresh out of steamy dialogue.

"Can we have George in, now?" calls Joaquin from behind the camera.

"Flyin' in," I cry and do.

The crumpled plastic was cold, but warmed quickly under me.

"Move up a bit more and a little to your right," requests Joaquin. The camera is set quite high up, shooting down upon the scene.

"Can you angle your legs more to the left?"

I do.

"OK, Jerry, I'm ready." Jerry climbs up and looks through the lens.

"I'm gettin' little kicks from that area near the corner," he points and looks to Joaquin for a solution.

Joaquin moves to one of the light stands and adjusts it downward a bit. "How's that?"

"Got it. Come look." Jerry climbs down from his perch behind the lens.

"Yeah. Good." Joaquin concurs. "OK. Let's shoot it."

As vividly as I can recall every shot done with Herman-the-boa that day, when I try to recall the sequence of events once Claire and I started our scene, it all just runs together.

Because it was being shot without sound, Joaquin was able to talk us through what he wanted to see. Claire was fucking me, but I was fucking Joaquin.

Claire ran through her repertory then began to invent new ways to expose, stretch, fondle and fiddle with every fold of flesh my anatomy had to offer.

After Claire's expert tongue brought me to about my third clitoral climax, I lay limp and panting. The set was absolutely silent.

Then Joaquin's soft voice quietly announced, "Out of film."

"We got it, Jerry," he calls over his shoulder. "We're in the wrong set, guys," he continues to the crew. This is the insider way of saying time to move to the next set. Very Hollywood.

"Hey! What about me?" Harry stands midway down the stairs, hardon in hand.

"Oh, Lord. I'm sorry," says Joaquin with true remorse. "I was so busy watching the girls, I simply forgot you were there."

"Jerry? What do you want to do? Should I load a fresh magazine?"

"Naw. It's fine. Leave it like it is. Sorry, Harry. You want some help with that thing?" Jerry laughs.

"What do I care?" shrugs Harry. "I get paid the same, in or out, up or down. Right, Jer?"

Jerry and the crew chuckle appropriately.

You could tell he did care, though.

Marc sidled up to where I stood beside the bed and chortled in my ear, "Now I don't feel so bad about being just another pretty cock. At least I didn't get left with an unused stiffy in my hand."

Jerry did get – and used – a very good close up of Marc's unmistakable kisser, but never told him about it. When it filled the screen at the New York premier, Marc nearly hurt himself smiling.

Water Sports

"WELL, BACK TO WORK." I help Claire up from the bed. "You want the bathtub first?"

"Why don't we double up," she replies, still in her seductive mode.

"Frankly, my dear, I need a rest. You go ahead."

I wipe as much of the oil off my body with a towel as I can, throw on my handy-dandy wrapper, slip into my shoes and head upstairs.

Nails go into their little box. (I didn't expect there would be any re-takes of any of the scenes in this film, but I filed everything carefully, just as if it were a real movie.) That done, I grab my jeans and a sweatshirt and head back downstairs to await my turn in the tub.

While I get the last residue of oil off my bod and out of my hair, Claire puts the finishing touches to dinner. Cranberry sauce, green salad, butter, rolls, green beans, cremed onions, candied yams, mashed potatoes, and loads of gravy are ferried from kitchen to table by all crew members not busy wrapping equipment. It looks like a scene from *Snow White*.

"Hey, you know? This is like a Thanksgiving dinner where all the relatives actually get along," proclaims Harry, raising a beer in salute.

Jerry carves.

The crew lingers over coffee – and yes – cigars! I stand at the sink doing dishes. Jerry slides in beside me and whispers, "You gonna be alright to shoot this last scene tonight? We can reschedule."

"No, I'm fine." I assure him.

> I know I've got another scene to shoot, for pity sake. Why do you think I ate practically nothing?

> And, oh boy, what a scene! You're gonna have to fish pretty deep into some weird corners of your psyche for this one, Kiddo.

Joaquin balances precariously: one foot on the tub, the other on the small hand basin. Marty has his hands anchored firmly on the cameraman's svelte hips to steady him. (Lucky Marty.) There are light stands in every available space; lights bounce off every wall.

Steamy water spurts from the hose attached to the faucet. The showerhead has been removed. Jerry has asked that I insert the hose into each of my orifices in turn. That would be a bit difficult with the four-inch wide spray nozzle in place.

The tub is about half full. I test the water with my toe. Almost too hot – just the way I like it. It takes me a while to get submerged.

"Georgie, you look so hot," says Joachin from behind the camera. I can tell by the way he says it, that he means I look sexy.

"Well, I am." My tone tells him I mean I'm about to melt. "Let's do this."

"Rolling."

Joachin handheld the camera for the entire scene, which, fortunately, didn't take very long. Jerry called for each action he wanted from outside the door. There was no room for him inside the teeny bathroom.

It was, again, just me and the camera as I poked the spurting hose into this, that, and the other hole. Well, not my ears. I was very careful not to get water in my ears. It's a bitch to get out. I wear ear plugs when I swim.

Miss Jones plunged into her frenzy of erotic ecstasy. The jet of warm water against her clit started her off, and she kept that happy thought going with one hand as she almost drowned herself letting the water rush through her open mouth. Then, of course, came insertion into the vagina from several angles, and eventually the ultimate enema shot.

We took a break after that one.

There's evidently a certain element in the porn demographic that gets off on that sort of thing. Jerry called it water sports. I've also heard that term used to refer to the practice of pissing on and being pissed upon – a rather more exotic area of erotica than I had ever encountered in real life. In one film I did later (*Confessions of a Male Chauvinist Pig*) my husband spurts beer over me to simulate his pissing on me. I smelled like a cheap dive for a week. Gave my hair a lot of good body, though.

After a few moments of blissful solitude, I let the gang know I'm ready for my closeups.

Joaquin leans against the basin and has me reprise the scene for the tight shots. After that I again relax in privacy until a light knock on the door is followed by Claire's voice.

"You OK? Whadda ya want on your..."

"All dark, salt and pepper, mayo, lettuce, and a dollop of cranberry sauce."

"Right."

"And a beer."

I'd earned it. Besides, Jerry said breakfast wouldn't be until eight. I could sleep in!

The scene in Hell is scheduled for the morning. There's no sex, so it should go quickly. Well, I jerk off, but that doesn't count as sex because you don't have to worry about getting a come shot.

Rick Livermore, my "son" in the witchcraft film is due to arrive about noon. He and Marc will make a sandwich of me in the afternoon: one on top, one underneath, me as the filling. That will be another first for me.

Propped in bed, I munch a perfect turkey sandwich and work on my lines for the scene in Hell. My dialog runs on and on and on. Unfortunately, I can't wing it. Jerry is playing the Lost Soul – the only other occupant of the room with no windows – I have to be letter perfect. I mean, after all, he wrote the thing. Claire's been sitting at the foot of the bed cuing me.

"OK. That's it. I can't keep my eyes open." I set my empty sandwich plate aside and down the last of my nice icy beer.

"Here." Claire hands me the script pages and flashlight. I set them beside the plate and empty beer can and blow out the lamp.

"That was some scene we did, huh Keed?" I murmur into the top of Claire's head as she curls into her familiar position: leg thrown over my hips, arm across my middle.

"Either you're a pretty good actress, or you're beginning to get the hang of this lesbian thing," she mumbles against my arm.

"I'm not gonna touch that. At least not now. I'm beat."

"Me, too. G'night."

About a half hour later, I feel the faintest pressure at the foot of the bed. Herman the night stalker is back. He works his way up under the covers until his head rests on my shoulder. The rest of him coils in my armpit

"Well, where have you been all evening?" I whisper. He wasn't talkin'.

I shift position slightly, to ease out from under Claire's leg. Herman takes that as his cue to retreat to his favorite spot – my crotch.

Claire doesn't stir.

Sartre and Sandwiches

JERRY LEADS ME under the set lights and peers intently at my face.

"Oh my gawd. You look awful!"

I'm thrilled. I'd spent over an hour on my makeup.

"Thanks. Wanna run lines?" I ask eagerly, script in hand.

"Just gimme a minute to get the camera lined up," he mumbles around an artful assemblage of lox, tomato and bagel. He then turns to consult with Joaquin.

I feel a filmed rehearsal coming on. Quickly, I skim through the scene one last time, hand my script to one of the ever-present production assistants, cross my mental fingers and take my place off camera.

"How does this look?" Jerry sits on the floor with his back against the stark whitewashed barn wall. He leans his arm on the only piece on the set: a small antique chest.

"That's good." Joaquin looks around the side of the ever-present camera. "Don't look quite that far down, though. I lose your eyes."

The script said very little about location or action but a great deal about Justine Jones' damnation. She has been condemned to endure an eternity of sexual frustration. (Yep. Sounds like Hell to me.)

"George," says Joaquin with that soft sensual "g," "walk in looking around, cross the camera then circle back. When you see Jerry, start your dialogue. Keep looking at him as you walk over to the chest, and sit down on it facing him. OK?"

"Piece o' cake," I flip the now-familiar phrase over my shoulder.

I wander into the bare limbo of the lit area. "About through here?"

"Yeah. That's good. Maybe a little closer to camera before you spot the geek in the corner."

"I resent that," chimes in our director with a big grin.

"She's gonna be too low for me to get any good shots of her pussy sitting down that way," Joaquin informs our director.

"George, can you get your left foot up on the bench?" asks Jerry.

> Of course I can get my foot up on the bench! I may be a good deal older than the average porn actress, but I'm not decrepit.

"That's good. Remember that position." Joaquin comes around into the set and has the crew make a few adjustments to the lights. He holds his ever-present light meter near my exposed crotch, turns to Jerry and says, "I'm ready."

"Me, too," replies our director.

I take his word for it.

"George?" They both look at me.

"Let's do it."

They smile. I love it when they smile.

"First position?" I ask Joaquin. He seems to be in charge, leaving our leader free to act his little heart out, I suppose.

"Please," he responds politely.

(Joaquin was always very polite. Hell. So were Jerry, Harry, Marc, Marty: every one I met on *Devil*. Well, OK. Mr. Makeup Man was a bit of a pain, but a very funny one.)

"All set? Rolling."

"Speed."

"Action."

I walk my assigned path, looking about with an air of resigned fatalism tempered with that itching hunger for more, more, more that defined Miss Jones' flawed character in my mind. Dissatisfaction was her true mortal sin.

I focus on Mr. D sitting on the floor, scrutinizing me as I circle, sit, and ask, "Am I... here?"

"Of course you're here. What a silly question." The hoarse voice slips easily from slack lips as eyes pierce into my soul.

Jerry knew his lines! He didn't just know them, he acted the hell out of them. I don't mean "acted" like bad actors "act." I mean he gave me goose bumps. I could really feel the empty pain he projected. This was a tortured soul in Hell more piteous than any skewered sinner in *Dante's Inferno*. He blew me away. I had to be just as honest or I would have looked like shit.

We did the whole scene non-stop twice in a wide master. Then Joaquin moved into place to get all of Jerry's lines in closeup. Every line matched the master: an editor's wet dream.

I must say that Jerry's portrayal of this lost soul would have made Sartre proud. (Jean Paul Sartre wrote the play, *No Exit*. Some have suggested it was the inspiration for Jerry's film. I doubt it. I don't think Jerry knew the play. I'm not sure he had ever even heard of Sartre.)

Now it's my turn.

Jerry has me do the screamin' meemies sequence in which I plead for the Lost Soul (who has other things on his mind) to help me achieve a climax. We shoot it over and over and over – until he gets exactly what he wants. He may have been willing to go with one take on the long shots, but when it came to wringing it all out of a really tight closeup, he was not stingy with the stock.

Finally, he is satisfied – even if poor Miss Jones isn't. All that's left to shoot are the closeups of the frantic twat twiddling that's supposedly been going on all along.

I call for the Jergens Lotion, having determined in advance that this porn film essential does not loosen the glue on false fingernails. The ones I have for this scene are the longest of the series. They're painted jet black. My biggest fear, after that of possibly lacerating my most tender tissues, is that I might lose one of the little suckers inside my snatch. Not that it would pose any real danger, but I sure as hell didn't want to fuck up a take and have to do it over.

Luck is with us. I manage fully five minutes of uninterrupted masturbation with no manicurial mishap.

Just when I think I may never take pleasure again in the bruised and abused area between my thighs, Jerry steps back and bellows "Cut! Print! Lunch!"

I collapse on the bench in mock exhaustion. Joaquin hurries over and rests a hand on my back, asking with genuine concern, "You OK?"

I sit up, grinning ear to ear. He smiles back in relief.

"That was some incredible scene, you know." He did know how to warm a weary heart – among other things.

Lunch is even more casual than breakfast had been. The boys all feel quite at home in the kitchen by now and proceed to help themselves to the remains of the ham and turkey creating their own sandwiches to taste.

Rick arrives in time to join us for lunch. Another friendly face: I was delighted when Jerry told me he would be the third of our threesome scene scheduled for this afternoon.

"How much stuff you gonna stuff in that sandwich?" asks Marc, watching Harry construct a tower worthy of Dagwood.

"As much as I can. A good sandwich must be properly stuffed, right?" Harry addresses the gathered male coterie with a twitch of his Groucho mustache. The boys around the table chuckle appreciatively. The blatant double entendre is not lost on me. Harry is making sly reference to the upcoming sandwich scene. Ha ha.

At the makeshift makeup table in the corner of the upstairs set, I begin applying my next to last look: Basic Drag Queen.

Out come the obscenely long false eyelashes, vivid electric blue eye shadow, and iridescent blue nails. I tease my tangled locks into as big a bouffant "do" as my skimpy tresses can sustain and check it in the mirror..

Am I ready for this? Do I have a choice?

No.

Stand up and hold your shoulders back!
Check your teeth for lipstick. Good. This

*is it. You're ultimate debauchery. Find
your inner slut, girl.*

Oh, you are such trash!

"Dazzle 'em with your footwork, Kiddo," encourages Claire, draping my wrapper around my shoulders. She punches me lightly on the arm with her fist. I feel like Jack Dempsey heading for the ring.

"Wait! Hold on a minute. Let him get his thing in my butt before you try to put yours in," I hiss at Marc who lies beneath me on the big brass bed.
"OW! Easy. Hold still. Gimme a minute," I gasp over my shoulder.
A breathless moment passes.
"OK. You can move now. S-l-o-w-l-y."

I have no idea if those were the exact words. What difference does it make what the dialogue was? Evidently, a lot. Savanna Samson – the gorgeous actress who recreated Justine Jones in the 2005 Paul Thomas remake of the classic – told me she was required to memorize everything I said in that scene! Paul had the whole scene transcribed. She was quite miffed to learn that we had been making up most of it as we went along.
"It's hard to remember lines when you're doing a DP," she told me. DP, I learned is the modern shorthand for double penetration – what they called a sandwich scene in the old days.
The pain was quite real, not some sort of perverted dramatic device. The position that Harry had me assume for our scene had made the anal insertion fairly easy. Now I was on my hands and knees. This was only the second time I had ever had anything that big up my ass, and I was still a bit sore from the day before. The childish chant that used to orchestrate my early childhood forays into erotica came to my rescue.
"You have to do it, whether you like it or not. It's your punishment. It's supposed to hurt."
Jerry's head suddenly appears between the tangle of limbs. "Verbalize," he rasps.
Right. Can't photograph thoughts.
Out spewed the dialog so treasured by Mr. Thomas thirty years later.

The two cocks fenced fearlessly within the supple walls of my interior. Again, the idea of doing something like that is probably more erotic than the actuality. Savanna was right. It does take concentration – and a large degree of detachment. It's absolutely amazing what the human physique will stand for if approached the right way. I learned that in ballet class. But I never learned how to isolate and completely relax a muscle until I did porn.

"Now that is what I call a sex scene." Jerry helps me up from the bed and places my wrapper around my shoulders.

"Eat my pussy," I chirp jovially.

"Let's get the room tone and groan track," he says to the room at large.

Room tone I understand. When all the footage of a scene is in the can, the sound department records several minutes of the "tone" of the room where it was shot. All the bodies that were there need to be there. For the breathing, I guess. But no one says anything or moves. It's for editing purposes. I have no idea what Jerry means by a groan track.

"OK. Got it," sings out the sound engineer. "Still rolling. Effects, take one. Go."

Jerry leans over and speaks quietly into my ear. "Just do everything the same way."

> Do what the same way? The whole
> scene? He's going to shoot the whole
> scene again? With the same guys? How?
> Simulated? New guys? What the fuck...

"You're going to shoot the whole thing again?" I choke out in stunned disbelief.

"No. No. We just have to get as much as you can remember of the dialog on a separate track."

He turns to the guys sitting on the bed toweling off. "When you run out of dialog, give us a couple of extra minutes of standard grunts and groans, plenty of heavy breathing. You know."

They do, and nod to indicate as much.

I pitch right in and spew forth as much of the dialogue as I can remember. The two guys respond with more audible enthusiasm than they had shown when we were shooting. I guess Savanna was right. It's easier to emote when you don't have anything else on your mind. When we get to the freestyle effects, I follow the guys' lead and almost hyperventilate myself into a swoon before the sound man calls cut.

"Good," says Jerry. "Set up for the Teacher's blow job as quick as you can, fellas."

One more scene to go. I check my script: lots of dialogue. I run downstairs for a quick bath. Then I check my notes and get into the makeup between slightly naughty exploration and utter debauchery. Harry and I run lines while the lights are rearranged. He has his down. I'm still fumbling.

"Don't worry about it. If we go off script, who'll know? Just keep sucking and muttering. If you go up (a theatrical expression meaning to forget one's lines), we'll fix it in the mix." Harry's confidence is catching.

I didn't go up. I did go down – and down, and down some more. By now I had a better idea of what a blowjob was meant to be. I even figured out why they call it a blowjob. Before you stick it down your throat, it's best to blow away any loose hairs.

Harry sat on his throne. I knelt before him in classic submission. No fancy moves, no extra devices, just good lighting and inspired sucking (if I do say so). I don't know how he did it, but by gosh he came right on cue. They shot the scene with both cameras so we didn't have to break stride. One could certainly understand the one-take rule in these circumstances.

I insisted Harry get into the bath first, not wanting to worry about hogging the one and only facility once I got in it. I used up all the hot water that was left.

When I emerged from the steamy bathroom, the big double doors were open and the crew was starting to load out the equipment. A brisk autumnal breeze cut through my wrapper. I hurried upstairs to find warm clothes. Marc was sitting on the bed playing with Herman.

I stopped to say hello. At the sound of my voice, the wily reptile's head turned my way. Marc let the snake slither on to my outstretched arm. Up he went, around my shoulders, down across my bosom and around my waist where he squeezed happily in a friendly boa hug. I began to gasp for air, so I lay back on the bed. Sure enough, the snake immediately loosened his grip and went right for my crotch. He curled up and plopped his sweet little head on top of my clit.

Don't tell me that snake didn't know exactly what he was doing. Marc nearly wet himself laughing.

When I got back to the kitchen, Claire was busy setting out hot franks, beans, kraut, some packaged meats and cheeses and everything else that was left in the fridge. The big tub was filled to the brim with iced watermelon and the rest of the fruit. Someone had made a run to the roadhouse so there was plenty of cold beer. Jerry called a halt to the wrap and had everyone chow down.

"Hey. Can I have a Georgina sandwich?" shouts one wag.

"Eat your weenie," I call back from the sink where I'm washing up everything not in use so's to get a jump-start on the final cleanup.

I sit down and fill a plate. Suddenly I realize how little I've eaten all day. The franks smell great – and they're gonna go great with beer.

Someone yells "Ouch" when I bite into my hot dog. That sets off another giggle fit. Oh, we are a raunchy bunch.

I was really going to miss this boy-scout camp full of just great guys. And yes, I had to admit to myself, I had been having a wonderful time playing movie star. But I realized it was time to get back to the real world. There were marches to be photographed, rallies to attend. Countless things were going on in the world that did not meet with our collective approval, and by damn, we were going to do something about it.

Try as I might, I cannot remember anything about the trip back to the city except that Harry and Marty sang that same damn country song featuring the consumption of peaches over and over. I don't remember very much about the next few days in town, either. I'm sure the constant search for gainful employment went on as usual.

Then Jerry called. I think it was Wednesday night.

"George. How ya doin'?" The slightly gruff voice of my favorite porn director warms the cockles of my heart.

"Fine. You?" I reply.

"I've been looking at the footage."

> Oh Lord, please don't tell me we're going
> to have to re-shoot anything.

"And?"

"It's all great. Can't wait for you to see it."

Whew, no re-shoot.

See it? Why would I want to see it?

"I don't have enough footage, though. I need another ten minutes or so. How would you like to work another weekend? Same pay, a hundred a day for two days and another twenty-five a day to cook. We can't afford to bring Claire, too, though."

She's not going to like that.

"Before I promise another moveable feast, what do you need in the way of footage?" I query.

I wasn't sure I could handle any more heavy sex scenes for a while, indeed, if ever again. I was damn sure I couldn't and cook, too.

"I want to get a long tracking shot of you and Mr. Abaca walking through that field behind the place. I've got some new dialogue for you. Can you come into the office tomorrow and pick up a script?"

"Sure."

That sounds like a piece of cake.

"And I need another really hot sex scene."

Why am I not surprised?

"How would you feel about playing around with some fruit?"

A gig for Corey?

"Have you hired anyone?" I ask too quickly.

"Real fruit," he clarifies. "You know, bananas and grapes and…"

"…other cold items I can shove in my snatch?" I sigh sardonically.

"Well, yes. More or less. It was Joaquin's idea."

Now how the hell does he know… Or does he? Fruit, hmm? Well, why the hell not – as long as it's carefully washed.

"Do we need the corset again?"

Would I be able to get the same stuff from Brooks?

"I don't think so. Unless you want to wear it. I just want you to look gorgeous and like you're having a great time. All the rest of the scenes are kinda heavy."

No shit, Sherlock.

"What time you want me to come in tomorrow?"

"Oh, any time after 10. I'll show you some of the footage."

That I could do without, but I don't say as much to Jerry. I didn't want to hurt his feelings. Nor would I have him think me a wuss.

Movie Magic

BEING TRULY FOND OF MY DIRECTOR (and wanting to fit in with the crowd) I stop for a small purchase on my way to the office. I'd seen ads for a doll with a tiny tape recorder inside. One could program the cute little thing to say what one wished. Far cry from the "Maaa-Maaa" of my first baby dolls.

Bursting into the office, I rush toward Jerry, package extended before me.

"Here, I brought you a present."

He looks a bit bemused as he unwraps and examines the toy.

"Pull the cord." I point to the small ring at the end of a string that dangles from the middle of the baby-doll's back.

Jerry pulls.

"EAT MY PUSSY," sings out the doll in a demanding squeak.

Harry, Jimmy, Jerry, and a couple of guys I haven't yet met, roar with gratifying guffaws.

"Come see your magnificent pussy immortalized for all time," insists Jerry, pulling me along into the small editing room adjacent to the office.

The editor works on a state-of-the-art Keller flatbed editing machine. There are three screens. The one on the left runs a wide shot of Harry the Teacher vigorously pumping his dick in and out of my snatch as I hold on to the railing at the foot of the antique brass bed. At several times the normal speed and running in reverse, it has a certain surreal quality. The screen on the right shows a single frame of a very tight closeup of his cock halfway in my pussy. The two reels of work print are wound through the machine's assorted spools and guides. The editor halts the wide shot and strokes a wax marker down the line between the frame sitting over the viewer mechanism and the frame preceding it on each of the two reels. He then pulls the film forward, and using a small mechanism called a splicer, tapes most of the footage from the closeup between the two pieces on either side of the marked frame in the wide shot.

And that, boys and girls, is how movies were made back in the dark ages. It also explains how the sex scenes in porn films last about twice as long as humanly possible.

When Paul was putting the final touches to his remake of *The Devil in Miss Jones*, he asked me to come into Vivid Video to do some commentary for the DVD "extras." I met the gal who was editing it – a delightful lady. She eagerly ran the trailer for me on her computer. Boy, what a difference digital editing has made. The fast zooms, fades, whirling effects, etc. would have cost a fortune to achieve the old fashioned way. These days, it just takes knowing which buttons to push – and how to edit film, of course.

The Vivid building is amazing: Hollywood to the hilt. A far cry from the walkup cubbyholes, grubby warehouses, and rented editing rooms of New York's porn productions of the '70s. Now it's all business – big business. There's none of that sense of naughty fun that characterized those early outlaw days. Has its legal acceptance ruined porn? Oh hell, sex is sex and it's always been about the money on the distribution end of things.

"So, whadda ya think?" Jerry asks as I watch and admire the skills of the young man cutting the film – literally.

"Amazing. The color is gorgeous," I enthuse. "I can't believe this is a work print!"

I was truly taken with the quality of the footage. So impressed was I that I forgot it was my exposed fanny up there before my eyes.

"Yeah. Now, how 'bout that big, glistening cock?" asks Jerry.

(I swear, he actually nudged me with his elbow.)

"Um HUM." I enthuse. "Beautifully lit!"

He rolls his eyes in resignation at my rude disregard for the erotic value of his footage. I can't help it. Doing it in the privacy of a film set is one thing, watching it embarrasses hell out of me.

"So, where IS the lighting artiste?" I inquire blithely, meaning, of course, the Brazilian.

"Working some other cretin's shoot. Don't worry. He'll be on hand for your big fruit fucking scene."

His tone tells me he is fully aware that my heart is all a-flutter. That's even more embarrassing than the flailing genitals still flailing on the screens behind him.

"Here's the script." He hands me a couple of typed pages. I know it's difficult to picture typewritten pages. They filled the gap between papyrus and PCs.

"Is Mr. Abaca coming in to rehearse?" I venture as I glance at the new dialogue.

Jerry looks at me with a slightly quizzical expression.

"Never mind. Whadda you want for supper?"

"Whatever you can wheedle out of your pals," he grins.

"Come on. You must have some budget?"

"Here's three hundred dollars. Let me know if you need more. We'll drive out Saturday morning. Can you be ready to leave by ten?"

"Sure. How many am I feeding?"

Jerry muses and counts on his fingers. "Eight. No, nine. I forgot me."

"We'll shoot the exterior just before sunset," he continues. "Then we'll shoot a safety Sunday afternoon. We'll have all morning for you to show us how artistically you can eat your own pussy."

"How I can WHAT?"

I'm still pretty limber and in fairly good shape for a lapsed dancer, but I can't see how I'm going to do THAT!

95

"You'll put the fruit inside your pussy and then eat it. It makes it sort of like you're eatin' yourself out. See?"

"Oh."

I have to think about this. So far, eating my pussy hasn't seemed to upset Claire's digestion. My prejudice against the fishy female fissure does seem a bit juvenile in the present situation. Maybe I could douche with cranberry juice or something.

"You OK?" Jerry catches my wandering attention.

"Hum? Oh, yeah. I was just thinking about how many ways I could peel a banana," I lie.

Our good neighbors Asia Meat, Stracce Produce, and Brookdale Butter and Eggs came up with a beautiful standing rib roast, a flat of eggs, half a crate of potatoes, some parsnips and carrots, salad greens and fruit for a grand total of fifty-six dollars. The rest of the provisions still didn't push the budget anywhere near my allotted three hundred dollars. There would be plenty left for the beer.

The yards of chiffon I had used to build my High Priestess costume adapted nicely into a great flowing cape. It would look just super on Miss Jones as she strolled through the Rockwellian field, the ominous Mr. Abaca at her side. I even invested in some fresh makeup. The fruit scene didn't seem to require any costume, so I was traveling pretty light.

Stella and her guy were bedded down for the night in her half of the front loft. Iron Mike and his brother, Charley (our carpenter and general Mr. Fixit) had left for the bike shop after dinner. Jimbo and Lurch were out on the town with some visiting biker club. With no production at the moment, things were pretty quiet.

Packed and ready for pickup the next morning, I finished up the supper dishes and sprawled happily on the makeshift couch with my roomies. As promised, Corey and I made a snuggly sandwich of Claire as we listened, not to opera, but the great Firesign Theater album *Don't Crush That Dwarf, Hand Me the Pliers*. Firesign was a big favorite at the PF. Right up there with the Incredible String Band, Moody Blues, CSNY, Santana, and, of course, Jefferson Airplane.

"I'm going up to bed," I announce, disentangling myself from my companions.

"I'll be up in a bit," Claire mumbles into Corey's neck.

"Goodnight," Corey adds, sleepily.

Halfway up the stairs to our loft, I look back over my shoulder to see Claire making very definite moves on the half-comatose Corey. He moans quietly and turns away from her. She shrugs, gets up and goes to the little refrigerator for another beer.

Good. She's not coming right upstairs. I can pretend to be asleep when she does.

Silly me.

"Are you asleep?"

Why does anyone ever bother to ask that?

"Hmm," I respond.

"I'm going to miss you," whispers my roommate, adopted daughter, lover, friend, sidekick, partner. I simply don't know what designation to use for this relationship that just grew like mushrooms after a rain.

"It's only for one night, kiddo," I remind her. I let her curl into her favorite position: leg thrown over my hips.

"Are you going to fuck Joaquin?"

"I didn't notice anything about that in the script."

"Well. If you do, will you tell me?"

"No."

"OK."

"So don't ask."

"OK."

That seemed to settle it.

Except for muffled street noises and the hum of the refrigerators, all was quiet.

You know that place where you're so close to being asleep you're not sure if you are or not? I'm really not sure if the next comment was actually made or if I dreamt it.

"I'll know if you do, you know."

I knew.

Bergman with Bugs

"SORRY, I CAN'T GIVE YOU A REHEARSAL. It would make a track in the grass," Jerry explains as we edge along the west wall of the old mill. "We'll just have to cue you when to start walking. After you're in frame, Joaquin will tell you when to start talking. Whatever happens, keep going. If you screw up the lines, don't worry about it. It's a long shot. We can fix it in the mix."

How many times have I heard that?

"Should we keep talking after we run out of script?" asks Mr. Abaca. "Yeah. That would be good. Stay in your characters..."

Hmmm. Is that some sort of problem in fuckfilms? Of course I'll stay in character. Mr. Abaca hasn't dropped out of character for an instant — on or

off camera. Geez Louise. Let's shoot
this.

"...and just keep talking 'til you hear cut."

Or we run out of field.

That's unlikely. The expanse before us is twice the size of a football field. A thirty-or-so-foot long track for the camera stretches over the rough ground at the south edge of the field. The grips are rehearsing the dolly shot with Joaquin aboard the camera rig, riding about six feet up in the air.

"Not so fast." Joaquin's usually soft tones are raised to a surprising resonance. It's even sexier than the usual soft tones.

"That's better. Keep it about there."

Oh, yes.

"Steady... Steady..."

Oh yes, yes, YES!

Stop that. He isn't talking to you.

"Good. Let's try it again."

"First mark," yells Marty. He and the other two guys on the rig haul it back to the top of the track near the building.

Talk about your Bergman long shots.
This is going to be spectacular.

"How do you feel?" asks Jerry, placing a friendly paw on my shoulder.

Is he concerned about my health or
checking on my understanding of the
scene?

"I feel fine. Miss Jones, though, is in a state of major anxiety, I assume?"

The script says nothing about how she feels. She's petitioning for more time in her mortal state, however, so I'd guess her to be a tad on edge.

"Whatever," says my director. He pats me encouragingly on the shoulder, swivels, and strides purposefully across the stubble to the first camera mark. He really should have have been wearing a monocle and had a quirt tucked under his arm.

"This isn't your first film, is it?" Mr. Abaca chuckles.

"You mean of an erotic nature, or in general?"

"Both. Either. Whatever. You do know your way around a camera."

"You're no piker, yourself," I reciprocate. "I've been working as a film editor the last few years," I state, in modest explanation.

"Ah. That would explain a lot."

"I was in my first fuckfilm a week ago," I continue, in a bid for cool. "For Beau Buchanan. Know him?"

"No. I don't know anyone else in porn films."

"I get the feeling you aren't particularly interested in doing so," I chuckle. "How did you end up in this one?"

"I answered an ad in *Back Stage*."

"When did you find out it was a porno?"

"When I walked in the office that morning we met. The *Deep Throat* posters sort of gave it away."

"That would do it. But you decided to read anyway?"

"My curiosity overrode my qualms, especially after I saw you."

What? Is this a come-on? Naaa.

"Were you really hired to cook before we did the reading?"

"Yup. And when this one is wrapped, I'll be back looking for any work I can find – hopefully in film, erotic or otherwise. In case you hear of any-one needing anything, I'll give you my number."

"Sure. I'd like to keep in touch."

"OK, guys. Stand by," Jerry shouts from his position beside the camera some 20 or so feet away.

"We couldn't be more 'by'," Mr. Abaca says under his breath. We both wave reassuringly.

The discussion by the camera goes on a bit longer. The light is starting to fade. I think Joaquin's waiting for it to reach just the right angle. What a perfectionist. In the cocksucking scene he spent more time lighting Mark's penis than most DP's spend lighting product on a class A commercial. Yeah. I've been there, too.

"You look familiar. Have you been in any regular films?" he asks.

"You mean non-porn? Yeah. A couple. Back when I could still make a living as a dancer."

"Which ones?"

Jerry calls, "OK, Guys. We're about there."

"Tell you later," I whisper.

"Go!" came the expected cue at last.

The brambly weeds almost rip the cape right off my back. I cling to it for dear life as we plunge purposefully along the indicated trajectory.

"Start talking," shouts Joaquin.

It was not easy going, coming through the rye – or whatever the long grass was. To add to the excitement, our progress disturbed an army of small bugs. They rose from the grass around us and circled our heads in a buzzing, biting cloud. I prayed they would not read in the extremely long shot. We dared not, however, obey our instincts and bat the shit out of them. We had no choice but to grit our teeth and press on.

I guess it was worth it. Critics mentioned the fact that there were scenes in the film where nobody fucked anybody. However, when asked (in a NY Times interview) how she liked the original, Savanna Samson, the Miss Jones of the 2005 version said, "I fast forwarded through most of it. There was sure a lot of talking." Bergman is not to everyone's taste.

"That smells wonderful," says Joaquin of the roasting roast as we re-enter the huge old mill.

I head straight for the kitchen to check on it. The thermometer indicates it has about fifteen minutes to go. Grabbing the baster, I suck up some of the juices and dribble them over the pan full of potatoes, onions, carrots, and parsnips sitting on the lower shelf of the oven.

Jerry and Joaquin head upstairs to block out the shots for the next day's schedule. I follow and change into my cook persona – jeans and sweatshirt. Everyone who isn't busy loading magazines, or unpacking and setting up lights, lends a hand in the kitchen. Mr. Abaca ties an apron around his waist and takes over the salad tub. We chop, we dice, we slice. Harry and a couple of the other guys set the table. Someone, I suspect Harry, brought a radio that actually works in this remote location. Of course, the country western station is playing the song about eating peaches. Not by accident, a peach cobbler stands by to go in the oven for dessert.

"So, what other films were you in?" Mr. Abaca places his plate and beer on the table and sits down on the long bench beside me.

"Funny you should ask," I reply around a mouthful of roast beef. The horseradish dressing makes my nose run. I grab a napkin and give it a good blow, "I was just thinking about a thing that happened with craft services on the Central Park set of *Sweet Charity*."

"The Shirley MacLaine movie?" asks my dinner companion.

"Yeah. I was her dance double and stand in for the New York scenes. I think Bobby Fosse gave me the job as a consolation prize."

"Consolation for what?"

"Well, you see, I went into the dance lead in the first musical he choreographed, *The Pajama Game*, but the show only ran another few months. At the closing night party, he said he was sorry I didn't get to do the role for a longer stretch but that he would use me again soon. When he needed a double for Shirley, he called me."

"I loved that movie. Did I see you in it?" asks Joaquin.

"Possibly. I was in some of the long shots, but, of course, the object was to make it impossible to tell it wasn't Shirley. When I saw it, even I couldn't tell when it was me."

"Anyway," I continue, "we were shooting in Central Park, and every morning the breakfast line got longer and longer. Word had gotten around. The homeless living in the park were joining the line each dawn."

"What did they do about that?" frowned Jerry, ever the producer.

"Well, craft services yelled at the bean counters and the bean counters yelled at production. I was standing near Bobby when one of the suits came up and asked him what to do. 'Buy more food,' he said."

The bed was cold – and lonely. I missed Herman. And yes, I missed having Claire's hot bod in its usual position: arm and leg thrown over me.

It suddenly hit me. I was sleeping alone for about the first time in twenty years. Clips of my soap opera life insisted on flickering through my head even though my body was screaming for rest.

> What would my life have been like if Fred
> hadn't already been married?

In memory, I could feel the way the arch of my foot would rest in the curve of Fred's ankle when we were cozily spooned after sex. That is, when we managed to have sex in a bed rather than standing up in a locked backstage restroom or on the floor of my dressing room between shows – first at the St. James Theatre on 44th Street and then in the Shubert, appropriately enough in Shubert Alley, when the show moved. As we snuggled, I would dream of staring in the musicals he would produce and of attending the opening night parties on the arm of some gay chorus boy because, as all the glitterati knew, our love would be forever clandestine – and frightfully glamorous.

Fred was the stage manager who hired me for the chorus of *The Pajama Game*, my first Broadway show. He mentored me into the lead role replacement. He had, most definitely, not been single. This did not stop us from having a torrid affair. Did I get the role because I fucked him? Possibly. I know I fucked him because I was nuts about him. Especially after he helped me get the role.

I flop around and find a slightly more comfortable position in the saggy old bed. A montage of scenes starring the gorgeous young British actor, known herein as CB, begins to roll. I feel again the excitement of our first encounter of a sexual nature – in a large closet of the apartment I shared with my best friend, Cherie, and a coterie of dancers that swept through in predictable tides possibly determined by the moon. Perhaps that tryst was so hot because my mother was sleeping just down the hall? (Mother was visiting New York to see her dancin' daughter in a Broadway show.)

One look at the gorgeous Brit and Mom was in love. I wish I could say that I was too, but my infatuation with that silver-tongued married stage manager named Fred still had me in knots. When roommate Cherie and her fella, Donald, got married, it just seemed right that they keep the floor-through-plus-basement-with-garden apartment that had become something of a theatrical boarding house. (There was the night I got home from the show and found every bed fully occupied and had to sleep in the tub.) I would find another place.

As it happened, CB also needed to find a place. We didn't start out thinking about moving in together. We were just apartment hunting together; saving bucks by sharing cabs.

When we stumbled onto a forty-five-dollar-a-month cold-water walkup a spit from Columbus Circle, neither had the heart to deny it to the other. The obvious solution was to share it.

The movie of my love life grinds on.

Lap dissolve: *The Pajama Game* closes. My mother phones from Texas and asks if December 7th is OK for the wedding! Well, why the hell not?

Our wedding night, when I gave CB what I'm guessing was his first blowjob, swims into my late-night reverie.

Next scene: Fred calls to ask me to choreograph and star in a production of *The Pajama Game* that will tour South Africa!

What a thrill. BUT, I had a brand new husband and a serious dilemma. No problem. Fred hires my new husband, CB, as stage manager.

Flying to London where the show would be cast and rehearsed, I'm sleeping lightly in the middle seat. CB's on one side, Fred's on the other. From one side, a hand inches across my thigh toward my crotch. A matching mitt starts creeping in from the other side! I grab both before they connect with each other. What a balancing act the next six weeks turned out to be.

After the tour, CB and I faced up to the fact that neither of us was really committed to a monogamous relationship. We realized we should be friends, not mates, so we fixed it. I would be in Los Angeles on my next job. I volunteered to make the trip to Tijuana for the three-hundred-dollar divorce. I even paid for it.

The fortuitously-timed job was a mammoth industrial show. I was one of thirty-two – count them – thirty-two dancers. We not only danced, we cavorted in flying rigs and roller-skated around dancing automobiles. We toured almost all of the U.S. of A. in a private train for three months. Six marriages resulted from that tour. My second, to M, was among them.

How the hell did I let that happen?

Let's see. From the moment I met the overly tall, incredibly sweet stagehand, we shared a bed in the motels and a berth on the train. We laughed a lot. He became my new best friend and, at his insistence, I moved into his apartment when we got back to New York. It meant relinquishing my gorgeous three-flight walkup on Riverside Drive with a BALCONY and VIEW, which I'd found upon my return from South Africa, but it's what I did for what I thought was love.

A two-week sail on a twenty-foot sloop bareboat charter through the Florida Keys went so well that M and I bought our own twenty-eight-foot sloop. Well, technically, *I* bought twenty-eight-foot sloop. I was rolling in cash from commercial residuals at the time. I learned to sail. I even made a sail for the dingy on a treadle sewing machine that I inherited from his mother's former governess. That's how committed I was to this new life.

Not unlike my feelings for CB, M and I, too, would probably have remained friends for a long time, but this time *his* mother, bless her pure Austrian heart, insisted he make an honest woman of me. She and M's actor dad hosted a lovely wedding for us at their Eastside brownstone home.

Big mistake. M's father knew it. He referred to me as The Buzz Saw. Not in my hearing, of course.

How right he was. Less than two years later, I fell in love with another man: Ian, the stage manager of a summer stock company where I was hired to play Lola in *Damn Yankees*. Ian and my husband were friends, for heaven's sake.

> Is it guilt about my sluttish past that's
> keeping me awake?

I tried not to let my infatuation show. Ian never gave any indication he shared my fervor. He was, after all, a married man. His very wonderful wife befriended me, inviting me on trips to the beach with their kids!

OK. I knew I wasn't really in love with my husband. But damn it, I did admire and respect him. I really wanted to be a good wife. I tried so hard that I broke out in a rash whenever we had sex. My mother-in-law was a marvelously intelligent woman whom I did truly love. She knew something was amiss and encouraged me to consult her next-door neighbor and friend, a Jungian psychologist. He had me write down my every thought and dream in a little notebook and we would then discuss them at length.

The following summer, Ian and I returned to that theater in Maine: he as the director, I as the choreographer. The producer thought it would be just swell if he, his wife, their two kids, and I shared a nice little house she rented for us since we'd all been such good friends the summer before.

Ian and I drove to Maine in my little Saab with their luggage for a family of four and mine stuffed into the trunk and back seat. What wouldn't fit inside, we tied to the roof. The hamsters rode on the floor of the passenger seat. Ian's wife and kids were to follow by bus.

They never made it.

I didn't know at the time, but their marriage had already dissolved. Those three weeks of sleeping alone, with only a thin wall between us, were the horniest of my life.

My cerebral cinema replays the night after the opening of our third show together when we feverishly destroyed the Seventh Commandment and most of a bottle of gin.

All the guilt from that summer of heady hedonism made its way into the damn journal. There was also a notation about the rash. The moment I walked into the apartment and saw M washing dishes – something he never did – with tears streaming down his sweet face, I knew the journal had been found and read. That was the absolute worst moment of my life.

He was about to go on tour with an industrial show that would take him to Los Angeles and offered to take care of the divorce. I gave him three hundred dollars and the name of the lawyer in Tijuana. I warned him not to drink the water.

It was an amiable settlement. He got the sailboat, the Greenbrier station wagon which was needed to cart the sails, the property in Westchester, and the Manhattan apartment on 56th Street – antique furniture and all. I packed my practice clothes and moved into a one-room sublet that reeked of cheap perfume.

Ian was officially still living with his wife and kids, but I slept alone very few nights in that funky space, and almost never once he and I moved into the apartment on West 72nd Street that we shared for the next ten years.

As sleep began to again fuzz my head, my vulva pressed into the soft down of the pillow and begin to purr – just a bit. Claire had seemed to understand my reluctance to fire up the old boiler after all the activity of the previous weekend. She hadn't made any overtures all week. A rested libido was stirring. The warmth began to spread through my groin and I felt the slow rocking that stirs the embers. My body wasn't asking my permission, or even participation. It just swerved and swiveled on the giving lump as it pleased. The tension rose in reluctant bubbles like fudge coming to a boil. There were no distractions. No partner to consider. No Director. No camera. No holding back. No kidding. Ka-thunk. Hmmmm. Whoo. Wow. Um. Hmm. Thunk. Thunk. Thunk.

> Oh-my-gawd! The bed has metal springs!
> The whole damn crew can hear me!

> Shit.

Well, you can't stop a barrel that's gone over the falls.
How fucking embarrassing.

A Fruitful Venture

CROWING COCKS AND CHATTERING BIRDS again announced the start of another day when it was still just a rumor as far as I was concerned. Flashlight in hand, I made my way to the kitchen.

I'd filled the coffee urn the night before so it was ready to go. I plugged 'er in then lit a fire under the big double boiler waiting on the stove. The top section held the oatmeal I had left soaking the night before. Nothing like a good bowl of hot oatmeal on a frosty morning – and this one was frosty. The pipes weren't frozen or anything, but my breath was visible. That's frosty enough for me.

While the rest of our motley crew snoozed on, I monopolized the lone bathroom for the next fifteen minutes or so, steaming myself open like an envelope. With two tee shirts under my big bulky sweatshirt, and three pairs of socks, I was almost warm when I emerged into the chilly barn.

By the time I got back to the kitchen, the coffee smell had rousted most of the crowd. Sleepy faces with grizzled cheeks poked around the corner and gratefully filled big china mugs with the steaming brew. The smaller cooler full of ice and fruit sat open at the foot of the table. As the parade of tousled heads made a circuit from kitchen to bath and back, I ladled out big bowls of the hot slimy goo to them as fancied it. There were wee boxes of assorted cereals out on the table for the sissies. Now I really felt like Snow White.

"Sleep well?" asks Harry in a smirking, teasing tone, Groucho moustache a-twitch. An undercurrent of snickers ripples around the table.

"Like a log," I reply in a tone meant to discourage further discussion.

I set a platter of crispy-grilled Canadian bacon down before His Bushiness, "Pass it along," I suggest firmly.

"George."

Oh-my-gawd. That delicious soft "g."

"You look lovely this morning."

"Sweatshirts turn you on, huh?" I reply, handing the Brazilian Bombshell a bowl of hot oatmeal.

"On you? Yes," he gallantly replies, kissing me lightly on the cheek.

"Careful. We have a long scene ahead of us. I don't want to lose it in the kitchen."

"Leave her alone, you lecher." Jerry comes up behind me and kisses me on my sweaty neck.

"Oatmeal?" I offer.

"Yuck. You're kidding, right?"

"You'll eat pussy, but you won't try oatmeal? Wuss. I'll fix you some eggs. How d'you want 'em?"

"Looking like a Playboy Centerfold, please."

"Sunny-side up it is."

I pull the biscuits out of the oven and plop them on the waiting warmed platter. "Wanna pass these around?" I hand them to Jerry.

"Hmmm," he inhales their aroma appreciatively. "Do I have to? I'd rather eat 'em all myself. Pass the marmalade," he pleads as he takes a place at the table.

"George," calls Marty from the far end of the table. "Can I have some eggs, too?"

"How you want 'em?"

"Scrambled, if it's not too much trouble."

"Anybody else want their name in the pot?"

Three hands go up. "Flyin' in," I assure them.

The fresh sheets on the big old brass bed smell – well – like freshly laundered sheets. It's one of the nicest smells there is.

"Can you lean in toward me more? Good. Drop your left leg a little. Good."

"Jerry," Joaquin calls over his shoulder, "you wanna look at this?"

"Just a minute," responds our director. He's in a heated discussion with Harry off in the corner of the set.

"Relax," Joaquin suggests. Good idea. I do.

We had been lighting for hours, but I wasn't about to complain. I had spent easily an hour on my makeup. I even used hot rollers in my hair. This would be my only real glamour shot in the film. Joaquin was welcome to spend all day getting the lighting just the way he wanted it as far as I was concerned. I loved posing for him.

"Marty, put that key just a little closer and more to the left," Joaquin continues to create his picture. "OK. Now open the flood a bit."

"How's that?" inquires the grip adjusting the doors on either side of the lamp.

"Oh, just another RCH," replies the perfectionist.

"What's an RCH?" I naively inquire.

The crew replies in chorus, "Red cunt hair." I was learning a wealth of technical jargon.

"OK. Are we ready to make history?" inquires Jerry striding up to the lavishly appointed brass bed where I recline in all my naked glory.

"Well, I don't know about history, but I'm ready to make a valiant attempt at forging a meaningful relationship with a banana. I should save it for last, I'm guessing?"

"Right. There's no sound so Jo can talk you through."

"Where are you going to be?" asks the cameraman.

"I'm gonna go make some roast beef sandwiches for lunch," replies the director.

"What should I do?" I ask both.

"Surprise me," says the departing Mr. D over his shoulder.

"Well, I guess it's just you and me," says Joaquin.

Be still my heart.

"When I start rolling, just take your time. Don't worry about position. If you go too far out of focus, we'll cover it with closeups. Try to keep track of your actions, though, so we can match the tight shots. What am I saying? You know that. Ready?"

"Where's the fruit?" I ask.

"Flying in," calls Marty as a grip places the bowl of fruit on the table beside the bed.

"I'm rolling," announces Joaquin.

Languidly, I stretch my arm over to the bowl and pluck forth a lovely bunch of grapes. I dangle it above my head in the classic pose immortalized by nude paintings above bars since the dawn of time. When I lower the wee morsel at the bottom into my mouth, I realize how cold the things still are. I hold the grape in my mouth as long as I dare to warm it up before I gingerly tuck it into my snatch.

"Oh, that's delicious. Do another one," Joaquin cheers me on from behind the lens.

I do. A small plum follows. Can't get it all the way in. More grapes. Next an apple and then a peach. The big stuff just gets a nice little pussy massage before I nibble it seductively.

Sensually, I pull back the skin of a banana. I stick it down my throat then try to stick it in my pussy. It breaks. I try another one. No luck.

"Leave the peel on," suggests Joaquin.

That works. I abuse myself gently with the hard, yellow phallic object and wait to peel it until it's time to felate it furiously.

We go through another bowl of fruit as I go through all the actions again. Joaquin moves his camera about, covering every angle in closeup – including coverage of my image in the makeup mirror which he has included in the set. There is something especially erotic about watching myself abuse myself in a mirror.

Throughout the whole scene Joaquin keeps me aroused with a never-ending stream of sweet talk in that soft, sexy accent. Oh what a silver-tongued cinematographer can do.

"We're going to shoot the walking scene the other way around," Joaquin informs me as he helps me up from the bed.

His hands linger on my shoulders for a nanosecond as he drapes my wrapper over them. A shiver goes down my spine and splashes into the puddle between my thighs.

There is one advantage to being a female; you don't have to worry about hiding a hard-on.

"You mean start at the foot of the hill?" I ask in an even tone as we walk toward my quarters by the head of the stairs.

He stops at the door to the bedroom. I go inside and pick up my jeans and sweatshirt. He waits at the door like the gentleman he is.

We continue chatting as we maneuver the narrow stairs and walk together into the kitchen.

"We moved the track a bit, so you won't be going through such high weeds. The wind will be blowing more toward you. At least it was blowing the right way the last time I checked."

"How long do I have to get dressed?"

"Take your time." He checks his watch. "It's about three now. I don't want to shoot before five or five-thirty. I'm watching some clouds though. If they start moving in and look great, we may go earlier. Can you sort of be ready and just stand by?"

"Sure. I won't need any makeup..."

"Not so. I'm going to be tighter this time"

> Not going to lose that Bergman feel,
> I hope.

"Jerry," he calls into the kitchen area where Mr. Damiano is putting the finishing touches on a plateful of roast beef sandwiches. "you gonna want any tight closeups of George on the exterior?"

"It's up to you. I don't know how much I'm gonna use of it – if any. Sorry, Georgie. I shouldn't say that in front of you."

"Oh, please. It's your creation. I am but putty in your hands."

"Don't sweet-talk me, you vixen. I expect supper on schedule."

"I'm gonna go check the dolly crew," says Joaquin, heading toward the door at the front of the building.

"I'll start dinner," I call to his back. "When you think you're about a half-hour away, sing out."

"Right," he says, never breaking stride.

My eyes are glued to his firm butt as his long legs swing along in those skin-tight jeans.

The second shot at the Bergman stroll was golden, as we say in the trade. The dialogue was relaxed and comfortable. Nothing like knowing one's lines. The new path had fewer and lower weeds, and practically no bugs. We did three full takes. I've never felt more like a real actress in my life.

The stuffed manicotti had but to warm in the oven while the sausages simmered in the thick, red sauce on top of the stove. Salad and antipasto platters came out of the refrigerator, and the bread went into the oven.

Mr. Abaca and I had become a well-oiled machine by now. We rivaled the slick, coordinated dance taking place around the set as the crew wrapped the shoot.

Jerry called a halt to the activity and had everyone sit down to dinner. He hauled out a small cooler that he had evidently stashed back in the little room behind the kitchen earlier. Out came several bottles of champagne! Talk about your class acts.

We toasted. We dined. We joked. A mild food fight with rolls erupted briefly. It suddenly hit me that I would most likely never see any of these guys again. A lump formed in my throat that made it difficult to eat. Difficult. Not impossible.

When the feast wound down, I grabbed a flashlight and went upstairs to pack my gear.

My footsteps echoed hollowly in the quiet, dusky loft. It looked huge with all the lights and props gone. Even the fancy brass bed was gone. It must have been a rental. How clever of Jerry to get such an icon of erotica for the major set feature of the film.

Possibly the strangest adventure of my life had just taken place in this silent cavernous space. I looked up into the soaring peaked ceiling now invisible in the dark except for the dancing light of my flashlight bouncing off the huge beams. A shadow fluttered across the light's oval.

Bat!

What more fitting finale?

I'm surprised a black cat hasn't materialized around my ankles.

So waddaya think? Have you consigned yourself to Hell for sure this time, Smartass?

What a question. If you don't condemn it in others, why are you feeling guilty? Hasn't your mantra since your wild and wooly teens been "What's wrong with sex? Why should photographing the reality of it between humans be less acceptable than those wonderful turtle fucks shown on wildlife documentaries anyway?"

Why are you asking yourself all these questions if you're so secure in your position?

Oh, shut up.

The undivided attention a principal actor in a film receives is indeed a heady brew. I doubted I would ever again experience its like, so I allowed myself to savor the dusty smell of my fleeting glory for another minute.

What of the sexy Brazilian cameraman? Would our paths ever cross again? Probably not.

Just as well. I was weary of longings.

The lump in my throat was getting really uncomfortable. I picked up my bags and headed for the kitchen.

Shadows danced around the walls as the crew moved the final crates of equipment out the huge double doors. The kitchen was bare of all but the last of the dinner dishes and a final beer that I sipped as I completed my craft services chores – washing the dishes.

The renowned director, Gerard Damiano, stood beside me at the sink. Unsolicited, he had volunteered to dry.

Turning to me, tea towel in hand, and with a solemn expression shrouding his soulful eyes, in the most heartwarmingly sincere voice, he said, "Years from now, when you speak of this, and you will, be kind."

Beer spewed from my nose, fortunately into the sink. Hearing the king of porn quote the closing line of *Tea and Sympathy*, Robert Anderson's sensitive play about a young man's struggle with homosexuality, took me completely by surprise.

Hmmm. I could be wrong about the echoes of Sartre.

New York to California – 1974

Playing Dress Up

"PENTACLE PRODUCTIONS, what can we do for you?" Corey always answers the phone like he's working at MGM.

"This is Gerard Damiano. May I speak to Ms. Spelvin?"

"One moment please." Corey puts his hand over the bottom of the headset – our version of hold – and yells, "George. It's Jerry Damiano."

I come down the treacherous stairs two at a time. It's been almost a year since we said goodbye at the old cider mill.

"Hey! How are you?" I gush.

"Good. You?"

"Fine. Thanks. What's happening?"

"We're having the world premiere of your movie in Toronto next week. Wanna come along?"

My movie? MY movie!?

"What kind of premiere?"

I still assumed this film, like the dozen or so others I'd done since *Devil*, would be seen on nothing more elaborate than an old sheet hung in some garage or the back room of a bar somewhere.

Jerry's jovial voice answers my query. "A premiere-type premiere. You know. Klieg lights. Critics. Reporters. Screaming fans. The usual stuff," he says casually.

He's kidding, right? Maybe not.

Geez Louise.

Signing autographs backstage at the St. James Theatre after a performance of *The Pajama Game* was my dream come true, true; but going face-to-face with reporters and (good grief!) fans?? In front of a PORN THEATER? That's something else again.

"Well, gee. Thanks. But I don't think so."

"We'll cover all expenses, of course," Jerry assures me.

Well, I should hope so... Still...

"You're the star. You really should put in an appearance, you know? Who knows where this might lead?"

Oh, please. Star, my Aunt Fanny...

"And in which of my two pairs of jeans would you like me to appear?" I ask jovially.

"You need wardrobe? We'll give you a budget. How's five hundred dollars?"

"I wouldn't even know where to shop," I counter, somewhat taken aback by the offer.

Why don't you just say no and let go of it?

At this point, Corey grabs the phone. He has, of course, been hovering close enough to hear the conversation.

"Hello. Mr. Damiano. We haven't met. I'm one of Miss Spelvin's associates here. I'd be happy to act as her stylist. What appearances, exactly will she be expected to make?"

My gawd. He DOES think he's working at
MGM.

"Oh, just a lunch with press, the premiere that evening and a TV interview the next morning. That's it for now," Corey holds the phone well away from his ear so that I can follow the negotiations.

"A comfortable travel costume, cocktail dress and a classic pants suit should do it," muses the newly self-appointed stylist.

Corey sounds like he actually knows what
he's doing.

Maybe he does.

"Let's see. Lingerie, shoes, accessories – we should be able to do it for under seven hundred."

Good grief. That's more than I got paid
to do the movie!

"You drive a hard bargain." I hear Jerry chuckle. "What can you do with five?"

"My best. I can only do my best," sighs Corey resignedly.

"Good. Can you come by the office today and pick up the money?"

"Noooo problem. We can be there in an hour..." Corey looks at me for confirmation. I shrug an OK. "How long do I have to get this together?" he continues into the phone.

"We'll be flying up day after tomorrow, but George doesn't have to get there until Friday," says Jerry.

It was Monday.

I grab the phone back. "What do I have to do when I get there?"

"Jimmy will meet you at the airport and take you to the hotel. You'll have a suite all to yourself."

What do I need with a suite?

I hope I'm not expected to entertain.

"How long do I have to stay?"

"We'll book you a return flight for Sunday morning. Is that OK?"

"I guess so. OK. Well, we'll see you in a little while."

"You're gonna be a big star, you know."

"Yeah. My dream come true."

The sarcasm was not lost on Mr. D, but he only laughed. Diabolically? Well, maybe a little.

"Try this one on," commands Corey, handing me a rampantly ruffled chiffon number with a bodice encrusted with colored rhinestones. In it, I look like a jeweled highball glass in a tutu.

"You know," I begin, "I really don't see why I need a cocktail dress that I will never wear again. The suit should be fine for everything."

The chic little number I speak of is forest-green wool, cut in elegantly simple lines. The flair of the legs over the monstrously tall platform shoes that Corey insists I must wear on this venture made me look six feet tall. That much taller looks that much skinnier — and that I liked.

"Well, if we skip the cocktail frock, we can get a dressier blouse for the suit and a different pair of shoes for the little wrap-around travel number.

"Let's."

"Good. I *hated* the idea of your wearing those green shoes with a beige dress." He actually shudders. "OK. Back to the shoe store."

Corey leads the way down Greenwich Avenue to the chic shop where we had purchased the first pair of these devices from Hell that were all the rage again.

A charter member of the Pickle Factory Auxiliary Social Club, a top-notch attorney whom we'll call Bernie, is just under five feet tall. He's paying one of his frequent visits to the Pickle Factory when Corey and I return from shopping. As I model my new costumes, he takes one look at the platform shoes and curses vehemently.

"I thought I'd seen the last of those &%#$ things in 1945! You're not wearing those things out with me anywhere."

"Don't worry. I ain't wearing them anywhere but to this gig. They're about to give me a nosebleed."

"You better take a sweater," warns Stella. "It may be hotter 'n hell here, but Toronto can be chilly in August."

"I'm taking two. Airplanes are always cold enough to hang venison, but I should be OK with them and the suit coat. It's pretty heavy."

"And beautifully lined," remarks Claire.

She opens the coat of the suit which she just had to try on and poses in imitation of a high fashion model.

"You look better in it than I do," I remark sincerely.

"It's more her style:" Corey murmurs into the back of my head, "butch."

"Bitch," retorts Claire, jocularly.

"Now kiddies, play nice." Stella places a huge bowl of salad upon the milk-crate table in the center of our conversation nest. "Help yourselves to the chili and rice on the stove. Bowls are on the counter."

"Soon as I can get out of this rig," I sigh, standing obediently still in the filmy travel dress while Corey places a huge chunky necklace around my neck.

"When is your flight?" asks our friend Bernie the attorney.

"Seven-twenty out of Newark."

"Want a lift?" he offers helpfully.

Bernie was always ready to help us out. One particularly hairy night we were cutting a film for Murphy, one of the filmmakers loosely associated with our commune. It absolutely, positively had to be ready the next day for a big presentation at the freakin' White House no less. Bernie, that rare New Yorker who owns a car, stayed with us through the wee hours of frenzied cutting in order to drive us through a blizzard to the Kodak lab in New Jersey to get the reel processed. He was that kind of guy.

"Thanks, Luv, but I'll grab a cab. Hey. They're paying for it," I remind one and all.

Indeed, the producers, whoever they were, covered all my expenses. It never crossed my mind to ask for compensation for my time. There's a very good reason I ain't rich.

Porn Chic and Publicity

THE FLIGHT WAS UNEVENTFUL. With only a carry-on bag, I avoided the baggage claim area and headed straight for the main waiting room. When I spotted Jimmy and a couple of suits I didn't recognize, I quickened my pace. Big mistake. The new platform shoes slid right out from under me, landing me squarely on my butt in the middle of the Toronto terminal.

I praised Corey for insisting on elegant tap pants for underwear. Most of the travelers in the area got a good view of the fancy drawers. Jimmy was too concerned that his "star" might be seriously injured to laugh, but I did. So hard I damn near wet those gorgeous step-ins.

The hotel was splendiferous: the suite, gigantic. You could have played badminton in the dining area backed by floor-to-ceiling windows. Jimmy and the two gentlemen with him conversed while I unpacked my gorgeous suit and hung it up in the bathroom. I turned on the hot water in the shower and left it running while I rejoined my escorts in the parlor of my la-de-fuckin'-da suite.

"I've got to get over to the theater and check on arrangements," says Jimmy, checking his watch. "Why don't you guys just relax? You're due at the press club at one. Did you get breakfast on the plane? Order anything you like. I'll see you at the luncheon."

He finally takes a breath, busses me lightly on the cheek, and whirls out the door. The man was a blur.

"Would you like coffee or anything?" I ask the two young gentlemen who turn out to be the theater owners.

They decline refreshments and suggest we take a quick tour of beautiful downtown Toronto on our way to the press conference. I turn off my steam pressing operation in the bathroom, take a quick pre-emptive pee, and join my escorts.

What a great city. What great guys. What an impressive building housed the press club – gray marble and deep, lustrous mahogany from stem to stern.

Holding my shoulders back, I strode in the door of the elegantly appointed private dining room. A humongous round, linen-draped table gleamed with fine china, sparkling crystal and polished silver. A frosty stemmed glass materialized in my hand. It had an olive in it. I surmised, correctly, that it was a martini. Shades of the three-hour corporate lunches I enjoyed while working at Penney's. I hadn't indulged in such luxury since. When the first swallow hit my solar plexus, that old familiar pink glow crowded out the last twinges of insecurity. Booze is great for that.

The reporters milling about ran the gamut from Vogue-elegant ladies in hats to scruffy road-warrior types in bush jackets and boots. I met and chatted with everyone before we finally sat down and I was served a chilled soup – and my third martini. I don't remember getting back to the hotel. I do remember the jangling phone waking me.

"Hey, Georgie girl," Jerry's booming voice snaps me back to where I am and why.

"Hey, yourself," I mutter. My mouth tastes like something really ugly crawled inside and died.

"How do you feel?"

"Oh just great. Really. Did anybody get the number of the truck?"

"Truck?"

"Yeah, the one that ran me over."

Jerry laughs.

"Ouch. Not so loud."

"You want to go get something to eat before the show?"

"I think I'll have room service send me up an aspirin milkshake, thanks. At what time am I supposed to be incandescent?"

"You know, I don't know what the hell you're talking about half the time, but you're cute." He affects something close to a British accent. "Shall I collect you about 6:30 then, Madam?"

"Whatever's fair. What time does the balloon go up?" During my tour earlier, I had seen that the theater was directly across the huge plaza adjacent to the hotel. We could walk over in about three minutes.

"The limo will be at the front of the hotel at a quarter to seven."

Limo? What were they going to do, drive around the block?

That's exactly what we did.

When we pulled up in front of the theater, someone opened the door for us, and Jerry and I marched up the red carpet. Flashbulbs flashed, and people with mikes screamed questions.

By the time we were seated in the only remaining vacant seats (two on the aisle of about row six or so, I think), the house lights were beginning to dim. The curtain warmers were washed out by the first frames of the film. The curtain whipped away under the image of Miss Jones' tortured face spewing forth a litany of erotic suggestions.

This was definitely not your average bachelor party setting. I knew I wasn't dreaming, because my head still throbbed from my ill-advised binge. Now I must watch myself doing all manner of obscene things on a thirty-foot high screen in front of hundreds of people with the tail end of a righteous hangover turning my stomach to lava, and not throw up.

I managed.

Knowing I was expected to appear on a TV talk show in the morning, I declined the champagne Jerry tried to hand me at the reception following the screening. Our hosts – the guys who had given me the tour earlier – kept introducing me to people and I kept politely answering more or less the same questions. My feet were killing me.

Finally, Jerry leaned toward me and whispered in my ear, "I think we can wave goodbye and head out the door."

The limo was waiting. We shot down the roped-off path and jumped inside. Back around the block to the front of the hotel we sped.

There was a bigger mob in front of the hotel than there had been at the theater! Of course, it might have been the same mob for all I knew. They could easily have run across the plaza in less time than it took us to drive around it. Who were these people?

We made it into the lobby as the doorman kept the camera-wielding crowd at bay. Jimmy invited me to join them for a nightcap, but I declined and headed straight for bed – alone.

Without the benefit of any booze to lull me to sleep, I lay pondering this weird turn of events in my life. OK. Any thoughts that this film would sink without a trace were put to rest. Would anyone who saw any of this coverage recognize me? I chose to believe no one I knew would ever see the actual movie. And I took comfort from the fact that in the film I look nothing like I do in real life. I was convinced no one would recognize me.

I tried to relax and get to sleep. I told myself it was all still just a passing whirlwind and my life would return to normal in a day or so. As to what I would say on TV in the morning, I hadn't a clue. I'd just have to see what the interviewer asked and try not to divulge any sensitive information – like my real name. After all, this was Canada. It wasn't like I was going on the freakin' "Tonight Show."

The week after the film opened in New York, I got a call from an old friend, choreographer and former gypsy, Jimmy Nygren.

"That's you in that fuckfilm, *The Devil in Miss Jones* isn't it?" he asks without preamble.

"Well, it's nice to speak to you, too. Yes. I confess. It is I."

"I *knew* it was you. When you turned off that faucet in the bathtub with your toes, I recognized your feet! I screamed. Right - out - loud. Right there in the theater. 'I know her!' My boyfriend thought I'd lost my mind. He doesn't believe me. Can I put him on?"

Judith Crist, considered one of the top film critics of the day, wrote reviews for the New York Herald Tribune (which later became New York Magazine.) Well, she reviewed the damn thing! She didn't exactly love it, but she was very kind to me, saying I "...touched the emotions." She concluded with "...for those whose taste it is, I say leave it lay." Thus was born a new film genre, "Porn Chic."

So much for anonymity.

About a week later, I'm home alone at the Pickle Factory – a rare occurrence – when another unexpected call comes in.

"Hello, Sister dear."

"Hey, BUD," I squeal in spontaneous enthusiasm. "How ya doin'?"

My brother rarely calls me. We have always been close, but rarely feel the need to talk to each other. My sensors start to quiver.

"I was reading *Newsweek*..." he begins. "There's an article about a movie, *The Devil and Miss Jones*..."

"In. *The Devil IN Miss Jones*," I correct.

"Oh? OK. Well. There's a picture of a lady in a corset sitting on the floor in front of a guy with a big mustache. Is that you?"

"Yup. 'Fraid so. I'm the one in the corset."

What should I say? Deny it and have him find out later that I was not only a slut but a liar, too?

I didn't know about the *Newsweek* article. I'd been holed up in my cave trying to avoid the splash of the "Porn Chic" torrent since Toronto.

"What does it say?" I venture tremulously.

"It says that you're a remarkably talented actress. Congratulations."

"Oh gee, thanks. Does it get specific about just what kind of film it is?" I press on, regardless.

"Oh yes."

"Oh." (Long pause.)

"Have Mother and Daddy seen it? The article, I mean."

"They haven't said anything. I doubt they would though, you know?"

"I know." Selective subject matter is the core of good family relations in the South.

"Well... I just wanted to be sure I wasn't imagining things."

(Another long pause.)

"Are you OK?"

I take a deep breath.

"Honey, what can I say?" Out spills our childhood caveat: "The Devil made me do it!"

He laughs, letting me know everything's OK in that quarter at least.

Out of the Pickle Factory and Into the Fire

WHEN NOT CUTTING FILM and running around to peace rallies, I plied my new trade as a porn star. Contrary to Harry's speculations, the going rate of one hundred a day did not increase with my new-found fame. That is, no-body offered me any more than that, and my socialist soul bought into some sort of "we're all in this together and should all be paid the same" mindset, so I never asked for more. But the offers poured in.

Remember this old joke?

A guy says, "Yeah, times are rough. Why, I lose ten cents on every piece I sell."

His friend asks, "How do you stay in business?"

"Volume!" he replies.

I made up for the paltry pay by doing a lot of films. It still didn't quite cover our expenses, but it helped.

On top of the new films I was invited to do, every piece of footage from the past that contained any image of me (and some were decidedly suspect) got pasted together and released under new titles. Now that the name was a household word, they all "starred" Georgina Spelvin.

In all fairness, I did get to do quite a few films with actual scripts. Some were even pretty good. And when Ted Paramour offered me a role, he actually asked what I wanted in salary. I was stunned. No one had ever asked me that. It was always a hundred a day, take it or leave it. I didn't know what to say, so I asked that I be paid one cent more than any other performer in the film. He magnanimously offered a dollar more. (I shall be forever grateful to Annette Haven for demanding, and getting, better pay.)

Ted lived in Los Angeles. Working for him and others of that era meant going to California a lot. Not only was the West Coast pay better, but the films were usually shot in Marin County near San Francisco. First-class accommodations were always part of the deal. It really was like making real movies, right in the movie capital of the world. These were the salad days.

Marilyn Chambers, the lovely Ivory soap model, starred in a film called *Behind the Green Door*. It was the third of the "Porn Chic" trio, Linda Lovelace's *Deep Throat* being the first. I wouldn't meet Ms. Lovelace until many years later when we were both guests on *Woman to Woman*, a TV talk show. I approached her with outstretched hand saying "So glad to finally meet you." She turned her back on me. I'd never done a film with Marilyn, but we did meet frequently at the annual company picnics (Adult Film Association award dinners). Once, she and I were invited to be judges at a nudist park beauty contest near Chicago.

"Professor" Irwin Corey is billed as The World's Foremost Authority. He of the never-completed ramblings punctuated by "however" was also a judge. After the festivities, he and Marilyn engaged in a boisterous coupling while Chuck Trainer (her husband at the time) and I shared a quiet drink in the adjoining room of the hotel suite the park's owners had provided for us. Ms. Chambers hit an impressive high C to the percussive accompaniment of a fortuitously sturdy headboard slamming the wall. Then we all went out to dinner.

A few months later I get a call from Marilyn. She insists I come up to the Warwick Hotel in midtown Manhattan.

"There's someone here who really wants to meet you," she chortles, mysteriously.

"I'm on my way to a Halloween party dressed as a witch." I explain my reluctance to make the trip uptown. Halloween costumes are de rigueur in The Village, but I'm loath to venture above 14th Street in fancy garb.

"Doesn't matter. You've got to come up."

She gives me a room number. I grab a cab.

Chuck opens the door. Altovise Davis is standing by the bar across the expansive living room of the suite. She and I had never worked together, but we knew each other from classes and auditions back in our Gypsy days.

As we are exchanging greetings, I'm grabbed from behind and lifted off the floor in a bear hug.

"See! I told you I knew Georgina," sings out the unmistakable voice of Mr. Sam Davis, Jr.

Now I remember. He and Alto had gotten hitched.

"Are you, or are you not," he asks, plopping me down and turning me toward him, "the little blonde dancer from Dallas, Texas, who showed us darkies where we could safely dine back in the early '50s?"

Before I can do more than nod, he continues.

"The same one we partied with in Vegas when The Pack was shooting *Ocean's Eleven*? Right?"

Let me here state, "partied" consisted of drinks and laughs – period. When I was introduced to Sam at the Sands in Vegas, he swore he remembered me from Dallas ten years before.

You see, the Will Mastin Trio was the opening act for The Jack Benny Review, first show of the State Fair Music Hall summer stock season of 1954. I was a dancer in the chorus for the season. After opening night, I cornered Sammy and asked for his autograph. He wasn't all that famous yet and said he was flattered. I'd never heard of him before. I just knew he was the best damn tap dancer I'd ever seen.

He asked if I knew where "folks of his hue" could safely dine. I told him about a couple of jazz joints (known as "black and tan clubs" back then) where folks of any hue were welcome to hear good music and pig out on pig meat and cornbread.

"If you joined us, would anyone get shot?" he smiled.

I didn't think so, so I did, and no one was – shot, or anything.

I was working in Vegas as choreographer at El Rancho Vegas in 1960 when the Rat Pack hit town to play the Sands and shoot the original *Ocean's Eleven* film.

One day I was whacking balls at a driving range when Shecky Green and Buddy Hackett recognized me from our show and struck up a conversation. They sort of adopted me and took me everywhere, including the show at the Sands – several times. They even took me backstage to meet "The Pack." When Sam remembered me from the Dallas episode, I made the A list for the pack's extra-curricular activities – including a benefit show they did at the Silver Slipper for the local children's hospital.

Sam and Alto, could not have been more gracious. They invited me to visit them in L.A.

When I did, Sam greeted me at their door with, "That's Pickfair across the road. Don't you know those folks just love watchin' me take out the garbage Thursday nights?"

On a later trip, they invited me to Alto's birthday party at Spagos. (The only time I was ever there.) Sammy came dressed as Superfly - and referred to himself as Superflea. He gave Alto a Rolls with the license plate ALTO in place. Her chin almost hit her chest when she saw it.

I visited them only a few times. We didn't exactly move in the same circles.

Variety interviewed me.

"Because..." the nice man who did the interview told me when I asked "why me?"

"...the name Georgina Spelvin is presently on more of the billboards on Broadway at the same time than any other name in history."

Dubious achievement award of the century. I suddenly felt personally responsible for the dreadful decline of The Great White Way if not the fall of Western Civilization.

Speaking of falls – the fall of the Pickle Factory followed shortly, due in large part to an invasion by the Red Clover Farm Collective.

Couldn't tell you where they came from originally, but we inherited them from Larry, the guy who rented us an editing room when we had any serious cutting to do. (Our own facility never got equipped with anything more elaborate than a table, bin, splicers, and a pair of rewinds.)

I'm in one of his editing rooms syncing dailies from a shoot we did of the Béjart Ballet Company. Larry sticks his head in the door.

"Let's make a deal," he says. "You let this bunch crash at the Pickle Factory until they finish their fershtunkina film and I'll give you a 10% discount forever."

"You must be desperate! How many of them are there?" I ask our pal.

"Hard to say. I've counted as many as eight in the editing room at a time, but it's rarely the same eight. They're costing me a fortune in toilet paper."

"Let me run it by the steering committee. I'll get back to you."

They came. They saw. They consumed.

We worked around wall-to-wall sleeping bags as we continued to put together our own documentary.

Murphy, the Irish firebrand who enlisted our services for an anti-war project of his, was a semi-resident for the duration. He had acquired some clips from the Viet Nam "Police Action" too gruesome to be shown on TV. These had been collected from the out-take bin by a menial at one of the major networks who shall forever remain nameless. We cut them into interviews Murphy did with returned service men and women, many of whom were amputees.

On the eve of the great May Day Peace Rally in our Nation's Capital, the Red Clover Collective packed their sleeping bags, granola, and reels (and reels and reels) of film into a pair of decrepit VW vans and disappeared in a cloud of eye-smarting exhaust.

Murphy, Claire and I loaded Claire's motorcycle, a rented Xenon long-range projector, three-day's rations, and a change of skivvies into a borrowed Greenbrier and headed south. We were going to show the world our horrifying reportage right on the face of the Washington freakin' Monument!

We couldn't get anywhere near the monument, of course, but we did get to screen our film.

Every underground filmmaker in the country was there. Each had a masterpiece they had planned to show somebody, somewhere. We were cheek-to-jowl in the park where Washington's finest confined us. Some major groups, bumped from their scheduled venue, set up a makeshift stage and their own sound equipment. Murphy mounted the platform and got the crowd's attention. He suggested we put together a huge screen from bed sheets. A plethora of textiles appeared from the surrounding vans. We collected every safety pin that could be spared, which led to some interesting fashion statements, and pinned the sheets together.

We stretched the billowing sail between light towers. One thing about hippie vans, there's never a shortage of rope. Our fancy-schmancy projector sat on top of the tallest available vehicle. We were later told that the projected images could be seen from the White House!

Some amazing films were shown that night, and a rousing good time was had by all, in spite of the grim images. Then the musicians took the stage and propelled us into the wee smalls.

Much levity was generated by the embedded agents working the crowd. They were carefully tie-dyed to the teeth, but still in their signature black shoes. Some wag suggested it was because they had phones in them – a la Maxwell Smart.

If the Red Clover Collective got there, we never saw them.

At the first whisper of dawn, bullhorns blasted us out of the deep slumber that follows such revels. The three-day permit had been revoked. All vehicles were to vacate immediately. Those on foot were to report to police vans which would transport them to a holding facility. This sounded a lot like jail so everyone without wheels was looking for a ride out.

Murphy had last been seen with a trio of nubile twits and was nowhere to be found. He was a big boy. He'd find his way home. We took four weary foot soldiers aboard and joined the line inching toward the exit.

We made it all the way to the freeway and were breathing a collective sigh of relief when the rear left tire blew. We unloaded the van and looked for the spare. There was none. Good thing we brought along the bike. Clare roared ahead to the nearest service area and returned with two canisters of that stuff you squirt into flat tires that'll take you a few miles. Without the weight of the motorcycle, we were able to make it to the service area before it went completely flat again.

New retread in place, we pressed on. The second tire didn't go until we were within view of the skyline of Manhattan. This time a kindly cop summoned a tow truck to haul us to the next service area. He didn't even search the van.

It was early evening before we finally pulled into the loading dock in front of our Pickle Factory.

The FBI was waiting for us.

The Clover crowd had been using a stolen FBI credit card to make calls from our phone! As if that weren't enough, they had run up over six hundred dollars in calls before they "found" and started using the illicit card.

It was the Red Clover bunch the FBI were looking for. They weren't the least bit interested in us. They took our statements, had several cups of coffee, and went on their merry way. Still, it was a bit unsettling. I admit to losing my enthusiasm for the movement about then.

Most Underground filmmakers work in Overground film to support their habit. Association with porn was the kiss of death when it came to getting work in "real" movies. Our film group quietly dissolved.

Claire, Stella, and Corey were the last left aboard. We owed the hardware store a fortune. The rent was two months past due, and now, thanks to the Red Clover Collective, the phone was history.

To get out of debt, we held an auction and sold off the appliances and editing equipment. The copper plumbing went for three hundred bucks!

Corey told us to gather up all the women's underpants we could find among our belongings. He began to auction them off, swearing they'd been "worn by Georgina Spelvin!" The fact that they were three different sizes didn't seem to matter.

That went so well, he sent out for a supply of razor blades. I was put to work autographing them. They went for ten bucks apiece even though they obviously weren't the blade used by Miss Jones to cut her wrists in the film.

Iron Mike's brother, Charley – he who had spent so many hours crafting the unique wood features of our failed factory – let us borrow his pickup: a lovingly restored 1936 Chevy. We used it to move our belongings to a series of crash pads and sublets over the next few months.

Stella referred to us as Doctor Yakalot's Traveling Space Circus.

Centrifugal force finally dispersed us. Stella and Corey ended up in San Francisco. Corey and his new boyfriend landed a gem of an apartment in the Haight. Stell moved in with her sister in Oakland. Charley moved to a farm in Connecticut with his lady. They soon had a son. Mike continued to tune spokes and freelance as a cameraman in New York. Jimbo returned to his old bike gang in San Diego. I have no idea what happened to Lurch or any of the other guys. I heard Murphy got a job as a guard at a federal prison just so he could help another revolutionary bust out. Can't swear that's true, but it sounds a lot like Murphy.

If it was her idea, or if I talked her into it, I honestly can't recall, but Claire went back to school in Florida. I put her on a bus with as much cash as I could scrape up. We promised to write.

Several folks in the porn trade insisted it was high time for a fuckfilm written from a woman's point of view, so I rented a typewriter.

They were either deluded or lying.

Busted

ABOUT THE TIME I began to seriously consider getting a day job, I was saved by the bell. Ma Bell.

"Hello," I try not to sound desperate.

"Hi, It's Vicki. I want you to come up and re-stage your productions of *Camelot* and *Oliver* for me this summer. Are you available?"

The signature husky rasp was unmistakable. I nearly dropped the phone.

"Vicki, have you any idea what I've been doing for a living for the past couple of years?"

"Of course I do. I don't live in a cave. But, what has that got to do with your availability?"

"Nothing, if you say so. I guess."

"If you want to fill out the season, I can find parts for you in the other shows. You'd be a great Bonny in *Anything Goes*. Ian will be directing that."

The tone of her voice asked if that might be a problem.

It wasn't for me, but I worried that it might bother him.

Not only was Ian not the least bothered about working with me, he asked if he might crash in my apartment for the week he would be there! Housing is always at a premium in Maine in the summer.

We hit the grocery store immediately upon his arrival.

"How many times have we set up housekeeping together?" he inquires in his light-hearted way. There was always a chuckle just beneath the surface of anything Ian said.

"Let's see?" I muse. "The first house here, the smelly sublet, the apartment on 72nd Street – what? Five, six summers here? And now this. What's that, nine?"

"Don't forget Vicki's cabin."

Our producer had this cozy little rustic place way up on a hill overlooking the bay. She invited us to stay there after one season. We spent a week hiking, sailing, stuffing our faces with lobster every night and just chilling out. It was the closest thing to a honeymoon we ever had.

"What year was that?" he asks.

"Hell, I don't remember. You want Cheerios?"

"Big box."

"Of course."

We settle into the familiar routine of 24/7 crises that is summer stock. Too busy or too beat to get into any probing conversations, we just enjoy each other's company and work our butts off.

Ian is a fantastic director. His quirky sense of humor makes the grueling rehearsals almost a pleasure. Well, most of the time. This last dress run-through of *Anything Goes* is proving a bit more grueling than most – for me at least.

"Five, six, seven, eight." The choreographer chants the traditional signal to begin. The finale is being polished for the opening that night. I am dripping with sweat and fighting for breath.

> What the hell ever made me think I could
> (puff puff) still do thirty-two time steps,
> (puff) twenty-four shoulder-high kicks,
> sixteen bars of (puff) trenchers (puff)

>and then sing a final (puff puff PUFF)
>chorus? Eight bars to go.
>
>Deep breath.

It goes well. That is, nobody bumps into anybody. The bows would now be set. Everyone would then run home for a quick bite and maybe a nap before returning to the theater for the half-hour (until show time) call at eight.

Ian walks down the aisle of the theater as the house lights come up. He stops a few feet from the edge of the stage, ever-present clipboard in hand.

"OK, everyone. Nice run-through." A buzz erupts on stage as everyone begins to exit.

"Hold on a minute." He raises one hand as he continues to look down at the clipboard in the other.

"Just one more little thing I need to fix."

A collective "Aw, nuts" murmur sweeps the gathered players.

"Go back to the opening scene where the Purser crosses to the Captain," directs the director still peering intently at the page shining under the little lamp on his clipboard.

We players reposition ourselves as required.

"Go," says Ian, signaling that the action should commence.

Purser: (crossing from down right to center stage and addressing the Captain) "Excuse me, Sir. There are a couple of FBI men waiting at the foot of the gangplank who wish to speak to you."

Captain: (to Purser) "Have them come aboard." (They salute. Purser crosses back to gangplank.)

Ian turns to the semi-dark audience area and calls out to the rear of the house, "OK. This is where you two guys come down the aisle and walk up on the stage over there."

He indicates the location of the ramp that reaches from the floor of the auditorium up onto the stage. He then doubles over in a futile effort to mask uncontrolled hilarity.

The producer comes down to the edge of the stage where Ian is sputtering and demands to know what's going on.

Two men in suits – nobody wears suits in the summer in Maine – are walking slowly down the aisle looking very uncomfortable. Ian waves me over to the edge of the stage where the two men come to a halt.

"I think this is the person you're looking for," says Ian in his deepest, most serious voice. You could hear the "dum-da-dum-dum" of a *Dragnet* sequence in the background.

"Are you Georgina Spelvin?" asks the taller of the two Suits.

"On occasion," I reply – not meaning to be sarcastic, just accurate.

Those still on stage are looking at us, and each other, with quizzical expressions. The rest of the cast and crew are peering from every drape hanging in the wings.

"We are here to serve you with a fugitive warrant for your arrest," explains Tall Suit.

"You can't arrest her now," rasps our producer, "she's opening in a show tonight."

This pronouncement is made in the authoritative voice of one who is not used to being countermanded.

"What do you mean 'fugitive' warrant?" I inquire. "I'm no fugitive. I'm right here with my name on the freakin' marquee!"

"I don't know," shrugs Tall Suit. "We got this on the wire this morning. Our directive says to apprehend you if found, and told us to look for you here."

My answering service in New York (good old Seven Arts) knew where I was. Hell, they know everything about everybody in show business. I'm listed in the Manhattan phone book. How hard would it be to find out where I was? Obviously not very; they did it. Fugitive. Geez.

"If I were a fugitive, how did they know where to tell you to look?"

"We don't make the directives, Miss. We just follow them," explains the G-man, sounding more like Sergeant Friday every minute. "Please come with us. We're to take you before the magistrate in Portland, according to the warrant."

"OK. Just let me change." I start to move toward the wings.

"Stay where you are, please," says the smaller of the two in a deathly calm voice. He starts reaching inside his jacket. I swear to God!

"Just a minute," says the producer, with more volume than I had ever heard come out of her before. "If my performer's presence is required at Jack's office, you are welcome to escort her there after this evening's performance. I'll give you seats right down front and you can keep an eye on her from the audience."

"Oh, I don't think..." begins Tall Suit.

"It's almost four now, anyway," she continues, checking her jeweled watch, "I doubt Jack's still in his office. (Jack, of course, is not his real name.) Look, I'll call... (she speaks the Governor's first name here — they, too, were close friends, it seems.) I'm sure we can work this out."

She spins on her very high heel and starts up the aisle in a determined stride.

Tall Suit speaks up.

"Wait a moment. That shouldn't be necessary."

He was obviously impressed.

"What do you think?" he asks his trigger-happy sidekick. "Can't we just leave her in the custody of her employer and let her appear in the morning?"

Short Suit shrugs.

"Good. That's settled," says Ian.

He turns to the still-waiting crowd on stage.

"Back at half-hour. We'll set bows then. Werger," he calls to the comic lead and mainstay of the theater, "I need you a minute."

The two suits are now in a heads-down conference with the producer. Ian is in a heads-down conference with the resident lead actor. I see no further reason to hang around, and, again, head for the wings.

"Just a minute," calls out Tall Suit.

What now?

I jump down from the stage and walk over to the lawmen.

"Yes, sir?" I respond politely, fearing the worst.

"Um," starts the tall one, glancing sideways at his sidekick, "we were just wondering if you'd mind signing a couple of autographs for us."

"Not at all," I smile, warmly.

Opening night is a smashing success. The fuzz who accepted Vicki's offer of free seats said they loved it. Next morning she drives me to the courthouse in nearby Portland.

Her old friend greets her warmly. He pores over the paperwork before him for a few minutes then peers up over the glasses perched precariously on the end of his nose and fixes me with a no-nonsense glare.

"They've got a nationwide fugitive warrant out for you. What in the world did you do?"

"I appeared in a sexually-explicit movie," I answer demurely.

"Oh? Which one?" he asks, straightening slightly in his big swivel chair.

"*The Devil in Miss Jones.*"

"No kidding? That was you?" He removes his glasses to get a better look.

"I'm afraid so," I reply.

"I didn't recognize you. You look a lot different on film."

I look askance at my producer. She stands quietly in a pool of non-committal calm

"Now, you're gonna need representation," the grizzled dignitary continues. "Do you have a lawyer?"

"No," I reply.

"Can you afford to hire one?"

"No." Vicki answers for me.

"Then you better get in touch with Lenny Shapiro over at the ACLU office." He hands me a card. "He'll take care of everything."

And indeed he did. I didn't even have to appear in court until I got to Memphis. I spent the last few weeks in Maine working for him in the ACLU office, not only on my own paperwork, but helping out in any way I could. Needless to say, I've been a card-carrying supporter since.

Lenny lined me up with another ACLU lawyer in Memphis who not only represented me, but showed me around town, hosted a luncheon for about twenty other activist lawyers in the area who wanted to meet me, and got me in and out of the machinery in two days.

Yes, I got my mug shot. Fifteen times. Every cop in the shop wanted his own autographed copy.

I was offered immunity if I would agree to testify for the prosecution. My lovely ACLU lawyer asked, "Immunity from what? Are you charging her with a crime? And if so, what crime?"

They were stuck for an answer. It seems it's not illegal to fuck. It's just illegal to carry pictures of people fucking across state lines.

I had never even seen a physical reel of the film since the day I visited the editing room with Jerry. They would have had a hell of a time proving I'd been smuggling it across state lines.

I was released from the witness warrant. My lawyer said to keep in touch, but he didn't think my presence would be required.

It wasn't.

I gotta say, the whole episode was actually quite pleasant.

According to the film *Inside Deep Throat*, Harry Reams did not fare so well. I didn't follow the trial and knew nothing of its repercussions or the persecution that dogged his and Jerry's footsteps for the next thirty years – if not still. We hadn't been in touch for the last couple of years, and I confess I made no effort to make contact.

It all seemed downright silly to me at the time. It seems even more so now as I look back on it. But then, I wasn't facing procecution and possible jail time.

Ian went back to New York after directing *Anything Goes*. I plunged into the task of directing the next one up, *Oliver*.

Picture it: well-known porn star now directing twenty-six little boys in Dickensian musical. It was enough to stir the curiosity of Norman Mailer. He came to see the show and invited me out for a drink afterward.

We chatted amiably. I'd ask about one of his books. He'd ask about this that or the other porn actress. Some I knew. Most I didn't.

"You seem to know an awful lot about the of ladies porn. Thinking of doing a book about us?" I smile, winningly.

"No," he replied amiably, "I was just hoping to get laid."

The Journey of the Dorabelladonna

REMEMBER CLAIRE? The waif who followed me home from the peace march? The Jane Fonda type who broadened my views of sex? The free spirit I had put aboard a bus to Florida less than three months ago?

Two days after Ian left, she walked into my apartment in Maine.

She had hitched a ride on a private plane from Ft. Lauderdale to Portland. Hitching on the highway from the airport, she got a ride on a produce truck that delivered her to my front door – which happened to be next door to the back door of this small town's best restaurant, and a scheduled stop for the trucker anyway.

Things had a way of magically working out for Claire that way.

I hadn't really thought much about what to do with the rest of my life. I didn't want to struggle along in grimy New York anymore. If I was going to be poor the rest of my life, I wanted to be someplace warm, and Texas was out of the question. California was looking good.

Now, thanks to a firebrand district attorney in Memphis, Tennessee, who was hell bent on putting all us perverts in jail, my plans were decided for me, at least the immediate ones. I would appear, as requested, before Mr. Parish for his trial of the century – the prosecution of all those involved in any way with "the transport across state lines of licentious, provocative, and filthy material" (i.e., the films, *Deep Throat* and *The Devil in Miss Jones*).

It being the fiftieth anniversary of the Scopes "Monkey Trial" in that same bucolic locale, perhaps Mr. Parish felt compelled to honor that seminal example of obtuse jurisprudence with something equally ludicrous.

From there, I would proceed to California. That was my plan.

But now I had my waif sideboard again. Two plane tickets? I had no money other than what I'd saved from my salary. A small summer stock operation cannot afford very splendid salaries. There wasn't much in the till. Claire had no money. None. Zip. Not even pocket change by the time she arrived on my doorstep. This was not unusual and never seemed to bother her very much.

Transportation was needed. Something big enough to carry the two of us and all our earthly possessions – which weren't all that much, but did now include the darling golden lab puppy that followed Claire home one day. Yes, we put up posters all over town, but nobody claimed him. We decided he must have gotten out of a tourist's car. She named him Rolph, because that's what he said when you asked him his name.

"Used school bus. Runs. Three hundred dollars. Call Opportunity Farm Boys Home," read the ad in the local rag. I had never driven anything larger than a minivan before, but I was getting the hang of it. Then a sickening crunch stopped us in our tracks. I had backed into one of the posts in the parking lot. Not a lot of damage to either the post or the bus, but it sort of sealed the deal. "You break it: you buy it." You know?

The next move was getting all the seats removed so there would be room to stow our gear and stretch out in our sleeping bags at night. A lovely man at a junkyard on the edge of town was willing to do the work in exchange for keeping the seats. It was typical of Maine transactions.

"How much you want for that foot-treadle sewing machine?" I point to a relic by the door of the huge old barn that was filled to the rafters with every manner of machine and furnishing imaginable.

"Oh, ten bucks, I s'pose," comes the welcome reply.

"Can you turn that seat around backwards?" I point to the next to last double seat on the port side of the unsightly yellow vehicle. "And bolt the sewing machine down between the seats?"

"Guess so," he says. "Makin' a nice little dinin' booth, eh?

"You got it."

"Would ya be int'rested in a little cast ah-yun cook stove I took off an ole trawlah? I can bolt it down on the stahbud side foah ya. Burns wood, coal, trash. Give ya good heat and ya can cook on it. I can put the smoke-stack out that hole wheah the flashah laht is. You won't need a flashah laht if youah not haulin kids. Fifty bucks. Wuth eva penny."

And thus sprang to life a most unusual RV. We christened her the Dorabelladona.

Vicki let us raid her prop and scenery warehouse where we liberated a rug, fabric for curtains, and even an old hammock that we stretched from corner to corner – a great place from which to watch the world go by.

Neighbors contributed pots, pans, utensils, and many jars of preserved fruit and vegetables from their gardens. Perhaps the most useful gift was a big galvanized wash tub. It was perfect for holding firewood or could be used for baths. A fifty-gallon plastic water tank was the only major purchase we had to make.

Our first stop on the way to the Great Memphis Smut Trial was Charley's farm in Connecticut. They welcomed us, let us help them string freshly harvested onions, fed us, gave us a place to sleep, and the Amazing Mr. Fixit (Charley) rebuilt our failing carburetor!

We acquired a passenger who needed to go to New Orleans. Not all that far out of the way, and we wouldn't be on any schedule once we got out of Memphis – if we got out of Memphis. Our new fellow traveler, Josh, was a guy we met when Claire and I went through one of those enlightenment courses called ARICA. (Oh yes. I've tried them all.)

After our brief, happy visit to the Halls of Justice in Memphis, and fond farewells to the coterie of young activist lawyers who had coalesced around my defense, we climbed aboard the Dorabelladonna and headed south.

New Orleans was as beautiful as I remembered from my childhood. It's that drippy moss. Makes you want to grab a mint julep, stretch out on the nearest chaise, and write a novel. Damn, where is my floppy hat?

We found the ARICA Ashram and enjoyed home-cooked veggie fare, good company, and some great music. Later aboard the Dora, the sounds and smells of "N'awlins" wrapped around me as firmly as my waif. I drifted into dreams of Southern Gothic novels, mint juleps, and California – not necessarily in that order.

Claire and I spent the next morning roaming the Garden District. Josh, our recently acquired passenger, decided to thank us for the ride by giving the bus a tune-up. While he was at it, he decided to fix the one light that wasn't functioning: the one that's supposed to go on at the foot of the front door step when the door opens.

It had never worked. We had never needed it. Still, Josh wanted to do something nice for us, so he fixed it.

He pointed out his accomplishments when we returned from our sightseeing. Indeed, the motor was purring.

We shut the door. We opened the door. The light worked!

We shut the door again, waved goodbye, and pulled into the tree-lined street and headed west.

We had topped off the tank before parking at the ARICA Ashram. The old bus got amazingly good mileage considering her age and size. Of course, we were running her with a much lighter load than she'd been built to carry. Whatever the reason, we got all the way to a nice roadside park somewhere in East Texas before nightfall with fuel to spare.

I pulled her in and cut the motor. We made a beeline for the facilities. Then we gathered up some twigs for kindling, fired up our stove, opened a can of stew, heated and ate it – all before it was totally dark. We could have lit our kerosene lamp, but why waste fuel when we couldn't keep our eyes open anyway?

The noisiest birds I have ever heard roused us before dawn. We stoked the fire, made coffee, washed up, stowed our sleeping bags, and enjoyed lush towering pines with pale light streaking down through them like a Seventh Day Adventist brochure.

Finally we're ready to hit the road.

I turn the key... nothing. I turn the key again... and again nothing, nada, zilch! Not a sound.

No. The lights weren't left on. The battery sparked just fine. Claire fooled around under the hood a bit – to no avail. Nothing to do but try and push-start the sucker.

I made Claire take the wheel. I figured my legs were stronger than hers. Leaning my back against the rear door, I pressed my feet into the ground firmly and slowly inched the thirty-foot-long bus into motion.

Pushing the vehicle until it started wasn't that difficult. Running to catch up to and jump aboard nearly killed me. Endurance has never been my strong suit.

Evidently, whatever Josh did to fix the doorstep light, unfixed the ignition. We were down to just the cash needed for gas to get to California. We had not factored in repairs.

Claire suggested that if we could make it through to Phoenix where her brother lived, he could fix it. He was good at that sort of thing. What a relief. Just what? Maybe four push-starts to go? No problem. We'd just park on a hill at night.

Have you ever tried to find a hill in West Texas?

We learned from some friendly truckers who guarded the door for us while we grabbed a shower at one of the truck stops, that on the CB circuit we were known as The Yellow Bus Nuns. Well, it was obviously a school bus, smokestack sticking out the back or no. We didn't disabuse them of their perception. We learned the waves and toots and I never felt safer in my life than on that marvelous, scenic trek.

We made it to Phoenix, and Claire's brother did indeed fix the ignition. We did a few peyote buttons in reverent obeisance to the native culture and spent an electric night watching stars in the clear desert air. Near dawn, an ambitious mockingbird took it upon himself to notify the pigeons roosting in the surrounding palm treees that the day was upon them. The pigeons dutifully flew to the nearby phone line in twos and threes to perform their morning toilet. In between swoops to the palms, Mr. Mockingbird did back flips from the wire and rehearsed his repertoire.

As the light went from pink to hot, we boarded our bus - which started on the first turn of the key - and continued on our way to California.

Crossing the border with our assorted boxes, two antique steamer trunks (one each, which served as closets and dressers in many locales for many years), one dog (Rolph), two kittens (acquired at the junkyard along with the cookstove), and six pots of philodendron. We had to surrender the philodendron at the border. You can't bring plants into California.

Corey and Stell were in San Francisco, so that was our next stop.

Picture this thirty-five-foot-long school bus with a smokestack sticking out the back, maneuvering the streets of San Francisco. Now picture this bus trying to find a place to park.

Next stop, Elysium Fields in Topanga Canyon, Los Angeles. This clothing-optional park was recommended by friends in San Francisco as being a place where we might find a place big enough to park our darling Dora and perhaps even find work.

Now picture this thirty-five-foot-long school bus with a smokestack sticking out the back winding its way up a rutted dirt road that is barely one-car wide and composed of one very sharp curve after another. See two very exhausted females on wobbly legs approach the kindly, white-bearded father figure who owns the park. Yes, we had spoken to him by phone and he had said yes, we could park our bus for the day and visit the park and he would see if there were any jobs we might do to cover our entrance fee. BUT... he thought we would be in a VW bus, not a thirty-five-foot-long school bus with a smokestack sticking out the back. We would have to move the bus to the rear of the buildings, out of sight of patrolling fuzz. Then we could clean the stable and spread fresh hay to pay for our stay. When we were done, we could spend the rest of the day by the pool. Dinner was included and we could sleep aboard that night. But... we would have to descend the treacherous drive the next morning and find a home for the Dora elsewhere.

It wasn't the first time I'd mucked out a stable. It was Claire's first time though, I'm pretty sure.

"You came all the way from New York in that thing?" asks Ed Lange, our host.

"We stopped off in New Orleans and Phoenix. Then we went to visit friends in San Francisco."

"How the Hell did you drive this thing around San Francisco?"

We reply in unison, "Veeeerrrry carefully."

He laughed. He was very nice. As were all the folks we met there. Well, one asshole had a momentary lapse of nudist park manners and started fluffing his semi-demi when we were introduced. (I was recognized, I'm afraid.) We ignored him. Even if he meant it as a compliment, that sort of thing is just not tolerated in nudist parks. Aside from that, it was a swell day.

"Where are you going from here?" asks our new friend, Mr. Lange.

"We have no idea," I reply.

"Have you ever visited The Swallows Park down near El Cajon?"

"Where's El Cajon?" asks Claire.

"It's a bit inland from San Diego. You do know where San Diego is?"

"South," I exclaim rapturously. "It must be warmer."

"Oh, it is. It's almost in the desert. In the hills, actually. Really lovely. The park is owned by a retired Marine Sergeant and her long-time room-mate." He looked at the two of us as if to say, "You girls know what I mean."

"How do I get there?" I was ready to roll. I liked the idea of heading south. It seems like you're going downhill.

"When you get to El Cajon, ask for directions to Harbison Canyon. There's only one road through it. The Park's on the southeast side of the road. You can't miss it."

But of course we did. Miss it. Several times.

We drove back and forth the length of Harbison Canyon Road until, on about the fourth pass, we were slowed by a combine making its lumbering way down the middle of the road.

There were two boys who looked about twelve aboard. One knelt on the floor, manning the pedals manually while the other stood on the seat, steering with his foot, hand on his buddy's head for balance, peering over a fence to our left.

"Can you see anything?" squeaked the kid on the pedals.

"That's it," I said to Claire, nodding toward the tall fence. We pulled into the next drive. Sure enough, there was a small sign that announced: The Swallows, A Clothing Optional Mobile Home Park.

The Swallows

"CAN I HELP YOU?"

A non-committal baritone issues from what is obviously a female. Her one (and only) huge bare breast rests cozily between her elbows on the fieldstone counter of the gatehouse. She peers from under the bill of a tennis cap and sizes us up – thirty-five-foot-long school bus with a smokestack sticking out the back and all.

"Ed Lange suggested we might be able to rent a space for our bus here," I purr in my best Fine Southern Lady.

"Well," she peers dubiously at our dear Dorabelladona and drawls, "we don't rent space to anything but regulation mobile homes, but if you just need a place to park for a bit, we can find some space, I guess. You'll have to get a membership though. How long do you expect to stay?"

"Depends. How much is the membership?"

"Depends. How long you want to stay?"

The details of the final transaction are hazy, but the gate slid open and the Dorabelladona sailed majestically forward with only a slight hiccup or two.

The residents gathered like friendly natives in a South Seas romance movie. They waved directions as I gingerly backed the old girl into a narrow space between the recreation hall and the laundry. She settled into the space like a broody hen. I checked her vital signs and turned off the engine. She gave one final shudder and breathed her last.

She never started again, no matter who did what. The noble beast had fulfilled her destiny. She had earned her rest. Long live the Dauntless Dora.

Her remains were donated to the good of mankind. Everyone in the canyon came to pay their respects and harvest any piece of her that they might be able to use. A colorful ageless neighbor known as Goat Annie got the iron cookstove. She insisted we take a small wheel of cheese in exchange. She makes the cheese herself from the milk she regularly extracts form her gaggle of goats, some of whom are house pets. It was fabulous.

The Dorabelladona's last bones became a chicken coop on one of the many nearby farms. Claire and I moved into a vacant trailer that I arranged to buy on time.

The Swallows was a gift from the gods – an oasis – yea, Khayyam's "Paradise enow!"

The trailer we moved into had been the home of a pair of extremely energetic seniors who had put in a vegetable garden at the top of a steep thirty-foot high bluff behind it. There was a ladder-like stair cutting through the solid ice plant that covered the cliff. We were told the former owners, paragons of bucolic virtue, had carried tons of chicken shit – acquired for free from the local egg farms – up this treacherous construction in bushel baskets. The cornucopia of fresh vegetables still growing came with the trailer.

The ice plant was in bloom. The purple was so intense it colored the walls of the trailer when the light was just right. There were two bee hives further up the hill at the top of the garden area. These winged fellows knew the ice plant was there for their benefit, but they weren't nasty about it. Indeed, once when a particularly stubborn weed I was attempting to extract suddenly pulled loose and sent me ass over heels over teakettle down that thirty-foot drop, I managed to flip onto my stomach and grab hold of the thick foliage. I hung on for dear life. Then those little buggers, who had managed to vacate the area I landed in before I did so, settled back down all over my back. I swear they each grabbed a hair and hauled my ass back up that fragrent precipice to safety. I never could have made it by myself. In all the time I lived there, and through two harvests of their honey, I was never stung.

Peach trees, cherry trees, and a walnut tree with big honking nuts on it also came with this prime location. Some of my childhood was spent on relative's farms, so I wasn't a complete city slicker. But the occasional avocado sprout from a seed in a jar on the windowsill was all I'd nurtured since puberty. Some atavistic urge now made me thrill at the prospect of eating produce from my very own backyard.

I had no idea how much work it would entail.

Big Sue ran the place. Her roomie (yes, they had been Marines together) was the single-breasted duenna who had checked us out at the gate. She was not the only lady there missing a mammary. I began to think I'd found the lost Amazon tribe of Greek mythology. This easy acceptance of the human form in all its shapes and sizes is one of the most endearing qualities of sun worshippers.

There are many different types of nudist organizations. This was a family park. Many of the residents had kids. Day visitors, too, were every age. Toddlers had their own pool. Octogenarians usually sat in the shade and played dominoes, gin rummy, and bridge.

A co-owner, Jim, was actually a duly appointed sheriff. He patrolled the place with a quiet authority, wearing a tin star on his vest, a forty-five in a holster on his hip, a baseball cap on his head, and wrap-around sunglasses. That's it. Vest, hat, sunglasses, gun belt. Oh yes. He sometimes wore sandals if it was really hot. I don't know that anyone ever disturbed the peace enough for him to take action, but it was comforting to see him on duty. Amusing, until you got used to it, but comforting.

The half dozen or so youngsters that lived at the park ran as a pack all over the place. Our trailer had an enclosed porch on one side. The kids turned it into their own personal playroom, which was just fine with their parents.

Most of the residents had nicknames: Big Sue, Tennis Bob, Dirty Mother (for the Kahlua and milk drink he favored). I became known as Granny Goose.

Though it was seldom the topic of conversation, everyone knew what I did for a living. They accepted me at face value. I was more than happy to conform to their standard of propriety. It pretty much matched my own comfort level anyway.

Every community has unwritten rules of behavior. Theirs solved my waif dilemma. One day Big Sue took me aside and told me that Claire's presence, since shaving her head and introducing her similarly tonsured, rather rowdy, baby-diesel dyke pals to the pool, was no longer welcome at the club. I could stay. She must go.

Claire wasn't even surprised. She shrugged and packed her backpack. That I might accompany her in her exile was never even suggested.

Her new gal pals picked her up that very afternoon. They were delighted to have her move in with them and join their basketball team. She was good. I think she may have been varsity in college. I sprang for some new jerseys for the team.

Now, wheels are a necessity in California. The first thing I did after moving into the park was prevail upon Tallie, a friend I'd met in New York who was now living in L.A., to sell me her old car. She wanted two hundred for it, but a hundred was all I had. Bless her: she said to send her the rest later.

When the front wheel fell off driving it home to San Diego, she said forget about the second hundred.

Tallie and her husband, Pat, were my first friends in California. They gave me a job on a soft porn film they produced called *Tarz and Jane and Cheetah and Boy*. (At one time it was called *Ping Pong* and I won a "Best Supporting Actress" award for my contribution. The donkey painted to look like a zebra should have gotten the award.)

That film was a hoot to work on. Another non-porn film she and I did for Al Adamson called *Girls for Rent*, wasn't nearly as much fun, but it did pay rather well.

I named the car Poor Pitiful Pearl.

That poor pitiful car was my lifeline.

Well, the girls were so grateful for my gift of the basketball jerseys that while I was off doing a film, they decided to thank me by steam cleaning my beloved Pearl's engine.

She never ran again.

I have the worst luck with Good Samaritans.

Stella came down to the park frequently to visit. Doctor Yakalot's Traveling Space Circus – the soubriquet she coined for our nomadic clan after the Pickle Factory Diaspora – was back in business. She and Corey had moved down from San Francisco, and from place to place in L.A., until Corey settled down with a new boyfriend in a cute little house overlooking the Rowena reservoir in a slot of L.A. between Hollywood and Silver Lake. Stell found a bungalow in Beachwood Canyon under the Hollywood sign. It was one of ten in a horseshoe around a narrow garden. Most of its tenants were in the industry – not the porn one, the real one. She dubbed it Rancho Beyondo.

Some steady editing jobs had finally begun to come her way. Her skills were becoming known in the business. Boy, it was good to see her again.

Another old friend I'd stayed in touch with through the years came down for a visit and brought his four-year-old son along. CB, the beautiful Brit I was married to for about fifteen minutes in 1957 had moved, first to Australia, and then to L.A. This son was from his third marriage, now dissolved. The two children from his second marriage were with their mother in L.A.

About a year after we were divorced, CB had asked me to go before a triumvirate of priests at St. Patrick's and swear upon my immortal soul that our marriage had never been consummated – i.e., that we had never had sex. He needed an annulment so that he could marry this good Catholic girl in the chorus that he'd knocked up while he was playing Mordred in the road company of *Camelot*.

Those three Fathers put me through a grilling I wouldn't wish on the worst serial killer – but they granted the annulment.

I'm not sure I did him a favor. They had a second child, so they must have had some sort of relationship, but stormy would be the adjective that comes to mind. His next wife was a real sweetheart. She bore him the enchanting blonde pixie the entire camp came to adore.

Even my mother came to visit me in my newfound paradise. She was on her way to join her GoGo Girls Travel Club in San Francisco for their cruise to Alaska. She and I went up to visit Stell in Los Angeles and did all the tourist things. From there we proceeded to San Francisco and did all the tourist things there. We stayed at one of the hotels that frequently housed porn film casts. The manager recognized me, but caught my look and didn't blow my cover. I waved a bon voyage as she sailed away with her pals to see Alaska. I think she had a good time. I still have a towel with our picture on it that we got at Grauman's Chinese.

One day, soon after Claire's departure, Dee, the darling dumpling of a lady who runs the snack stand sits down beside me after the lunch crowd disperses.

"Can I come down to your house and play this afternoon? Carlos is in one of his ugly moods and I don't want to go home."

"Of course," I reply. "You know you're welcome anytime. I'm gonna make a run to the market. You wanna come with, or hang out at the trailer?"

"All my clothes are in our trailer and I don't want to get into another argument while he's drinking. I'll just bring my book and hang out, if that's OK. I'd sit out by the pool, but my skin can't take any more sun today."

"No problemo. Do you need anything from the market?"

"No thanks. Don't forget to put some clothes on," she calls to me as I trot off toward my trailer. You'd be surprised how often we did that; start out the gate forgetting we hadn't a stitch on our backs.

That afternoon, I suggested she crash at my trailer until they worked it out, which they did.

He kept their trailer.

They remained friends.

She and I became trailer mates for the time I lived at the Swallows, and friends for life.

She also became my costumer – filling the role my mother had played in my early life.

Mother had lovingly built all my tutus, baby bee, snowflake and other costumes. She also built those of most of the other baby ballerinas in whichever little town we happened to be in at recital time.

Dee, the swap-meet maven, also a welcome customer at every thrift shop in Southern California, found and fitted me into several elegant outfits for my new career as a stripper.

Here's how that came about.

Many of the theaters that show porn films present the added attraction of ecdysiasts – ladies who take off their clothes to music. As Georgina starred in so many of those films, this agent, Jay, a delightful little guy who reminded me a lot of my Nate, my first boyfriend in New York when I was a kid trying to break into Broadway, assured me he could get big bucks for Miss Jones' strip act at these venues. *Devil* was in its third or fourth go-round by then. Adding a stark naked appearance by Miss Jones herself could only add to its shelf-life, I suppose. He had caught one of my personal appearances and got in touch.

At those gigs, the many such appearances I made when *Devil* opened, I would speak briefly, answer a few questions from the house, and sign autographs in the lobby after the film. The questions were pretty predictable, but the audiences were not exactly what I had expected.

Due to the Porn Chic phenomenon, couples had starting coming to these films. One time, a pair of nuns appeared in the line for an autograph. I almost fainted. They said they thought the moral message of the film – that suicide was the "one thing He would not forgive" – was well-stated and that they thought I was courageous. (I checked with the manager standing next to me. Yes, they had said courageous, not contagious.)

Strip? Well, why the hell not?

My idea of what a strip act should be came right out of the musical, *Gypsy*. Specifically, from the song, "You Gotta Have a Gimmick." In this hysterical number, three veterans show a young Gypsy Rose Lee the ropes as she prepares to make her debut in the "art." That was really about all I knew about stripping, and it bore little resemblance to reality.

Jay said the Q&A thing could form the basis of an act. I need only add some disrobing. This canny agent even gave me my gimmick, suggesting I handle a snake as part of the act. Herman had evidently made quite an impression in his debut role.

I knew I could handle a snake. I knew I could dance – though that didn't seem to be required. I'd proven I could talk to an audience. All I needed were a few tasteful gowns and a basket big enough to hold a snake, but small enough to fit under an airplane seat, and, oh yes, a snake.

"Marc? It's Georgie. Yeah, I'm fine. You? Oh, I love it here. You gotta come out and visit. It's paradise. Really. Listen. I need a snake. Yeah, for a strip act I'm putting together. Fang and Claw? The one on 14th Street? Yeah. I've been in there. Creepy place. They rent? That's great. Thanks. I'll call you when I get to town."

Jay even advanced the money for costumes and tapes.

Tapes, I learned, had replaced the piano players and drummers of an earlier age of stripping. The standard procedure of the day was for the girls to bring tapes with them to each venue. These contained the songs they wanted played while they disrobed, danced, and otherwise tittilated the audience.

There were a lot of very sensual songs going around at that time, but that wasn't what I had in mind.

An album of the score from *The Devil in Miss Jones* was still available. It had sold remarkably well, and was another testament to Jerry's artistry at putting together a film. I heard he paid as much for the score as the actual shoot had cost. Then he used only a small portion of it. He replaced much of it with the signature wind effects that were music in themselves.

Paco, a pal at the park, helped me transfer selections from the album to tape. He segued from these into the very popular instrumental that had swept the bedrooms of America recently – "The Stripper."

It was harder to find a good recording of "Stars and Stripes Forever," but he did, and laid it in for my finale.

He then made several backup dupes for me. Wouldn't take a cent for his efforts, of course.

The costumes didn't cost much either, what with Dee's knowledge of local thrift shops and bargain stores, plus her considerable skill with needle and thread, I was ready for prime time in no time.

I'll have to admit, it's an exciting thing to fornicate in the privacy of a film set. Yes, a film set is a very private space. That bubble of light in front of the camera is the whole freakin' universe when you're in it

When I got a film job, I would go on the wagon and stay sober throughout the shoot. I had – and have – great respect for every form of the biz of show. Just like those who labor to create live theater, those who work on and in film, whatever the genre or content, are dedicated professionals. They work hard to improve their craft and are fiercely determined to make every project a success. I'm proud to be a card-carrying member of this club.

Discussing fucking and sucking and taking off my clothes and shaking my booty in front of a live audience however, was a whole 'nother story. Don't laugh. It made me feel cheap.

I didn't mind it as much when I was drunk.

Atlantic City to Texas – 1976

The Intervention

TAKE OFF WAS A FILM I really worked my butt off getting in good shape to do. It was a very elaborate big-budget production. My scenes were shot on location at a huge estate upriver from Manhattan. I played a super-rich flamboyant socialite of the Roaring Twenties – complete with Silver Ghost Rolls driven by the requisite tall taciturn Man Servant of swarthy hue.

Armand Weston called me a full two months before I was needed in New York. My drinking problem obviously had become common knowledge in the trade by then – even though I had always been on deck and sober when shooting. He was giving me time to prepare. And I did.

Not only did I climb resolutely on the wagon, I did a ballet barre every day, swam like an otter, ran all over the camp, and even climbed the thirty feet up to the garden almost every day to pull weeds. My close encounter with the benevolent bees was a direct result of this resolute endeavor.

By the time I got to New York for the shoot, I'd dropped ten pounds and could see my eyes in the morning without the aid of toothpicks. Frankly, my dear, I looked maaahvelous.

Yeah, I looked damn good for an old broad. But the male lead, Wade Nichols, took the comeliness cake. He was gorgeous – simply gorgeous. I heard he went on to do non-porn films in Europe. He was also very, very nice: a Rolex, as my favorite Brazilian cameraman would say. Our steamy-gauzy-twenties-picnic-romp is some of the prettiest fucking footage I've ever seen.

The wrap party was as elaborate as the location: hot hors d'oeuvres, champagne – the works. In the space of three days, I parlayed that into drinks with friends, drinks with strangers, and drinks alone from a paper sack while sitting on a piling at the end of the Christopher Street pier. Fortunately, the Hudson is too dirty to jump into. Hell, you'd bounce right back off the floating condoms.

So I spent my last $2.95 for another pint of blackberry brandy and sat down on the curb outside the liquor store on Greenwich Avenue. I wanted to be near the gutter in case I threw up before I could get the bottle open. Marc Stevens walked by. He didn't recognize me at first. Not surprising. I hadn't bathed in three days.

He hauled my ass to County Rehab and waited the hours it took to get me admitted. He held me tightly when my brandy fix wore off and I began to shake. When I told him I was going to start puking, he stormed the desk and got me moved to the front of the line.

After the requisite three days of darting to the sink to upchuck then crawling back into bed to curl into a quivering ball of misery, I was able to take nourishment. The second week, I went to my first ever AA meeting. When we were called upon to recount how we had landed where we were, I mentioned that my last binge had started with a single glass of champagne. The gutter-hardened men laughed me from the room. I did forge lasting friendships with the only two gay guys there, and won twenty-three packs of cigarettes playing gin rummy.

At the next company picnic (AFA Awards), I won best supporting actress for *Take Off*.

I stayed sober for nearly a year after that.

Then the Pussycat Theater folks mounted a musical review in San Diego called *Take It Off*. (Not to be confused with the film, *Take Off*.) The idea was to showcase La Spelvin's long forgotten musical comedy skills. The only problem was they'd been forgotten for a good reason. They were the lamest skills in the show. Doing a barre occasionally does not replace regular class, and I never could sing for sour apples.

It was very depressing. Still the show must go on. The obvious solution? Dutch courage. Booze. Specifically: Brandy Alexanders. I thought all that milk would be easier on the gut. It wasn't.

The show didn't go on very long.

It was back to the strip joints.

The next tour delivered me once more into the arms of the Big Apple. Specifically, "naughty bawdy fawty-second street" – blocks from the scene of my triumph in *Pajama Game* in 1954. Back then I was the cutest new kid on the block. Now I bantered lewdly and danced nudely for a crowd of horny guys in a sleezatorium up a long flight of filthy stairs.

I'd graduated from Brandy Alexanders at the bar to a flask of vodka in my purse.

An intervention – sort of verbal dodge ball – was arranged by the two kindest people in the world: a couple who always let me crash at their Greenwich Village apartment when I was in town. It was set to roll the minute I stepped in the door.

Several people were seated around the long narrow living room. My eyes landed first on the man seated at the far end of the room. Light streamed through the French doors behind him making it difficult to make out his features, but the casual slouch was unmistakable.

It was Ian. Remember him? The man I left my second husband to pursue? The one I callously abandoned when the happy-hippie-peaceniks marched by?

He nodded a polite greeting. My heart skipped several beats. Then it stopped completely when my eyes adjusted to the light and I realized the woman seated on the couch to my right was my mother!

My benevolent hosts had called Ian to ask what could be done about me. He then called my mother. She was on the next flight to New York with the firm intention of hauling me back to Texas to wring me dry.

When that plan was mentioned, I explained I had committed to an appearance in Atlantic City the following week. I said I would fly to Texas at the end of that engagement. Mother said she would accompany me to Atlantic City and we would both fly to Texas at the end of the week. Mother was not unfamiliar with the workings of the alcohol-soaked brain. She wasn't letting me out of her sight until I was sober.

Trying to get to sleep that night without the aid of booze was futile. I was sore all over from lying as still as possible and listening to my mother's soft snore coming from the bunk beneath me. About four, I gave up and climbed carefully down and found my flask. A good swig let me snooze for a couple of hours.

As dawn spilled through the iron gates across the window, I sneaked back down for another quick swig before Mom woke. When she did, we packed and slipped out quietly.

Next stop, Fang and Claw: the exotic pet emporium where I rented snakes for my act. The one I'd been using for the last three weeks had gone in for refueling the night before. They were a little tetchy to handle after a meal, so every few weeks I would leave the hungry one there to be fed and pick up one that had eaten a week or so before.

The owner had opened early for me and had my new co-star in a case ready to go. We exchanged brief pleasantries and were out the door.

From there, we hightailed it uptown to Port Authority and hopped the next bus to Atlantic City.

Opening Night of a Closing Act

THE PACKED THEATER IS HUSHED. Not even heavy breathing can be heard. The soundtrack bounces off the old theater's unpadded walls in eerie echoes.

On the screen, a woman sits on a plain chest, scruffy black velvet dress pulled up over her thighs. She masturbates frantically, trying to bring herself to a sexual climax. There's a strange introspective male sitting on the floor. She addresses him in a throaty conspiratorial rasp.

"Just touch me. If you touch me, I can get off. Look. See how wet my pussy is? Put your cock in me and we can get off together," hisses the woman on the screen. The extreme closeup of a ravaged face is replaced by an extreme closeup of female genitalia. Frantic fingers tipped with long black nails diddle and probe the exposed flesh as the hysterical wail continues. "Just touch me so I can get off," the husky voice hammers in desperate insistence.

I stand at arm's length behind the screen. I would have to crane my head back to see the top of the image. I don't. I don't need to. I've seen the film.

The familiar dialogue continues to reverberate through the empty backstage area.

"Look! Here! See my dripping pussy? Come on. Don't you want to put your tongue in my pussy?"

The actress abandons her seductive whisper and screams in frustrated anguish, "Help me, Goddamn it. Please help me. I can't do it by myself."

That more or less sums up the moral of this cautionary tale that is the film *The Devil in Miss Jones*. To wit: abuse it; you lose it – that wonderful ability to plunge into the luscious spasm of a sexual climax.

I take a deep breath, lift my chin, straighten my shoulders and thrust my hip to the proper angle to make the slim navy crepe gown fall into the proper 1930's drape. The figure on the screen is held in a freeze frame of eternal damnation as the ironic tinkling lilt of the Fruit Scene music plays over the rolling credits.

As the final notes fade, a deep, mellifluous voice intones, "And NOW-ooh-uh, ladies and gent-le-men, Mzzzzzzzz. Georgeeeeeena Spellllllvin."

The stage managers who hold the tinseled threads of strip houses together are a breed apart and very special. All seem to be endowed with deep rich baritone pipes. The first of these paragons of patience I was to meet was known as "Old Velvet Tongue." He held court backstage at the century-old Trocadero in Philadelphia.

No sooner had I set down my little green makeup kit, than Mr. Velvet Tongue informed me confidentially that Edwin Booth, brother of Lincoln assassin John Wilkes Booth, had trod the very boards upon which my dressing table sat. I do not think they had been washed since.

There was one very nice thing backstage though: a box of three-week old kittens. I was playing with one when I heard my cue. I had no idea what I was supposed to do for an act, so, as I'd done in the sex films, I made it up as I went along. Walking into my spotlight with the kitten cuddled in my arms, I nodded my appreciation for the wave of applause, paused at the microphone until there was silence, leaned in and purred, "You guys came here tonight expecting to see a little live pussy, right?"

The roar of agreement almost blew my wig off.

"Well, here you go." I lifted the adorable fuzzball up into the spotlight and was rewarded with my first laugh as a stripper.

The Troc – once a Grand Legitimate Theatah, then an early Vaudeville House, later a Classic Burlesque – had become a porn emporium and was the first such theater to book me in my new career as a stripper.

My current engagement in Atlantic City would be the last.

The screen flies up into the loft of the theater, a follow spot hits the mike rising from the stage floor, and I step into the light. A gratifying wave of applause rises from the dark theater.

"Thank you," I say with true sincerity. Hey, I could have been met with icy silence. It's happened. Applause is nicer.

I pull forth a slip of paper from the small collection of notes in my trembling hand.

My hand trembles not from nerves, but the need of strong drink. With luck I will get through the next ten minutes of Q&A, another twenty or so of disrobing, dancing, re-robing, exiting, returning for a smashing finale and bows without tossing my cookies all over the first row.

I lift my chin and and speak into the microphone. "I really appreciate all the nice compliments you guys sent back, but I'm not gonna read them out loud. I'd be too embarrassed."

I shoot a sultry look out to the audience and use the very lowest note in my limited vocal range.

"I'm easily embarrassed, you know."

That gets a slight titter.

"I would, however, like to thank (I check the name on the slip of paper) Marvin for his comment."

I shade my eyes with the paper and peer into the dark beyond the spot.

"I'm glad you like small tits, Marvin."

The audience responds with scattered, good-natured chuckles. It takes a while for porn-house audiences to realize it's OK to laugh.

Not everyone likes my act. "They don't come to a porn show to laugh," the owner of one of the more urban theaters once said. "If they wanted to laugh, they'd stay home and watch television."

So, they come to a porn house to – what? If it's to jerk off, wouldn't they rather be in the privacy of a loop booth?

I never asked, so I still don't know.

I address my Atlantic City audience. "I'll try to answer as many questions as we have time for."

There's a bit of mike feedback. It's quickly adjusted. I select and read a question printed in large block letters.

"How did a nice girl like you get into porn?"

"Hmmm, how did I get into porn?" I needlessly repeat the (obviously) setup question.

Pensive pause – big smile.

"Just lucky, I guess." (Badda ching!)

"I can barely read this one." I turn upstage, holding the slip of paper up into the spot. This gives the audience a good look at the back of my gown which is cut down to my crack.

"Who had the biggest... what's this word?" I turn back to the audience in wide-eyed curiosity, "Ego?"

"Erection! What's the biggest dick you ever did?" is shouted from the second row. Porn film audiences do get straight to the point.

"I've heard John Holmes holds the title for Mr. Big in the trade," I demurely reply, "but I can't vouch for the merits of his claim. I've never done a scene with him. (This was true at the time.) I know Marc Stevens wrote a book called *Mr. Ten and a Half*. (A nod and a wink.) "I don't think he was talking about his shoe size. (Chuckle, chuckle.) You just saw the film, what do you think?"

I pick another question.

"Did you have to audition for the role of Miss Jones, and if so, what did you have to do to get the part?" leers a heavy baritone from the second or third row.

"Well, in a way I did, but I didn't know that's what I was doing at the time."

A few chuckles from those sensing a double entendre. Then the audience sits quietly as I tell my tale. This is the fourth show of the day. The first show was at noon. The Businessman's Special. Sure enough, there was a solid shelf of attaché cases across the laps in the front row. The six and nine o'clock shows were full of tourists, judging by the garb and abundance of cameras. Lots of couples. Even a gaggle or two of giggling girls. This, the midnight show, has a crowd that was, at first, a bit rowdy. They now seem to be hanging on my every word.

"...then Jerry offered me the role of Miss Jones. They were gonna pay me twenty-five dollars a day to cook, or one hundred dollars a day to fuck."

Pause. Smile.

"I'm not crazy."

"A hundred dollars a day to fuck." Jezus H Keerist! My mother's sitting backstage in earshot.

I press on regardless. What else can I do?

After a few more exchanges the follow spot blinks, signaling me to move on.

"Time for one more." I spread the scraps of paper out like a hand of cards and pick one.

"Would you rather get screwed in the ass or suck cock?"

Ah, language. Doctor Ruth, that pert, pint-sized psychologist whose frank talk about sex made her a TV star in a more permissive age, spoke easily of fellatio and cunnilingus – even anal penetration. To my knowledge, no one got a major harelip. But this was a porn house, not a talk show. Early on, I was admonished by management to *not* use language that would make me sound like a snob. Still, cocksucking and buttfucking are hard to say when you know your mother can hear you.

Again, I face the audience with my baby doll look.

"Do I have to pick just one?"

I do wish there were a drummer
in the pit.

"OK. I know you guys didn't come here tonight to listen to me talk, right?"

Murmur of assent.

I continue in my oh-you-naughty-boys voice, "You're waiting to see me get naked."

A nice roar follows me to the wings where I trade my handful of notes for a small, antique leather suitcase. The *Devil* theme music fills the stage. The lights dim, leaving a warm puddle in the center of the stage.

So far, so good. I'm shaky, but the gut's not heaving.

I set the case down, reach up and pull out the two long pins that hold my hair in a neat swirl. It cascades around my shoulders. I slip the straps of my dress off of my shoulders. With a barely perceptible shrug, the gown falls in a small circle around my feet.

Standing (I like to think, majestically) in my altogether, I marvel at the audience response. Dead silence. No catcalls, no whistles, just dead silence.

I dance. My routine is based on ballet: my native tongue. The music segues from the happy lilt of the Fruit Scene to the sensuous strains that accompanied my love scene with Herman, the boa. Out comes my secret weapon, my gimmick, the recently rented stand-in for the now famous Herman. I coax the five-foot snake up my arm and around my shoulders. Snakes head for any warmth they perceive and boas love to climb. I lay on my back, hike my hips up as far as I can and stick one leg straight up in the air. The little ham scoots up my erect member to get as much of his length into the spotlight as he can. (I think he thinks it might be warm.) I coax him back around my arm and we whirl and swivel around the stage. As the snake music ends, I carefully coil him back into his little round basket and secure the lid.

The spot changes from deep blue to Shubert pink.

I begin to dress. Right. Dress. Remember, I'm naked. Most gals take it off. I put it on. Out of my case I pull black silk hose which I play with in traditional stripper style – pulling them through my crotch and like that – ending with them on instead of removing them. Next I don the garter belt. Then I slip into the spike-heeled shoes.

The slow, rhythmic strut of that all-time classic "The Stripper" pulses around me. Fastening the hose to the back garters on the belt is the high-point of this segment. Facing upstage, I lean over and reach between my legs. I fumble and fondle around my bare bottom to find the dangling garter, snap it provocatively (which can be dangerous) and finally secure it to the stocking. I straighten up to rest my tendons and allow a bit more by-play with the bald-headed darlings in the front row. Then I do it again for the other leg.

By the end of the second chorus, I'm dressed in a conservative business suit with a wrap-around skirt. I pick up my suitcase, now with crepe gown and snake safely tucked inside, strut to the wings, and hand it to Bill the stage manager. I grab the curtain and do the final bumps, grinds, squats, nods, looks and winks of a traditional stripper exit.

In the wings, I rip off the suit and don a tee shirt emblazoned with the interlaced arms of males and females in a circle around the legend, "The Great Bi-Centennial." It's 1976, remember?

Bill pours a pitcher of water over the shirt as I slip into my toe shoes and grab my baton with little American flags on each end. Bill slams my Uncle Sam hat on my head and I march on top of my tippy toes across the stage, flags whirling, "The Stars and Stripes Forever" blasting away.

I stole this idea from Dick Shawn. As the in-house choreographer at the long since burned-to-the-ground Rancho Vegas resort in, where else? Las Vegas, I set the dance routines for the ladies of the ensemble around his act. For his finale, he asked me to twirl fire batons on top of this six-foot high platform. He came onstage in a monk's robe. This he threw off, revealing a transparent Uncle Sam suit over red and white striped boxer shorts. One night, I was twirling away when he threw the monk's robe over me, bringing me crashing to the stage floor. My tall feathered hat had caught fire. Brought the house down.

Thank gawd by now the audience knows it's OK to laugh, and do.

Blowing a final kiss, I exit and sprint for the lavatory in my dressing room.

Mother is waiting with a cool damp cloth for my forehead and a big fluffy towel for the rest of me. As soon as I stop throwing up, she hands me a Mason jar of beef bouillon mixed with vodka. A sip of this excellent concoction (known as a Bull Shot) provides just enough alcohol to keep me from retching and the benefits of some serious nourishment.

Mom confiscated my flask upon arrival. It was empty by then anyway. She now doles out doses of her magic brew as needed. Only as seriously, no kidding, needed.

"Got some good laughs," she says.

"Yeah. Full house again. Hope it stays that way through the week," I respond between sips.

"Hungry?" Mother gently takes the jar from my grasp and replaces the lid. Into her voluminous carryall it goes to rest amidst the knitting, tape measure, crossword puzzles, pencils, paperback books, scarf, collapsible umbrella, sewing kit, coiled nylon clothesline (complete with teensy plastic clothespins), Swiss Army knife, and assorted cosmetics.

Bill sticks his head in the door.

"Great show, Georgie. You gonna do autographs out front?"

"Sure. Give me five minutes."

It's more like ten, but a goodly crowd is still gathered. Mom circumnavigates the swarm and heads off down the boardwalk. We meet at the restaurant.

"Need another shot?" she asks, offering the jar as I slide into the booth.

"Thanks." I sip gratefully at the salty brew. She peruses the menu.

"How 'bout the halibut?" she suggests.

"Just for the hell of it? I'll drink to that," I raise my jar of Mother's brew.

"Feeling sick?"

"No."

"Good."

She grabs the jar and returns it to the seashell-bedecked tote bag that touts Galveston as the Riviera of the Gulf.

It was going to be a long week.

The Morning After

"OK. I'VE GOT THE TAIL," says Mom.

She is perched gingerly on the edge of the old-fashioned bathtub, feet braced firmly on its bottom, holding tightly to one end of the snake, her brow puckered in fierce concentration.

Slo-o-owly, I stretch the boa out along the bottom of the tub and place my foot gently on the area just behind his head. (I'm not sure snakes have necks.) This frees a hand to retrieve the tube of ointment held firmly in my teeth. I squeeze out a squiggle along the reptile's broad flat head and begin to smear it gently around the scaly surface.

Our big comfortable room is on the second floor of a Grand Old Dame of a hotel on the boardwalk. The gracious Spanish structure is probably about like it was when it was built over seventy-five years ago. The bath fixtures aren't quite that old, but they are far from new. Thank heavens. In a modern enclosed tub-shower combo, our current operation would be damn near impossible.

A current of salty air carries the sounds of surf and children through huge open windows. The breeze sends a pleasant ripple of coolness across our bare skin.

Yes, that's bare, as in butt naked. After much discussion about how to cover five feet of snake and ourselves with ointment and keep it there for ten minutes until we could rinse it off, we settled on bare butts in the tub.

Mom's little round belly begins to shake with suppressed laughter.

"What's so funny," I ask, truculently.

"Think about it. I'm stark naked in a bathtub in Atlantic City, hanging onto the tail end of a snake, and there ain't a damn soul in the world I can tell about it."

I see her point.

Father would not appreciate the humor of the situation.

None of the ladies at the Petroleum Club Bingo Nights would ever hear about it. Nor would her co-workers at the office where, as secretary to the Comish, she runs the Parks and Recreation Department of the quaint town where she and my Dad now live. Dad's company had finally bumped him up to a permanent post there after his twenty-odd years of faithful service in the fields. Permanent post or no, Mother never hung any curtains in the living room because she said every time she did, they moved.

Why are we butt naked in the bathtub with a snake?

Yesterday we picked up the boa from Fang and Claw on our way to the bus station. When we got to Atlantic City, there was no time to do more than drop our bags in the room and hightail it to the theater.

Management had an aquarium all set up in my dressing room as promised. The kid had his own private dressing room where he could relax between shows, safely contained. Mom and I unpacked and explored the restaurants in the area. There were several rather good ones.

The shows went well. The boa was a natural. He really seemed to enjoy being handled and was easily persuaded into the various positions I used in the act. It was a long day and we were all glad to get back to the hotel and crash.

About four a.m. I woke needing a drink and reached for my Mason jar. Suddenly, I felt little bugs crawling all over me. I thought I must have the DT's though I had only heard about them. I hoped a dose of booze would fix it: took one, flopped into my fetal curl, and tried to get back to sleep.

My tossing and scratching finally woke Mom. She flipped on the light, took one look at me and proclaimed the place infested with bed bugs. Indeed, upon close examination, little black specs could be seen moving about on the sheet.

She was about to call the desk when a slight rustle in the snake's case caught my attention. I looked inside. My poor little prop was as restless as I had been. I lifted him up and let him coil around my arms. Holding his head near the lamp, we could see wee black bugs crawling around his eyes.

During the course of our close dancing, the little critters must have crawled from his body to mine.

I quickly returned him to his quarters.

The worst part was waiting for Fang and Claw to open. Several hot showers filled the time. We washed the bedding in the tub while we were at it, hanging the sheets in front of the large open windows on a rigging of coat hangers hooked into the louvered shutters and the length of clothesline Mom always carried with her when traveling.

Ta DA! Instant porn theater. All we needed was a popcorn machine.

We watched the clock slowly approach the hour of 8 a.m. The instant it did, I put through a call to the pet store. The hotel operator offered to redial them every five minutes when I told her it was urgent. About 8:20, the phone finally rang.

"Oh geez, I'm so sorry," the proprietor of Fang and Claw wails when I tell my tale of woe. "That guy came in day before yesterday. I never got a chance to check him out. Bring him over. I have a slightly smaller female I can give you."

"Thanks, but I'm already in Atlantic City. He worked the shows yesterday and, except for the bugs, he's just fine. Good dancer."

"So, what are these things?" I continue. "How do I get rid of them?"

"They're reptile mites. Don't worry. They don't bite people."

The hell they don't!

"Just dose him with some Barc ointment," suggests the snake man.

"What's that?" I ask. "Do I have to find a vet to get it?"

"Naw. They sell it at any drugstore. It's for crabs."

Crabs I knew about.

Once, a friend sublet my apartment while I was out on the road with a show. A few days after I returned, he came by for lunch. We dined on the terrace. Yeah, terrace. What a wonderful apartment that was: a one-flight walkup with a separate bedroom. Double doors in the living room opened onto a small terrace that bulged out over Riverside Drive. You could see the George Washington Bridge if you leaned way out and looked to your right. You didn't even need to lean out to see all the way down to 72nd Street on the south side. Of all the ill-advised things I did that led to my disastrous second marriage, the stupidest one was giving up that apartment. At least it passed down through many Gypsy hands before I lost track of it and most of my Gypsy friends.

This particular Gypsy friend sat on the side with the view down to 72nd Street. Had I not observed him scratching his eyebrow until a small speck fell onto the table, and had I not then looked closely at that speck as it tried to head for the border, it might have been weeks before I itched enough to discover my new roommates.

I'd heard about crabs, and I knew how you got them. I hadn't slept with anyone for the last six weeks. Yes, that was unusual for me – especially on the road – but I was carrying a big torch for Fred, the married stage manager. After CB and I divorced, Fred, now managing a new musical, devoted the time between shows on matinee days (Wednesday and Saturday) to our relationship. The rest of the week belonged to his wife.

It was totally unfair that I should get crabs in this secondhand manner. Thank goodness Fred hadn't been able to visit since my return.

I'd never actually seen body lice before, but I recognized the speck immediately when I looked at it with a magnifying glass. There's a good reason they're called crabs. That's exactly what they look like.

My only other encounter with the beasts took place many years later after the motley crew of filmmakers from the Red Clover Collective crashed at the Pickle Factory. Yeah, the ones that left us a six hundred dollar phone bill and a cursory investigation by the FBI. They also left us an infestation of crabs. Fortunately, I knew what to do about them by then.

"What do I do with the stuff, if I can find it?" I ask Mr. Fang and Claw.

"Smear it all over him, especially around his eyes. After ten minutes, rinse him with tepid water. He should be fine. You might let him swim a while afterwards. They really like that."

"I know. I just hope he doesn't harbor resentments."

"I'll give you a fifty percent refund. You wanna trade him in for the little female next week?"

"No thanks. I think this is going to be my last gig with a snake."

"I hope not because of the mites?"

I assured him that I did not hold him personally responsible for the end of my career as a stripper, and told him I'd return the boa at the end of the week.

Mother and I set out to find a drugstore. The friendly desk clerk told us there was one a couple of blocks down the boardwalk.

Our hotel and the nearby theatre both faced that famous esplanade. This was back before Atlantic City became Vegas East. The boardwalk was still as it had been for nearly a century. Close your eyes and you could hear The Gentry taking the salty air in the hand-pushed wicker chairs. The chairs were still there, but now they were motorized and cost a small fortune to rent. We walked.

A young man was just opening the doors of the establishment upon our arrival. We exchanged the usual banalities about the weather (nice), tourists (many), Mets (shoo in), and so forth.

Reaching his station behind the counter he asked, "What can I do for you?"

"I have a pet snake that seems to have gotten himself an infestation of reptile mites. The vet told me to use Barc ointment to get rid of them. Do you carry it?"

"Barc? That's a treatment for body lice, isn't it?"

"So I'm told."

"Let's see. Yeah, here you go. That'll be $4.95."

As we walk rapidly back to our hotel, Mother, who had spent the exchange gazing at magazines in the front of the store, begins her signature chuckle.

"Now what's so funny?" I ask.

"You think that guy actually believes you have a snake, don't you?"

The snake has been successfully covered in slithery white ointment. We've now but to wait the requisite ten minutes. Have you any idea how long ten minutes can be?

We talk of this and that. Anything but porn films or strip acts.

"How long has it been?" asks Mom, wiping her perspiring brow with her forearm.

I look at the travel clock sitting on the lid of the toilet.

"Five minutes," I reply. "Five to go."

The boa suddenly starts to coil. He gets one loop under him, but I'm able to calm him down and persuade him to stretch out again. He's such a docile pussycat. He almost seems to be purring.

"Have you ever been bitten by one of these things?" asks Mom.

"Just once. Not onstage. Jay needed some publicity stills for the act. I called Marc and asked if I could borrow Herman. He said the kid had grown to over six feet and was getting really heavy, so I went to Fang and Claw and rented one."

Mom shook her head. "Now, you know, my daddy didn't raise no sissies, but damn, I don't know how a person can work in a place like that," she says with a shudder. "Isn't your friend afraid one of those tarantulas is gonna get loose and drop down the back of his neck someday?"

"I've seen you pick up tarantulas," I chide.

"That ain't the same as having one down the back of your neck!"

"Yeah, it's daunting. But I love the place. Some of the critters are amazing. We got a pair of Kenyan chameleons for the PF once. They used to ride around on top of our heads. Freaked out the clients."

"I can't imagine why."

"The thermostat in their tank went on the blink, though, and they got too cold and died. It was a cruelty I will never repeat."

"Well, you live; hopefully, you learn." Mom gives the snake a friendly stroke or two.

Is there a subtext there? Do I want to go there? No. Not right now, anyway. Will I ever be able to talk about my post-Broadway career choices with her? Does she even want me to? There's probably a good reason she hasn't broached the subject.

I return to the original question. "I looked over their selection of boas, and picked the littlest. That was my big mistake."

"How so?"

"Babies are more easily frightened."

"And you scared him?"

I shrug, "I guess. The photographer was shouting, 'Turn this way; lift your head, 'hold him up higher,' and stuff. I was probably gripping him too tightly. You gotta keep control, but you can't squeeze too hard."

"Sorta like raising kids," murmers Mom.

Nope. Not going to get into that discussion, either.

"I guess. Anyway, he struck me. Bit me right on the lower lip. Almost like an overly ardent kiss. Drew a little blood was all. I stuck him in his basket while I repaired the damage, and when I picked him up again, he was fine."

"You picked him up again after he bit you?" Mom is more puzzled than aghast.

"Well, I had to finish the shoot," I explain, quite reasonably.

"You do have a strong Puritan work ethic, that's for sure," she says wryly.

She's talkin' about my insistence on doing this gig, I suspect. I don't feel like exploring that subject, either.

I crane my neck around to check the clock.

"Time?" she asks.

"Close enough for streetwear. Let's rinse."

Stage Mothers

STAGE MOTHERS ARE A BREED APART. How many moms would help their dancing daughter delouse a snake for her strip act?

Like most little girls who were lucky enough to see one, I had decided to become a ballerina by the age of three.

It all started when I won first prize in a Woolworth's Most Beautiful Baby contest at age two. Everyone who had their baby's picture taken at Woolworth's was automatically entered in the contest. First prize: free dancing lessons! I suspect first prize may have gone to everyone who bought into the deal. It was a pretty big class.

Dad was not thrilled. He said then and there that dancing lessons would lead straight to Hell in a handbasket.

I doubt he got much satisfaction out of being right.

Because I could do a cartwheel, I got to be Dopey in the Snow White ballet. I'm afraid Father felt I had been singled out for ridicule. I probably got the part because Mom could make the costume. Well, I could do good cartwheels. Still can.

After dazzling the crowd with my cartwheels at that first recital, I was standing in the wings and noticed that nothing was going on in front of the curtain while the set was being changed! That didn't seem right. So, still in my Dopey costume, I did my off-to-buffalo tap steps (which I also did quite expertly) back and forth across the stage until the teacher reached out from the wings and dragged me offstage – to thunderous applause, I might add.

Poor Dad. He ran from the auditorium hoping no one would realize he was the father of the showoff. He never attended another recital.

Mom did everything in her power to make my dream of ballerinahood come true. When we'd get to a new town (the oil company sent us to a new one every month or so) she would find a good butcher, the library, and the dancing school – in that order. Surprisingly, there was almost always a dancing school though there wasn't always a library. As soon as I was old enough to be trusted on the street alone – about six, in those golden days of yore – a Sunday school of any flavor within walking distance was also in the picture. I gained a broad perspective on religion and a baby brother as a result.

Mom built all my recital costumes. She ferried me many miles to see ballet companies whenever such marvels came our way. She loved the stuff as much as I. One of her fondest memories from childhood was seeing Anna Pavlova dance. Grandmother, too, had done all she could to expose her children to any cultural event that came anywhere near their small Gulf Coast town. There were lots of touring companies back then. No TV. No Web. No wonder.

Nikita Talin, formerly of the Ballet Russe de Monte Carlo, moved to Dallas and opened a dance studio. The two dance teachers in our little burg a hundred miles or so to the east pooled their students and engaged him to come to town and teach a master class on Saturdays. When he announced he would conduct a summer dance camp in nearby Dallas, Mom and I started pestering Dad to let me attend. I held my breath, waiting for his decision.

Christmas morning I opened his present to me. I knew it was a doll. He always gave me a doll for Christmas even though I hadn't played with dolls for years. It was a very small doll but it had a tutu-style skirt made of five accordion-pleated hundred-dollar bills. Tuition for the dance camp just happened to be five hundred dollars.

That summer, I met Jerome. He lived in a little room at the back of Nikita's studio. Two other students and I shared an apartment with Nikita's mother across the street. The four of us danced, dumpster dived behind the local market for food (we were all on very tight budgets and always hungry), danced, cooked, danced, ate, danced, slept, dreamed of dancing, danced, and washed our practice clothes in the bathtub while we discussed – The Dance.

Jerome became my best friend. He still is. He was the first boy I ever met that didn't want to fuck me. I'd never had a best friend before. (Unless you count my imaginary playmate. She went away when I found out I was the only one who could see her.) Girls were mean. Boys were... well, boys. Jerome was gay.

I didn't quite understand what that meant until well into the next summer when he and I both landed in the chorus of the Dallas State Fair summer stock musicals. The choreographer and the other male dancers were, surprisingly enough, all gay. They were a lot more fun than the girls.

Dad never came to see any of the shows I was in that summer. Mom and her posse made them all. The only other time my father saw me on a stage was when I was doing the dance lead in *The Pajama Game*.

The town's postmaster had seen the show when he was in New York on vacation. Even though they'd never met, he called Dad to congratulate him on having such a talented daughter. Small towns in Texas are like that. When Dad said he hadn't seen the show, the respected elder of the community offered to buy him a ticket to New York. Father nearly popped a blood vessel and assured the gentleman that he just hadn't had time as yet and planned on going soon, thank you, and did. (The expense was a factor, but Dad wasn't about to admit that to anyone.)

He flew into New York on Saturday morning. After he watched the matinee, I asked him what show he'd like to see that evening.

He answered, "Why would I want to see another show? I came up here to see you."

Fred, the stage manager who owned my heart, got him another house seat for the evening show. Dad flew back to Texas Sunday morning.

It's autumn in New York: as bewitching as the song by that title says it is.

Mom and I barrel up the steps of the IND subway on 8th Avenue, dash down 44th Street toward Broadway, turn into the alley just short of Sardi's, and arrive, slightly out of breath, at the stage door of the venerable St. James Theatre.

We're not late. We're cold. A cloud of expensive perfume rises from the sea of furs in front of the theater as we swim through. It trails us into the musty hallway.

"Hey, Otto," I greet the rotund doorman.

"Goot eefnink, Headliner. Hoo poy, you got lots of pipple vishing you vell," he says as he hands me a stack of notes and telegrams.

Otto was a dead ringer for S.Z. Sakall. Ever see him? Round, rubbery face he squished every which way when things went inevitably awry in those madcap movies of the '40s.

"You remember my mom?" I smile my broadest smile. "She's gonna watch the show, but I wanted to show her my dressing room first. Is that OK?"

"Sure ting, Peanut."

That was his nickname for me. He had a different one for each of us kids. Chorus dancers were called kids. Of course, as of tonight, I was no longer a chorus kid. I was now a principal player – a headliner. My name was on the marquee. A six-foot high photo of me in the merry widow costume I wore for the "Jealousy Ballet" stood in front of the theater. This is what I had come to New York for; what I had danced my little tootsies to a bloody pulp for all those years; why Mom had sewn her fingers to bloody nubs making costumes for me. This was our dream come true.

"I'll valk her out front at five minutes. Whoosh. All doze telegrams. Any offers from Hollyvood?" Another more current Otto look-alike was Schultzie on *Hogan's Heroes*. No, there weren't any offers from Hollyvood.

"Nervous?" asks Mom, solicitously.

"Why should she be nervous?" booms Fred, my knight in shining armor, emerging from the backstage area. He puts a reassuring arm around my shoulders.

Fred, the stage manager, had hired me for the the show.

The ponies (dancers) were in a rehearsal at The Latin Quarter when word reached us there was a call for replacement dancers for the road company of *Damn Yankees*. My best pal Cherie and I ran to the theater as soon as we could leave rehearsal. I didn't have time to go home for my sneakers, so I danced the audition in high-heeled shoes.

Fred was there to find a replacement for the show he stagedmanaged, *The Pajama Game*. He thought I was the tallest girl there and hired me on the spot to replace Carmen Alvarez, a taller-than-average dancer. When I reported for my fitting, the wardrobe mistress about took Fred's head off. She would now have to hem all the costumes. It took me six months to get on her good side.

Fred's mentoring didn't end with hiring me for the chorus. He encouraged me to learn the lead dance role, Gladys Hotchkiss, and audition for the understudy spot when it became available. (Shirley MacLaine had been the understudy to Carol Haney, the original Gladys, but they were both long gone to Hollywood by the time I got into the show.)

"This kid's the best Gladys since Carol," my booster, Fred, declares as he squeezes my shoulder and ushers us through the mysterious dark backstage area of the theater.

"Really. If she'd been the original understudy instead of Shirley, she'd probably be in Hollywood now," he assures Mom.

Is it any wonder I'm madly in love with the man?

He leaves us at the foot of the circular metal stairs that rise to the "star" dressing rooms above the stage left wings. Annie, my dresser, arms loaded with costumes, vaults up the more conventional stairs leading from the wardrobe department in the basement. The evening's poker game can be heard getting under way below decks. Ruth Gillett's piercing baritone rings out, "Seven-card stud, nothing wild. A buck to play."

"Oh, your mom's here!" Annie gushes in genuine delight. Reaching from beneath the pile of garments, she shakes Mom's hand. "The kid was afraid you might not get here for her big night."

The signature derby for the "Steam Heat" number bobbles precariously atop her frizzy mop of hair. I take it and place it on my own head.

Eddie Foy, Jr. comes through the stage door with his son, Eddie III. (Eddie Jr. was the eldest of the vaudevillian Eddie Foy's famous "Seven Little Foys": the offspring Eddie Senior put on stage as soon as each could reliably execute a buck and wing. Eddie III is an assistant stage manager on our show. Eddie, Jr. plays the comic lead Heinzie – an efficiency expert at the

Sleeptite Pajama Factory and the madly jealous lover of the boss's secretary, Gladys. That's me.

"How's my new little Glad Ass?" asks my leading man, patting me paternally on the appropriate part of my anatomy.

"And, how's Mom?" He shakes her hand.

"Thrilled to death, of course!" she replies.

"Enjoy the show," he commands as he deftly executes soft-shoe steps onto and across the stage toward his dressing room. Next to it, John Raitt can be heard running scales up and down the range of his magnificent baritone.

"Half-hour," calls Eddie III.

Mom and I scurry up the circular stairs after Annie.

"Was this really Gertrude Lawrence's dressing room when she was starring in *The King and I*?" asks Mom.

"That's what they tell me." I begin to untangle my false eyelashes curled up like little sleeping centipedes in their box.

"Hey, Kiddo. How ya doin'?" Julie Wilson, the leading lady, calls through the open door between our dressing rooms.

"Just great. You? This is my mom. Mom, Julie Wilson. She plays Babe now." (Janis Paige, the original Babe, had been in the role the year before when I joined the show and Mom had first seen it.)

"Pleased to meet you. Watching the show?" asks Julie.

"Oh yes. I'll hang around backstage the rest of the week, but tonight, I'm in the third row."

"Fifteen minutes," bellows Eddie III.

"More flowers," he adds as he plops a huge bouquet on the floor inside the door. There are others perched precariously on the shelf above the clothes rack. Mother looks at the card.

"These are from someone named Zoya," she says.

"That's the dance captain, Bob Fosse's assistant, Zoya Laporska. She's the one who's been beating me to death since I got this job. You'll love her. She'll be around before curtain to remind me to keep three fingers straight when I tip the damn derby in 'Steam Heat.'"

No sooner said than we hear her strident voice.

"It's the Shreck!" she cries as she pounds up the stairs.

(Long before Disney used the name, Zoya would announce her appearance in this way. Her appearance in the dressing room was usually to correct mistakes or sloppiness on the part of us dancers. That was her job. She termed it "shrecking.")

Tonight she has only this to say, "OK, you little fireball. Break a leg."

She is not suggesting I injure myself. That's the way show folk wish each other luck. Don't know why.

I thank her for the flowers. We hug and kiss. She boots me in the butt with her knee saying, "merde." (This is a French word: slang for shit. How or why it also is a good luck talisman when accompanied by a boot in the butt, I couldn't tell you, but it is.) She whirls to leave and nearly collides with Otto as he squeezes in the door.

"Ready to go out front, Madam?"

We all clatter our way down the spiral stairs to the stage level.

Fred is there to walk me to the stage right wings for my first entrance. I clutch my steno pad and pencil props so tightly my fingers are numb.

"Just remember that if you aren't having fun, the audience isn't either," Fred whispers in my ear. Then he kisses my neck just below it as we hear the last of Eddie's monologue and song in one. The curtain rises on the frenzy of the opening number. The boss, Mr. Hassler (played by Ralph Dunn), charges like a bull moose to center stage, stops and bellows with all of the considerable power of his amply-girthed lungs, "Where's my secretary? GLADYS!"

That's my cue! Will I be loud enough? My heart beats so hard I can barely hear the music. I need to hear the music so I come in on the right beat. Shit. I rush onstage. "Yes, Mr. Hassler."

Oh, thank God. My voice comes out loud and clear. Well, loud and raspy. That's all I ask.

And, it lasts through the whole show: songs, hysterical screaming scenes and all.

After the final curtain, when I take my solo bow, the applause swells! To top that heady brew, the cast onstage gives me an enthusiastic hand!

We dined next door at Sardi's after the show, of course. Mr. Vincent Sardi himself sent a complimentary bucket of champagne to our table. Now that's the kind of evening a Stage Mother deserves. Not deli sandwiches backstage in a strip joint.

Nudity and The Latin Quarter

"WAS DEVIL YOUR FIRST FUCKFILM"

Instead of the flimsy slips of paper with scrawled pencil notes seen yesterday, I now hold four-by-six file cards. Perhaps Management was impressed with the four full houses yesterday? Today's noon show is packed, too. I confess to a warm sense of satisfaction.

"No, it was the second," I reply. "The first one was – ready?" (I use my hoity-toity voice), High Priestess of Sexual Witchcraft."

Applause? I was sure that one had sunk
without a ripple.

"You saw that?" I ask incredulously.

The spotlight winks to let me know it's time to move on.

"Last question." I say and read aloud, "Do you enjoy sex?"

I look at the audience for a long time before I answer. "Not really. I just grin and bare it."

To prove my point, I drop my dress and go into my routine.

I love to dance in the buff. It's almost as good as skinny dipping – which not only feels good but just makes good sense. Can anyone explain to me the logic of putting clothes on to get wet? I guess the modesty gene just never kicked in when I was fashioned. I have never understood why folks make such a big deal outta gettin' naked.

Pictures of boobies and weenies were the major attraction in The National Geographic magazines I devoured in my youth. Nobody as far as I could see raised an eyebrow. BUT ? pose for a picture with one little titty barely showing through a diaphanous veil – as I did in a publicity still for Lou Walters' Latin Quarter supper club in New York in 1954 – and the sharp clamp of pursing Texan lips could be heard all the way to Times Square.

Now what would make a nice girl like me pose practically nude at the tender age of 18? Let me tell you a little about The Latin Quarter.

She was the queen of Supper Clubs, and reigned supreme from the triangle formed by the crossing of Broadway and Seventh Avenue at 47th Street – that sacred ground known as Times Square. The entrance to the club was on 48th Street. My scandalous portrait hung right in the front lobby. You could see it from the street! It was part of the decor until the place closed though I worked there for only a few months. It was a very classy picture, if I do say so.

Working there was like living the musical, Guys and Dolls. The dapper gents who met the chorus girls after the show had names ending in y for the most part: Joey, Vinny, Tony; the occasional Sal – sometimes called Sally (with no hint of humor). The owner, Lou Walters, however, was never called "Louey." No one addressed him as other than Mr. Walters.

He was always very proper and fiercely protective of "his ladies." No foul language was ever heard backstage. The girls' dressing room was another matter altogether.

Rosie, the wardrobe mistress, would holler a warning whenever Jackie, Mr. Walters' younger daughter was seen climbing the coil of stairs to the chorus dressing room. Everyone watched their tongue when she was there. I remember her as a very sweet teenager with a charming lisp and a terrible crush on Johnny Ray; he of the crying songs. One night, she flew up and down the narrow aisle behind our dressing tables to show us the paper cigar ring he had placed on her finger telling us shyly of their engagement.

It was said her sister Barbara didn't particularly care for show folk – least of all celebrities. I guess she got over that. I don't remember ever seeing her at the club.

Nate, aka The Counselor, was responsible for this happy turn of events in my life.

We met when he walked up beside me at the corner of Broadway and 57th Street. When the light changed, we started across the street almost shoulder to shoulder. He said he had seen me there this same time every day for the past week. From the way I walked he could tell I was a dancer, and would I mind if he just talked to me as we crossed the street (which we were doing) because he had a bet with his friend who said I wouldn't give him the time of day.

He was so intense and had such a cute Noo Yawk accent that I couldn't help giggling as we were swept along in the stream of pedestrians. He won his bet. I even made a show of looking at my watch for the benefit of his distant companion. He then suggested that since I was responsible for the windfall he had just won, I should share in it, and how about dinner?

He had thinning dark hair, was barely as tall as I, and rather slight. Frankly, I was pretty sure I could take him if it came to a struggle. Free food? Why not?

Our first date was dinner at Lindy's, complete with their world-famous cheesecake for dessert. Nate seemed to know everybody. Our second date was a trip to The House of Upsets in Brooklyn to watch prize fights. One dose of that was more than enough for me. Not to worry. Our third date (he promised) would be elegant.

Jerome takes it upon himself to see to it that I am properly dressed for this occasion even though he isn't all that enthusiastic about my new beau. Yes, Jerome from Nikita's. After the summer of fun and bruises in the Musicals, we came to conquer Broadway together. We share a garden apartment on West 76th Street at this juncture.

Nate picks me up in a taxi. The lights swirling past us as we zoom down Broadway to 48th thrill me to the bone. (They still do.) A doorman opens the door for us at the entrance of The Quarter. There's quite a crowd. Nate grabs my elbow and steers me through the press. A rather large man in a tuxedo nods as we pass. We climb the carpeted stairs to the club floor. My image in the mirrored wall facing our ascent startles me. In a silver lamé sheath and matching pumps (courtesy of one of Jerome's transvestite pals) I look more than elegant. I look fan-fuck-n-tas-tic.

"Good evening, Counselor. Ringside?" asks the tall man behind the reservations desk.

"Thank you, Vinny, that would be very nice," replies Nate.

Nate always spoke very politely, albeit with a thick Noo Yawk accent. His vocabulary was impressive. I don't know if he was actually a lawyer, but I don't know that he wasn't. I never really got to know him all that well.

The dining area of the Quarter is indeed elegant. Linen, crystal, a wee little lamp, and a vase with a rosebud grace each table. An army of uniformed staff stands by.

We dine. I have the steak. It's enormous. (There was enough left over to feed me and Jere for a week – even with guests!)

The orchestra ends its medley of quiet dinner music. A rousing fanfare announces that it's Show Time!

"Come on along with me. We're stepping out to see, the life in gay Paree – the Latin Quarter" sings the parade of gorgeous girls – more or less on key.

I'm so enthralled that Nate has to shout right into my ear to get my attention.

"I said, 'you can do all that stuff,' right?" He nods toward the dance routines taking place on the stage that looms directly above us.

"Blindfolded," I shout back honestly.

"They're looking for dancers. You wanna audition tomorrow?"

"Are you kidding?"

"Hey, Arty," he calls to a passing suit, "my friend Georgina here is a dancer. She's gonna come in to see Madam Korova tomorrow, OK?"

"Sure thing, Counselor," growls the size 48. Then he sticks a ham of a hand in my direction. "Pleased to meetcha. Come to the stage door on the Broadway side and give Benny your name at ten, OK?"

Twenty or so girls show up for the audition. The choreographer demonstrates some pretty basic steps, and ladies are dismissed with a "thank you" until only three of us are left. The choreographer has me do some high kicks and my ever popular cartwheels. There's a confab in the dark area beyond the stage where a few suits sit at one of the dining tables. The shortest of the group comes up to the edge of the stage and motions me over with his head.

Madam Korova (the choreographer) walks up behind him, looks at me with her head tilted to the side and says, "You see Jojo do can-can?"

I nod. It had been the highlight of the evening as far as I was concerned.

"His partner must leave act to have little Jojo. Vould you like replace her and do can-can spot?"

Vould I?

"You get extra fifty dollars. OK?"

"Sure," I gulp. (Hell. I would have paid them!)

She nods and moves back into the dusk of the dining room. Short Suit tells me to report to the photographer's studio for publicity stills and gives me a card with the address.

Publicity stills! Was this it? The Big Break?

As soon as I can change back into street clothes and phone the news to my roomie, Jere, I hurry to the address on the card, puff my way up two flights of narrow stairs, and search out the right numbered door. The other girls, who left at the end of the audition, have just arrived and are being greeted by a large, blowzy woman with a huge mop of frizzy hair. She says to call her Midge.

"Help yourselves to any makeup you need. There're some donuts and stuff in the kitchen through there," she says in a pleasantly smoky baritone nodding toward an open doorframe beyond the mirrored makeup tables.

Putting a friendly paw on the shoulder of the knock-out strawberry blonde who sat through the audition near the table of suits, she growls, "You're already madeup. Wanna go first?"

"Sure," replies the slender beauty. She does look like she might have just come offstage: copious eyelashes out to here. She and Midge head out into the studio area, letting the swinging door flap shut behind them.

"Cherie worked at the Quarter last year," offers the tallest of our group, indicating the willowy dancer who had just exited. "She left when she got a gig in Italy. She's a terrific dancer. I'm not surprised they hired her back."

Amazingly, while filling me in, she is able to add a stick of gum to the wad she already has going.

"I was with her yesterday at the Quarter when she was getting fitted for wardrobe. This guy's just sittin' there watchin' and he asks me if I wanna be in the show! I told him I couldn't dance, but he said he wanted me in the show anyway. I say, 'Yeah? Who are you?' He says, 'Lou Walters.' I say, 'Sure. And I'm Ava Gardner.' He says, 'No really. I'm Lou Walters and I'm offering you a job.' and I say, like, 'Well, sure, why not?' So here I am. I can't dance for shit."

I'd noticed.

"They're going to use me as a model, though. I wish I was tall enough to be a showgirl," she sighs, and begins to add dramatic eye lines to her makeup.

Midge sticks her head in the door and motions for the quiet kid who'd been doing her makeup in the corner to follow her. I can just see the first girl in a brightly lit set doing very professional girlie poses in a sequined corset costume. She is truly gorgeous. Legs forever. The swinging door closes behind the quiet girl. It's just me and the gum-chewer.

The attractive brunette motions for me to sit down beside her at the makeup table. I take advantage of the supplies and copy her skilled use of them.

"Are you an actress?" I ask.

She laughs a warm, open denial.

"Student. I'm going to NYU. Sort of. I still live at home, but I try to spend as little time there as possible."

She flips her long dark hair back over her shoulder and nods toward the door. "Cherie dates my brother. She is an ab-so-lute doll. You're gonna love working with her. Even my sister gets along with her. My sister's the dancer in the family. She's worked at the Quarter since about forever. Cherie's really funny. I mean funny, 'ha ha,' not funny 'strange.' I hope they get married. My brother and Cherie, I mean."

"What are you studying?" I inquire.

"Men," she replies without hesitation.

"You mean anthropology?"

"Anthro who?

"Anthropology. The study of man."

"Just where is your home planet?" she chuckles, then sticks out her hand.

"My name's Jan, but everyone calls me Zelda. That was F. Scott Fitzgerald's wife. My brother says I'm her reincarnation."

"She was sort of the poster child of the Anything Goes twenties, right?"

"Yeah. I relate to her worldview: 'We're only here for a visit. Enjoy yourself.'"

Midge and Cherie return from the studio before I can point out the sad end of Zelda's saga – incarcerated in a loony bin and all.

"That was painless," declares the shapely redhead. She turns to me. "Hi, I'm Cherie. I see you've met Zelda."

"Yeah. She tells me you worked at the Quarter before."

"Did a three-month stretch. Then I got a show that toured Italy. I fell in love," she sighs dramatically. "With Italy, I mean. Stayed until my money ran out. Can't wait to get back. Where're you from?"

"Texas," I reply. "And you?"

"Pennsyltucky. You're gonna love the Quarter." There's a definite hint of sarcasm in her tone. "Four shows a night and all the pastrami you can eat."

"What's pastrami?" I ask. (I was really new in town.)

Midge motions for Zelda to follow her into the studio. The quiet girl passes them coming through the swinging door and joins us.

"Hello. My name's Turalura Lipschitz."

"Hi," I answer with a totally straight face. Cherie doesn't do quite as well.

"Ma had a thing for the Irish," she shrugs. "You can call me Tulie."

(Which we did. Come on. You can't think this stuff up. That, she swore, was her God's-honest-truth name.)

Going into the studio for my turn, I pass Zelda. A bicycle clip between her legs grips her torso. It is festooned with feathers that cover the front and back of her crotch. That painful-looking device and a couple of pasties barely covering the points of her ample tits comprise the sum total of her costume. No wait. There is also a headdress – about a hundred times as big as the rest of the outfit. Zelda is just getting the hang of balancing the thing. Tottering backward, she slowly loses to the forces of gravity and lands on her ass. She regains her footing with true showgirl grace and with headdress still in place, flashes her dazzling smile. Zelda's smile always got her out of as much trouble as it got her into.

When asked to pose seated on an ornate garden bench beside a Doric pillar with naught but a gossamer drape covering my tits (I do believe the gentleman behind the camera referred to them as bosoms), I voiced no objection. Why would I? I was now a Broadway Chorine; part of a sisterhood that dates back to Flo Ziegfeld. They write songs about us.

And that is how and why I got my picture taken with my tit showing at the tender age of eighteen. My ride to Hell in a handbasket was well under way, and I was loving every minute of it.

Wedding Bells

MUCH AS ZELDA PREDICTED, I fell in love with the witty up-beat Cherie. She became both mentor and best friend.

Jerome had gotten a job that took him on tour. I couldn't swing the rent on our lovely garden apartment alone, so I was temporarily housed in a bizarre sublet. It was a basement apartment with black walls, black furniture, black bath and kitchen fixtures, and black drapes covering the lone window that barely peeked above ground to a rather nice garden in the back that could not be accessed. The tenant of record was a Shakespearean actor of some renown. Oh yes. There was one spot of color: a blood-red round throw pillow on the couch.

Cherie suggested we become roommates and look for a place to share. She was currently crashing with some pals in a room above the China Bowl restaurant on 44th Street. They invited me to join them there until Cherie and I could find our own place. I was quite willing to leave the crypt.

The two girls worked during the day. Cherie and I got the sofa bed from 6:00 a.m. until we had to get up and get to rehearsals or auditions or whatever. We had both found supplementary work after the Quarter's shows let out: hawking cigarettes (Cherie) and minding the coat room (me) at an after-hours joint called The Key Club. We worked from two till five, so we didn't get home until six anyway. Manhatan Babies don't sleep tight until the daaaaaaaawn.

The Box and Cox arrangement was only needed for a couple of weeks. Cherie and I found a great apartment on West 84th street at Riverside Drive in that part of Manhattan that became known as the "Yupper West Side." There were sometimes as many as ten in residence on any given night. It was that big. We had the entire ground floor and basement – plus a garden in the back.

Not long after we got the apartment, I got the job in *The Pajama Game*, and Mom came up to New York to see her dancing daughter's debut as a chorus girl on Broadway. She loved our 84th Street theatrical boarding house. Mom adored New York, and she most definitely adored CB (that beautiful blond Brit) on sight.

About a week into Mother's stay, my pal Deedee, who sits next to me in the chorus dressing room says, "Hey, my boyfriend's roommate wants to date you. Wanna go out with us after the show tonight?"

"I don't know. What's he like?"

"Adorable. Blond and British. Come on. It'll be fun."

"I don't know… I'm in slacks."

"No problem. We're just gonna get a bite at Joe Allen's or something."

Instead, we pick up deli and beer and have a jolly good party with Cherie, Donald (Cherie's beau – brother of Zelda), and Mom. When the rounds of drinks and jokes wind down, we walk Deedee, Rob, and CB the blonde Brit, to the front door.

"Alright then," says the Englishman to me, "may I knock you up tomorrow?"

I'm speechless. We have, after all, just met. The well-traveled Cherie quickly clarifies.

"He means he wants to come by tomorrow morning."

"Oh, well…sure. By all means, please do."

It was well into Mom's third week there and about our fourth date, I think, that CB and I sneaked into the small room in the center of the apartment after the rest of the world was asleep. This room had been requisitioned to serve as everyone's closet – there being a dearth of the real things in the place. Several rolling clothes racks from a clearance sale in the garment district held wardrobe enough for a summer stock theater. Suitcases, boxes, and what all were stacked around the walls. Donald called it the Thrift Shop. At times it served as yet another spare room for temporary guests, so there was a nice pile of bedding in one corner. There, as quietly as possible, the gorgeous Brit and I took each other's measure and found it much to our mutual liking.

Mom went back to Texas. Cherie and Donald set a date for their wedding. All agreed that they would keep the duplex apartment. I would find another place to live. Rob's regular roomie was coming back from touring, and CB needed to find another place to hang his hat as well. We didn't really set out to move in together, we were just hanging out together looking at apartments.

When we came across this treasure of a cold-water fourth-floor walkup – across the street from what would become Lincoln Center some ten or so years down the road – for forty-five dollars a month, neither of us had the heart to deny it to the other. The obvious solution was to share it.

This was still the 1950s. Couples didn't live together until they got married – at least not in Texas. Mom probably assured Dad that we were planning to get married just as soon as the show closed. We just wanted to wait so we could have the wedding in Texas. I may well have given her that idea. Hell, I thought the show would never close. I was totally unprepared for her response when I told her we had gotten our two weeks' notice.

"Oh, that's too bad. How's December 18th for the wedding?"

CB was on the extension. We looked at each other, shrugged, and said almost in unison, "Sure, I guess that's OK. Sounds good."

The wedding was spectacular. Mother made my dress, the matching bridesmaids' gowns, and even a spiffy coordinated outfit for herself. I think it may have been the first time since I was a toddler that she built something for herself. She was always way too busy running up fluffy tutus for all the budding ballerinas of East Texas. She had a full-fledged costume studio going by the time I left for New York. After that, she added a new line: creating amazing, bejeweled, long-trained gowns for the royalty of the annual local flower festival - year after year after year.

I bought the dress for wedding number two off the rack.

In glamorous Atlantic City, it's the first show of the second day and I'm fighting nausea. Mom holds out the jar for me as I plunge into the dressing room at the end of my turn. Another close one. A quick sip restores my composure.

"Want to go to the beach?" Mom stashes the jar in her tote. "I had the hotel pack us a lunch."

I set my wig on its little Styrofoam head and glance in the mirror. There's a large shopping bag sitting beside the ever-present straw tote. Several inviting pieces of fruit sit on top of wrapped sandwiches. There are even a couple of frosty beers stuck down on the sides!

I assume these are for Mom, but no. As we settle on the sand, she hands me one with my sandwich.

That was the best feeling beer I ever drank. You feel beer, you don't taste it. It's the cold sting as it goes down that brings on that aaaahhhhhh. Is there anything better than lying on warm sand, skin tingling with fast-drying salt water, munching crab salad on a roll and swigging down ice cold beer? Well, yeah. Actually there is, but. I didn't know it at the time.

"I'm always surprised at how cold the Atlantic is," says Mom as she enjoys her own crab roll and suds. "The bay down at Padre Island was always so nice and warm."

"And oily," I remind her.

"Yeah. Lately, that's true. But I can remember when you could see the bottom at thirty feet or more."

"I wish you could have seen the water in the Yellow Flats off the Bahama Islands. It was so clear and green – it looked like a swimming pool. You could see the bottom even by moonlight. No kidding. It must have been twenty-five or thirty feet deep," I recall. "And talk about warm..."

"When were you in the Bahamas?"

"Don't you remember when Jim Kimberly invited me to go sailing on his eighty-la-dee-two-foot-dah ketch? It was right after *The Pajama Game* production I did in West Palm Beach."

"Oh, yeah – Kimberly Clark paper mills. Jim Kimberly, the Kotex King. Whatever happened with that?"

"We dated whenever he came to New York for a year or so. Then he started seeing one of the pilot beauties from that James Bond movie. Not Pussy Galore. One of her chums. I can't remember her name."

"He was the one with you in that nightclub picture that was in all the papers, wasn't he?"

"Yeah. Some gossip columns were all a-twitter because I had, at his insistence, pierced his ear for him when we were on that cruise. He invited me to spend a weekend at the family's getaway estate on Lake Michigan. They weren't that thrilled with the earring."

"How surprising."

"He was such a sweet guy. Did I ever tell you he introduced me to Hunt Hartford when we were down in Great Exuma on that sail?"

"Who's that?"

"Huntington Hartford? The jillionaire? You know. The Huntington Hartford museum?"

"Oh. Right. So?"

"Well, he did. About a year or so later, Mr. Hartford called me to say he had heard that Jim and I weren't seeing each other anymore, and would I honor him with my company at a tea dance."

"A who?"

"Tea dance. It's one of those charity things 'that set' does on a regular basis. I blew nearly a hundred bucks on a dress for it."

"Was it worth it?"

"Well, almost. He gave me fifty dollars for cab fare home. While we were dancing, he asked if we were going to make it. I was a bit taken aback and stammered that I didn't think so. I was still in that not-on-the-first-date mode. So he said would I mind, then, if he sent me home in a cab so he could cruise the rest of the talent. I took the subway and saved the fifty."

Mom looks out to sea, shaking her head bemusedly. "You primly decline to put out for a multi-millionaire, then turn around and become a porn star." (It was the first time I had heard her use the term – porn, not star.)

"There were about twenty hard-knock years between," I reply in my defense.

"Yeah." After a long pause, "Well, chilly or not, I'm going back in," she says pulling on her bathing cap. I watch her tuck her silver curls under the edge as she runs down the sand and plunges headlong into the surf.

When I was a kid, Mom could sit on her sleek, mahogany-colored hair; I always thought my transparent blonde wisps would darken and grow as long as hers some day. Hah!

Ron Sullivan (aka Henri Pachard, director of innumerable fuckfilms) decided to do a sequel to *Devil* a few years after the original came out. He got Jack Wrangler, who was a star in both gay and straight films, to play The Devil. To create this director's version of Hell, huge bursts of stage smoke made of dry ice fumes were blasted onto the set. These intensified the heat from the lights and made the crowded area a true hell. The delightful gay hair stylist was doing his best to give my character a lofty, bouffant hairdo. Between each shot, he would drag me back to the dressing room to set, blow-dry, and tease my poor wisps back into the shape of his vision.

"Good Lord, George," he fumed as he back-combed at a furious rate, "your hair falls faster than Jack Wrangler's hardon."

I wear a wig for the act.

The long, chestnut tresses sweep over my face. I peek coyly at the front row as I draw the black stocking slowly up my leg and secure the front with the clasp that dangles from my garter belt. I face upstage and do the old "reach between the legs" to fasten the back strap. The audience is properly encouraging.

Thank goodness. After three shows, I need all the help I can get.

Mom has decided to trust me with the jar and stay in the hotel room for this last show of the day.

After swimming hard between shows all day, she was pooped.

Boy, could my mom swim. She had me and my brother swimming be-fore we could walk. He became a speed swimmer, went to college on a swimming scholarship, then became a Navy Seal. I couldn't out distance a crippled carp, so Mom organized a Synchronized Swim team allowing me to participate in the swim meets. She made the fancy bathing suits for the fourteen of us. I choreographed the routines. We won something – medals, trophies, plaques – at every meet. Of course the speed team boys called us the Stinkchronized Swimmers, but what the hell. Our little statues were just as good as theirs.

The pounding beat of "The Stripper" propels me through the steps.

Only a few more bars to go. I bump and grind my way to the wings. Bill grabs my funny old leather grip. I grab the curtain and make violent love to it. It's a wonder it isn't in shreds by now.

I'm off and moving fast.

Off comes the breakaway jacket and skirt. On goes the Uncle Sam hat and toeshoes; I tippy toe back onstage before the applause dies.

Good laugh. Nice hand.

The heaves begin to seriously threaten as I rush to my dressing room.

Just make it.

WHERE'S THE FREAKIN' JAR?

I look frantically around the small room.

Bill steps in the door, closing it behind him.

The jar is in his hand.

"We can't let you keep booze in the dressing room. The cops'll shut us down." His voice tells me he is really sorry.

"Bill, if I don't get a swallow of that brew down my gullet in the next fifteen seconds, you're going to have puke all over you."

I reach for the jar, which, he wisely relinquishes.

"OK," I say as soon as I can speak. "How do we solve this?"

"Let her keep the jar." The theater owner says stepping in the door. To me he says, not unkindly. "Just keep it out of sight. OK?"

"You got it," I croak.

I had left the damn thing sitting on the dressing table. Yes, it's an ordinary Mason jar. Not a fifth of Jack Daniels or something.

Who the hell felt the need to sniff out the contents and blow the whistle? Most likely, whoever it was could smell me anyway. Drunks do have a very distinct odor.

Well, so much for keeping my condition from management.

Life can get so damn complicated when you're a lush.

Binge

WHAT'S WRONG? WHAT WOKE ME?

I open my eyes to a pre-dawn splash of peach on the ceiling. Everything seems OK. Mom sleeps in the bed to my right. The smell and sound of the ocean reach in from the open window.

Something is definitely strange. What is it?

The clock says five thirty. I'm electrically awake. I was whipped when I hit the sack about two. Three and a half hours? That's longer than I can usually sleep before I wake up needing a drink to keep my insides from trying to get out.

That's it! I don't need to throw up! That's what's different.

Ah, but the back of my arms are starting to do that tingly thing. I'm not sick yet, but it won't be long. By now, I know the signs. The only sensible thing to do is get a jump-start on it.

Shit! The jar's empty.

Mom must have a refill stashed somewhere. I need just the teensiest, weensiest sip to stave off that worse-than-the-flu ague that makes everything hurt and shake, and soon leads to the Vesuvius effect.

Carefully, so as not to wake her, I open Mom's suitcase on the floor of the closet. I feel around the back lingerie pocket. Pay dirt! A pint bottle of vodka. A can of bullion is stashed beside it. I don't want to risk waking Mom by trying to open the can. The bottle's already been opened.

Just one little nip. She'll never miss it. Ah, that's better.

I'm wide awake. I get my paperback book from beside the bed, grab a pillow and retreat to the bathroom, quietly closing the door behind me. I bring along the bottle – just in case I start to feel sick.

"Oh, for crying out... I ought to yank you baldheaded!"

Mother's voice reaches me about the same time her hand reaches the empty bottle on my stomach. The sounds from the beach are in high gear. It must be fairly late.

"Thank the Lord I didn't get a fifth," she states as she sits me up, pulls off my tee shirt, throws it, the pillow, and my paperback on the floor and turns on the shower. Full force. Cold.

"You've got about two hours to pull yourself together and do a show, you know."

Of course I know. I'm not feeble minded, just drunk.

The cold water feels like bullets hitting my head.

"It's my own fault," laments Mom. "I never should have given you that beer at lunch."

I'm too befuzzled to argue. Was it having the beer that tipped the balance? I remember that the slight buzz from it lasted through the six o'clock show. I didn't even throw up after it. Then Mom said she was pooped and was going to go back to the hotel if that was OK, and left the jar with me.

That was her mistake. My sips were bigger and – yeah – more frequent without her supervision.

"Are you going to make the show?" she asks.

I nod my head. This is a mistake. The pain hits the back of my eyes like hot bricks. This triggers the regurg-a-matic. Dripping, I dive for the porcelain throne.

"I gotta lie down for a minute," I whimper when the heaves let up. I'm cold and clammy from the sweats as much as the dousing.

Mom helps me toward the bed, drying my back on the way and my front once I flop down.

"It's nine thirty. I'm gonna go get us some coffee. There's not any more booze in the room, so don't even bother looking." She picks up her wallet and heads toward the door.

"Here, in case you're in a hurry." She picks up the wastebasket by the desk and places it by the bed.

"I'm sorry," I moan.

"That's a masterpiece of understatement," she says under her breath as she closes the door – well...forcefully.

And here comes the toenail express again. (You know, when you barf so hard your toenails come up.) I grab the wastebasket just in time. Afterward, I slip into merciful unconsciousness.

I don't hear Mom come in, but I hear the pfsst of the can opener! Then I smell the booze. She sits on the bed and holds my head as I sip the magic potion.

"There's more bullion to the bite this time. I think I was making it too strong," she muses. Trust Mom to find some way to make it her fault. She's a Pisces – like me.

Lox, bagels, and about a gallon of coffee later, I'm ambulatory. When we get to the dressing room, the snake seems happy to see us. "You gonna hang here?" I ask Mom.

"I'm not letting you out of my sight until we get your head screwed back on straight," she states with quiet determination.

"You're up," calls Bill with a rap on the doorframe.

"Who was the woman that gave you the oil rub? Is it true you and she were lovers off screen?" The printing on the card is very precise. Not signed. Male or female? I wonder.

"That was Claire Lumiere, and yes, we were lovers."

"Was she your first lesbian lover?" a bass-baritone from near the front calls out.

"First, last, and only, I'm afraid. In spite of my many sterling portrayals of lesbians on film, I confess: I'm a closet heterosexual."

A few chuckles.

"Look, nobody's more of a live-and-let-live gal than I. To each his own. Whatever floats your boat, you know? But I gotta tell you, the trouble with lesbian sex is, there's just no place to stop. With a guy, you know when the fat lady has sung. The way girls can come, and come again, things just keep going and going and going – like a damn Energizer Bunny – until somebody either remembers an appointment or falls asleep. Or, as in the case of Claire's and my lesbian scene in *Devil*, the camera runs out of film."

The spot says it's time to move on. I do. "One more once" and it's back to the dressing room.

"Well, you made it." Mom says as she hands me a towel and the jar.

"Beach?" she asks, retrieving and stowing the brew in the ever-present tote.

"Definitely," I reply as I peel off my eyelashes. It's well worth doing a fresh makeup to get in a quick swim.

"I'll go pick us up a lunch and meet you in front," she says, grabbing the tote from which she extracts a small dark bundle. "Here's your suit."

"Thanks. I'll be right out."

As I park my wig on its Styrofoam head, I hear voices in the hall.

"Oh, please," rings a sarcastic soprano. "Artistic, my ass. Who the hell comes to a strip joint for art, anyway?"

It's the voice of the tall, blonde stripper billed as "Tawny."

"What's wrong with spilling a little culture on these clods?"

That's Roberta's voice. She is a swell gal and a great stripper. She picked the name "Roberta Redford" as her stripper name because she adores the actor. From afar, she will assure you.

"I mean, she's really dancing out there, you know!" Roberta insists.

"OK, sure. I guess she's had a couple of ballet lessons, but Margot Fonteyn, she ain't."

Well, of course she ain't – I ain't. If I were, would I be dancing in a burlesque show?

"Hey, Roberta," I call as I lean out the door. "Wanna hit the beach?"

I look directly at the tawny Tawny and smile – as sweetly as I can.

"Thanks. I'm gonna nap with the paint in place, I think. It was a wild one last night," says Robbie with a delightfully salacious grin.

"Anyone I know?"

"Wouldn't tell if it were."

Roberta is a standup gal. She does all the classic burlesque "Talking Woman" bits in the show's comic sketches. (They still did those at this particular theater.) She's been working here for several years, so she's sort of a Mother Superior to the other girls who are booked in for a week or so at a time.

"See ya," says the tawny one. She turns and heads for her dressing room swirling copious yards of chiffon in her wake.

"Don't mind her," whispers Robbie, "she's got more legs than brains."

Mom is striding up the boardwalk from Irving's Deli as I round the corner from the alley that leads to the stage door. She pauses at the stairs leading down to the beach. I hurry over to her.

"What's for lunch?" I ask.

"Pastrami on rye. I wish I'd known about Jewish food years ago."

"Yeah. Good stuff. Did I ever tell you about gaining twenty pounds my first three weeks at the Latin Quarter?"

We descend to the beach.

"How the hell could you gain twenty pounds in three weeks?"

"Hot pastrami on rye – and beer."

We kick off our shoes at the foot of the stairs.

"My first night there," I continue, "the delivery from Harry's Delicatessen arrived just as we ladies of the ensemble barreled off stage after the finale of the first show. Cherie told me to order hot pastrami on rye with mustard when they called in the order. Well, I fell in love. Three shows a night; pastrami and beer in between each; twenty new pounds in three weeks. Those huge sandwiches…"

"And, of course, the beer…"

"By the quart."

"…might have had a little to do with the weight gain. What happened after three weeks?" asks Mom.

"The wardrobe lady got tired of letting out my costumes. She asked if I was preggers. I was so embarrassed, I stopped cold turkey."

"Or more precisely – hot pastrami," giggles Mom.

She pops open a beer and hands me a coke. It feels almost as good going down as a beer, but I hate the aftertaste and the way Cokes leave you thirstier than when you started.

"Can I ask you something?" Mom licks the beer mustache from her top lip.

Oh Lord. I hope we're not through tiptoeing around the subject of my career moves.

"Only if you want an honest answer." (This has been my stratagem for avoiding questions from my parents since my teens.)

"I can hear most of your talks onstage, you know."

"I know."

"You make it sound like you were having a pretty good time making those movies. I just wonder why, if you were having such a good time, you were drinking so much?"

Not exactly what I was dreading.

"I thought drinking was part of having a good time, I guess."

Lame reply. After some real reflection, I venture, "I think my drinking problem really started while I was producing films for Penney's. That's where I met the three-martini executive lunch."

"I seem to remember that you weren't very happy in the corporate world. Isn't that why you quit and went to work for that Greek?"

"He was from Yugoslavia. Well, there were several factors involved."

"Claire being one?"

"Claire being the catalyst, perhaps, but I'd been getting itchy britches for some time before she came on the scene."

I think about it some more and say, "I think maybe I was looking for something – anything – that would make me feel as good as I used to feel when I was doing *The Pajama Game*."

"You did a lot of shows after that."

"Yeah. But I always felt like any minute someone was gonna tell me I'd been hired by mistake. I never, ever again, felt the assurance I felt when I was in *The Pajama Game*. Doing that show, I felt for the first time in my life like I really belonged where I was and was doing what I was meant to do. I felt like a real Broadway Gypsy you know? I felt like somebody special."

"Aaaaah, so," breathes Mom. "Realizing you're only as special as everyone else drove you to drink, eh?"

"Yeah. That was it. Come on. I'll race you to the float."

I leap up and push her playfully into the sand, thus affording me a good head start. Of course, she beats me anyway. She not only beats me, she's up on the float catching her breath by the time I finally reach the ladder. She's on her second dive by the time I catch my breath enough to stand.

"I'm floatin' back," I wheeze.

"Boy, you really are out of shape. Come on. You float. I'll push."

Floating on my back with my feet on Mom's shoulders I almost doze off. Her strong strokes propel us through the waves, and my memory machine goes into high gear. I'm back when I was two and we were living in Houston. The 1938 hurricane that devastated Galveston had created an alarming flood in our suburban neighborhood.

"Put your bathing suit on," Mom tells me. She hands me the tiny terrycloth garment she had made from a hotel towel for my two-year old frame. We stayed in hotels a lot as we moved about with my dad, the geologist.

I do so eagerly, though I can't see how we're going to get to the swimming pool. It isn't raining, but it's almost like nighttime and the wind is blowing so hard it's making the house shake. Water is almost to the top of the steps outside the door! It's splashing over the tops of the cars!

"Go get my jewelry box," says Mom. She starts pounding out the pegs that hold our front door on its hinges.

When I get back from the bedroom with the case, the door's down flat on the landing; one end sticking out over the muddy water.

Across the yard (a space of about thirty feet), Mom's friend Helen is leaning out the window of the big brick apartment building where she lives.

"Shouldn't you wait for the firemen?" she yells. "The radio says they're picking up folks along the bayou now. They should be here in an hour or so."

"In an hour or so we'll be under water," Mom yells back.

She parks me and the jewel case in the middle of the door.

"Hold on tight now."

I crouch with the small wooden case between my knees and hold on to the knocker thing in the middle of the door. She peels off her dress, hands it to me, and shoves us off into the water wearing just her panties and bra.

I can hear her grunt with each kick that gets us closer to Helen's hands reaching out the window. One more big push, and the hands grab me and lift me up through the window. I hang on to the jewelry case for dear life. Helen sets me down inside the hallway and reaches back for Mom. I can see her hand hanging on the windowsill. Helen grabs it and helps Mom scramble through the window. Our door boat goes swirling away with all the other stuff in the water. I was too excited to feel scared until later.

We couldn't get back into our apartment until real late the next day. The bed was scooted all the way across the room and the mattress was jammed almost through the window. The sheets and pillows were all washed away. So was most everything else in our house.

Dad got back around noon the day after that. He and his crew of doodlebuggers (oil workers who drill holes in the ground much as the little bugs they're named for do) had been stranded out in the fields north of town since the storm.

When he asked Mom what happened to the front door, Helen told him all about how Mom had swum us to safety even though Mom was trying to shush her from behind Daddy's shoulder the whole time.

When Helen left, Dad gave Mom hell. I never understood why.

After the six o'clock show, we join Roberta for dinner at a vegan enterprise housed in one of the lovingly restored Victorians near the theater. Lots of ferns and wicker, and the best bread I ever met.

"Are you from Atlantic City?" Mom asks my new friend.

"No. I grew up in Trenton, but we used to come here for vacation every summer. I always loved the beach, the boardwalk, the carnival atmosphere and everything. When I flew the nest, I headed south and landed here."

I begin, "How did..."

"...a nice girl like me get into stripping?" she finishes. We both laugh at the cliché. "I was working at the record store down the block. Al (the theater owner) used to come into the shop a lot. One day he asked me if I could dance. I asked him if he was asking me out. He said no, he was offering me a job."

"I went to see one of the shows. The movies sort of freaked me out, but the show was really funny, and the strip acts were within the limits I could handle, so I went shopping for costumes."

"Yours are fabulous, incidentally," says Mom – and she should know.

"Thanks. I design them, but I don't have room where I live to sew. There's a woman who makes most of the stuff for the girls. She has a rummage shop a few blocks from the walk. You can find anything there."

"Maybe we could go by there tomorrow after the first show?" suggests Mom, ardent rummager.

"There's a great rib joint just a block from Mama D's," enthuses Roberta. "They've got other stuff, but the ribs are to die for; the kind that fall off the bone and stick to your fingers."

Even my delicate booze-ravaged gut likes the sound of that!

We're on.

Ribs and Revelations

"YOU GONNA SLEEP ALL DAY?" Mom holds a steaming cup of coffee under my nose. The room is awash with bright sunshine. The beach is in full swing.

"What time is it?"

"Nearly ten."

"Ten? I can't believe it. I've been asleep since, what?"

"About two. You actually fell out before I did. I finished your mystery novel. Feel like some breakfast?"

"Could you stand a quick swim first?"

"I've already had a shower. You go. I'll pick up some breakfast and meet you at the theater."

What's this? She's going to leave me unsupervised? I could grab a beer at the stand on the beach and she'd never know!

She'd know.

I don my suit and wrapper, and we head down the grand marble staircase to the lobby. There is an elevator, of course, but the single flight takes less time. Mona, the day clerk at the desk, waves a hello as we pass.

Mom leaves me at the wooden steps that reach down to the sand and heads on down the boardwalk. I drop my wrapper and towel on the sand and run headlong into the waves.

The water is icy and leaves me tingling. I actually feel almost good. A little weak, like after a bout of the flu, but no aching shakes. I try a coffee from the stand. It does not sit all that well in my stomach, but it stays there.

The soundtrack from the film buzzes from the speaker above the dressing table. I've only a couple of minutes before my turn.

"Need a hit?" asks Mom, jar in hand.

"Please." The euphoria of the beach is fading. The need for alcohol is beginning to make me shaky. I gratefully grab the jar. The closing theme of the film begins, and I rush to my place behind the screen.

"I just watched the movie. I really liked what you did with all the fruit. Whose idea was that, and how did you feel doing it?"

I chuckle softly, remembering the soft chocolate-brown eye on the other side of the lens during the filming of that luscious scene.

"Jerry swears it was the cameraman Joaquin's idea," I respond. "How did I feel? Well, gorgeous, to tell the truth. But just between us, I can't stand the smell of bananas to this day."

I go to the next card.

"Did you ever fuck Jamie Gillis? I don't know if I spelled his name right."

"Don't worry about it," I offer. "I doubt if it's his real name anyway. Could be, though, come to think of it. He's a very straight-forward guy who seems to take a justifiable pride in his work. Yes, I did one sex scene with Jamie, but I can't remember in which film. That's one of the big problems with this quasi-legal business, you never know where footage you're in is gonna show up."

"What does 'kwahz-eye' mean?" someone shouts from the back of the house. I suspect it's the manager reminding me to use little words.

"Not quite." I speak to the back of the house. "As in 'I got a quasi-boner for you, Baby' meaning you're holding it up with both hands, hoping for the best," I reply, sweetly.

"Did you ever fake an orgasm?" comes from my front-row gallery. It's a familiar voice. Not that I could put a face to it. There seems to be a growing cadre of regulars.

"On camera? You bet. Not all, but some. In real life? None of your business."

"Which orgasms were real?" Same voice.

"Can't tell? Good. Neither will I."

Card. "Why do women scream so much having sex on film? It's sure not like that in real life much."

"Well, of course it's not. Especially not on the couch of the living room with your parents hopefully asleep upstairs! Lord knows it was a foreign concept to me. The exaggerated yelling and stuff is acting."

"You mean faking," shouts some smartass.

"No. I mean acting. When you're making a movie, it's acting."

"OK. Enough of this chitchat. Let's get it on." The crowd concurs.

When I get to "The Stripper" section, strains of a wonderful number from the musical *Pal Joey* fill my head. A stripper tells us what's going through her head as she systematically disrobes. "Zip," it goes, "I was reading Schopenhauer last night, and, zip, I've a feeling Schopenhauer was right..." People seem to hate it when strippers talk like they've read a book.

"Gimme," I gasp as I reach for the jar. The shakes had started about halfway through "The Stripper" routine. The first two slugs made return engagements immediately. The third stayed put.

"Robbie's waiting for us," says Mom, screwing the top back on the jar. "You feel up to making this excursion?"

"Sure. Just let me sponge off," I reply as I set my wig on its stand and grab a towel.

The emporium of Mama Dulea was several blocks inland from the beach but only a couple of blocks south of the theater. The local business establishments, restaurants, et cetera, gave way to residences of decreasing splendor as we progressed. The building that housed the shop had a bay window filled with sparkles and feathers alive, alive oh. The old three-story clapboard hadn't seen paint in a long time. Robbie bounced up the wooden steps and stuck her head in the screen door that faced at an angle onto the porch.

"Hey, Mama D. We're going to Uncle John's for lunch. Wanna go?"

"Hey, girl," says an ageless giantess around a mouthful of pins. "Yawl go on ahead. Order me a beef on a bun. I just got to finish pinnin' up this baby's hem."

The "baby" in question is a six-foot-plus drag queen festooned in several dozen yards of shimmering tulle. Her makeup's a bit over the bar for streetwear, but not unattractive.

"You're Georgina!" the towering figure explodes. A bejeweled finger points toward my nose as I peek around Robbie's shoulder. "I caught your show yesterday. You are too, too fabulous. Are you having lunch with this lady? And you didn't tell me, bitch??" she inquires, not unkindly, of Mama D, playfully hitting her on top of her nappy head with a six-foot long chiffon scarf.

"You hold your ass still, Miss Thing, or you gonna get it stuck. Heah?"

"Oh, don't say that unless you mean it! You're such a flirt," giggles the towering figure.

"We'll save you both a chair," says Roberta, backing out the door and leading the way down the block to the rib shack.

It wasn't much to look at, but the aromas emanating from its unpretentious façade made your head swim. My stomach was growling audibly by the time one of the four cable-spool tables was vacated, and we found and placed five chairs around it.

"That was Fanny Folderol," Robbie explains to Mom as we settle in and scan the chalkboard menu. She's the headliner at The Toy Box. That's the local gay bar and cabaret."

"It was male, right?" asks Mom, tentatively.

"Technically," I reply.

"Amazing."

That was all she had to say on the subject.

The ribs were perfect. Mom and Mama D hit it off as expected. They soon began to speak in tongues of gussets and darts and selvedges, and cabbages and kings. The chatter went on all through lunch and back down the street to the shop. Roberta, herself a seamstress, held her own. Fanny had waved from the door as she passed, but declined to join us, pleading a constant battle of the bulge. I just kept eyeing the tote bag.

When will Mom dole out another dose?

Probably not until we get back to the privacy of the dressing room.

Waiting for my last turn of the day, I listen to the sensual strains of "Love to Love You, Baby" drip from the speakers like treacle. It was the music used by the featured stripper, Tawny, for her floor work. Floor work: the final segment of the style of stripping of the day; precursor to the pole. Once everything is off, the performer places a mat or rug (fluffy sheep skin is a big favorite) as near the audience as the stage or runway (if there is one) allows. Here she gyrates and poses as if giving herself to an invisible (your fantasy here) partner. It's the...well, climax of her act.

"When a girl's doing her floor work, she's sort of 'doing it' with the audience, isn't she?"

As soon as I can get my jaw back in place, I answer Mother's probably rhetorical question with my own.

"Where'd you pick up the term floor work?"

"I've been here nearly a week. Did you think I was deaf?"

"I thought you were...disinterested."

"You can be disinterested in a passing cement truck and not miss it."

"Right. Yeah. Well, that is probably the intended effect."

"It's probably all the love life most of those guys have, I guess."

Mom was always one to grant more benefits of a doubt than most.

"It's probably healthier than hookin'," she sighs. "Do you think it cuts down on prostitution or encourages it?"

This was not the first time I'd heard my mother discuss prostitution. Her view was that it should be state-controlled with frequent health exams, and kept out of the nicer neighborhoods.

"Do you want to watch her turn?" I ask, again side-stepping any deep philosophical discussions.

"I'm not sitting out in that audience!"

"No. I mean from the wings."

"Well...not really." There was silence between us as I finished brushing my costume and putting it into the suitcase for the next show.

"I'd like to watch Roberta next show, though," says Mom.

"Me, too. She does a classic, old-fashioned strip," I assure her. "No floor work."

After several more minutes of silence…

"Well, if I haven't died of embarrassment yet, I guess I'm not going to. Let's go watch Tawny."

Tawny finishes her turn to thunderous applause and exits past us as we stand in the wings. We, too, applaud vigorously. The long-limbed beauty looks back in surprise then smiles.

Later she stops us as we're leaving for the night.

"That was really nice," she says. "Applauding me from the wings like that."

"You were very good," says Mom. "I started watching you because I'm interested in costumes. Yours are splendid, by the way. Then I got caught up in your, ah…dancing and – everything. You're very graceful."

"Well, thanks." To me, "You're lucky to have such a cool mom."

"I know."

Mom puts down her paperback, takes off her specs, rubs her eyes, stretches her arms out to the side and places them behind her head. I'm reading my own trashy novel but can see her in my peripheral vision. Her classic profile is framed in the glow of the elegant old reading lamp beside her. She looks like something you'd see on the side of an urn in a museum.

"Do you remember when you asked me if I was a virgin when I got married…" she begins.

"And you answered," I reply without looking up from my book, "'Questions like that are why parents don't discuss sex with their children.'"

"Yep. I do believe that was my reply – or close to it." She looks at me across the gulf between our big double beds.

"Which effectively ended the conversation, as I recall," I conclude.

I set down my book.

"I couldn't tell if you didn't want me to know if you were or if you weren't," I continue. "Or if you were afraid I was leading up to a confession you didn't want to hear."

"All of the above. I've always wondered if by not giving you an answer I sent the wrong signal. I mean, we had just moved into town. You were what? Fifteen? And of all the luck, we get a duplex next door to the town whore."

"What made you think she was the town whore?"

"Well, the red light bulb on the porch, for a start."

"That was just a gag the local hotshots pulled."

"And why do you think they chose that particular joke for that particular house?" she asks rhetorically.

"I thought," she plows on, "when you became pals with that overly large girl who lived in the big expensive house down the block... What was her name?"

"Charlotte."

"At least she was in the right crowd."

"Too bad her friendly overtures turned into passionate love notes," I remind her.

"Yeah." (Pensively.) "And she came from such a nice family. I was really sorry when they sent her off to boarding school at Hockaday."

"Oh boy, yeah. That made a lot of sense. Daughter too much of a tomboy? Send her off to an exclusive girls' school. That'll straighten her right out!"

Mom goes back to her book. I glance at mine, but can't get back into it. Finally, I put it aside.

"You were very open with me when I asked you if you'd ever done it with anybody besides Daddy," I pursue.

"That was after you were married – a couple of times. It's OK to talk about things like that with a grown daughter."

"Also, you had no problem telling me you hadn't. Though you did confess to having thought about it," I try not to smirk.

"I did. A couple of times."

"But just with Carter, right?"

"And the funny thing is, I didn't – don't – find Carter sexy, especially. Not a Clark Gable, exactly. He was just so nice and easy going. I think I just wondered if it would be – well – different with someone else."

"Different, as in better?"

"Well, yes. The truth is, actually doing it turned out to be a lot less exciting than thinking about it was. With Daddy it was always, 'Well, looks like old Bill wants to play,' and on he'd hop. There was never any touching or stuff like in novels."

I don't know what to say so I go back to reading my book. After a few moments, Mom puts down her book and continues.

"You hear all this stuff about having a climax. I just wonder if I've ever had one. What's it like?"

"Mom, if you have to ask, you haven't."

I don't want her to think I'm being flippant. I'm really sorry but not surprised to hear her ask such a question. I try to elaborate.

"It's kinda like a sneeze; when it happens, you'll know."

"That's what I thought."

We read a while longer.

"Pop once said that the only reason you wanted to get married to him was because your cousin Joyce was gonna marry Carter. Were you secretly in love with Carter?"

"When did he say that?"

"When I was in the hospital with my neck in a sling. He came in one day and told me you guys were talking about getting a divorce, and asked what did I think about that?"

"What'd you tell him?"

"That I loved you both, and always would, whatever you did. Tell you the truth, I was kinda hoping you would split up. I figgered you might come back to New York and live with me."

"Maybe I should have."

Don't want to go there.

"If you had strayed, you mightn't have been so candid," I parry.

"Well, that's probably true."

"So were you?"

"Was I what?"

"A virgin when you got married."

"Does it matter?"

"No," I laugh. "Did you know when I no longer was?"

"Was what?"

"A virgin."

"Well, I wondered why you took a long tub bath after your first real date. I was afraid to ask you about it, though."

"I guess I was pretty adamant about not having my privacy invaded," I granted.

"Most teenagers are. So, was it that trombone player?"

"Yup. I'm surprised you let me go on all those band trips if you knew – or suspected."

"I thought you loved band."

"I did. The worst mistake of my life was dropping it for Blue Brigade when we moved."

The Blue Brigade was a high school pep squad. Don't think Dallas Cowboy Cheerleaders here. Our uniforms had calf-length skirts, sported white Peter Pan collared blouses, button-up vests, jackets, pillbox hats and, yes, white gloves. Most nuns showed more skin than we did.

"OK. I'll take the blame for that one," says Mom. "I guess I should have known you would never fit in with the debs no matter what I did. If you'd stayed in the band, maybe you would have had something to take your mind off boys."

"They had trombone players in that band, too," I chuckle.

"True." She doesn't seem to have anything more to say on the subject.

"OK, then. Well, good night" I switch off the bedside lamp.

Mom turns hers off almost simultaneously. She squiggles herself into a more comfortable position facing toward the window. Her murmur is barely audible.

"Y'know." Pause. "Sometimes I've wondered if it wasn't something in the water around Jasper. Your cousin Jo became a lesbian and you turned into a nymphomaniac."

"I'm not a nymphomaniac. Just overly accommodating," I protest.

"Hmmm. Well, at least you've left a trail of very happy little boys in your wake," she mumbles as she makes a final adjustment to her pillow. "Maybe you should get a humanitarian award of some sort."

"Night," came a last, muffled murmur. Her soft snore begins almost immediately.

Mom could fall asleep faster than anyone I ever knew. Well, except for her father. Granddaddy can nod off, snore a snort or two, wake up, and pick up a conversation right where he left off.

Mom says he's narcoleptic. Swears she inherited the gene. Wish I had. I toss and stretch and wiggle, and finally give up and knock back the rest of the medication in the jar.

The resultant warm buzz settles me into a comfortable semi-doze.

> Stop worrying about how you're going to make a living. Think of something nice. Find a happy place.
>
> Nikita's ballet studio?

When Jerome and I were dishing, I was happy. I don't think I ever laughed like that before – and rarely since. But happy? Nikita was such a sadist. Stomping, demanding, blowing smoke in your face, slapping your legs so hard it left marks, ridiculing every attempt to achieve those impossible positions until he reduced you to tears... God, it was wonderful.

The apartment Jerome and I shared just off Central Park? Yeah, that was a happy place and time. Especially my 18th birthday. Who made the Brandy Alexanders? Oooh, were they good. How many did I have? I think Jere said five. I don't remember but three. He said when I stood up I crashed to the floor like an ironing board.

Jerome's shack in Hawaii! Now THERE was a really happy place. His batik studio took up most of the tiny hut, but the beach was expansive and all his, being on a private plantation. You could skinny dip, eat a mango, take a nap, take a walk, then do it all again... all day and night. That week's visit was way too short. I should write Jerome. See how he's doing and bring him up to date on my life.

Maybe not.

Cashiered

THE CRYSTAL GLOW OF A PINT OF VODKA slowly materializes as I blink the tears from my eyes. My peripheral vision reaches to the hem of Mom's robe on my left. My hand shakes so badly as I take the small bottle and try to get it to my lips that Mom has to guide it with her own.

Waking with not a drop at hand, I had tried in vain to fall back into what had been a rather nice sleep. No luck. The sounds of my morning retch had brought Mom to the rescue like a St. Bernard in the Alps.

"Sip it. Don't gulp or you'll just lose it."

I sip.

"Let it slide down your throat."

The scant mouthful of vodka hits my gut just at the height of a spasm and spews into the bowl. Fortunately I'm still on my knees before it in my usual posture of worship. The spate hits dead center. I'm getting good at this.

"Ready to try again?"

I nod. She hands me the pint of vodka. I guess she got tired of wasting so much expensive bullion waiting for the alcohol's fake enzymes to kick in. This time I sip even less, trying to think good thoughts as I let the fire slide down my throat. Ah. I can feel the wires start to slacken. Once more with feeling. Yes. Better.

I look up at my Guardian Angel in her blue robe. By gawd, there's a halo around her head. OK. It's tears and the backlighting. Acknowledging this doesn't diminish the effect. She carefully puts the toilet seat down and sits on it. I find my head in her lap and everything I need to say erupts in unintelligible sobs. But that's OK. Words wouldn't help, even if I could find them. Would I ever be able to? Does she wish I could or hope I won't?

"OK. You can cut the dance stuff. I'll run a short before *Devil* to fill. You sure you're gonna be OK with the talk?"

Bill picks up his intercom to the booth and begins to bark out instructions to the projectionist without waiting for my answer. If he could see through my story of a slight cold, he was enough of a pal to say nothing.

As I turn to leave, however, he adds, not unkindly, "If anybody asks for their money back, they'll take it outta your pay, you know."

"Seems fair to me."

I would gladly have forfeited my entire salary to leave right that minute. However, that damn sense of somehow owing it to Jay, the sweet little guy who got me into this, would not let me suggest it.

It was obvious the audience was largely repeats. I would still do the dress-drop. Then I would just walk offstage, dragging the sucker behind me a la Gypsy Rose Lee. Bill so advised the follow-spot operator.

Mom handed me a still-warm fried egg sandwich as I sat down at my dressing table. Small nibbles of this interspersed with small nips at the jar sustained me and kept the whoopsies at bay.

On with the show.

"Were you ever busted?" is written in a barely legible scrawl on one of the question cards. Not the first time it's been asked.

"Just once. In Milwaukee. In the dead of winter..."

I'm freezing. I can see a truly matronly matron passing within earshot of my cell and call to her.

"Excuse me, Miss?"

"Yes?" she replies in a friendly enough voice considering the surroundings.

"Don't I get to make a phone call?"

"Nobody's let you make a call yet?" She seems genuinely shocked.

"No, ma'am."

I do my best to look like a Margaret Keane huge-eyed waif painting.

She spins on her heel and mutters something that sounds very much like "assholes."

In a trice she's back with a phone on a long cord – and a BLANKET.

I'm still in the wet tee shirt and toe shoes of my grand finale. The Uncle Sam hat has disappeared along with the flag-festooned baton. (I later learned it was being held as evidence. The arresting officers, I also later learned, said they thought I intended to do them bodily harm with it.)

The blanket is a bit threadbare and doesn't smell very good, but it is welcome as flowers in May. I clutch it tightly around my shivering shoulders and reach for the handset the matron pushes through the tray-size opening in the cell door. The phone is an old rotary dial that doesn't fit through the slot. The matron holds it against her ample bosom.

"What number you wanna call, Hon?" she asks. Her voice is warm; her face, kind.

"I don't know. Does a call to information count as my one call?"

"Not in my book." She chuckles and dials 411.

I realize I have no idea what the name of my current place of work is.

"Do you know the name of the theater where they show the X-rated movies?" I ask hopefully as the instrument makes its connection.

I was asking the matron, but the operator answers.

"That's the Bijou," intones a neutral voice in perfect phone company diction. "Shall I connect you?"

"Please."

I try to remember the name of the manager whom I haven't seen since he jovially escorted me to my dressing room just in time for the 8 p.m. show.

I'm beginning to suspect the arrest was expected, if not arranged. A TV camera and crew were at the end of the block covering the action as I was escorted to the squad car. It's possible that I slipped and ended up face-down in a snow bank, hands cuffed behind my back, because I was looking at them instead of where I was going. It's possible.

Surely the manager will tell me that everything's being taken care of and that I can expect to see them there at any minute. I still have two shows to do!

On the fourth ring, the line connects.

"Good evening, and welcome to the Bijou, home of Milwaukee's finest adult entertainment. This week, Georgina Spelvin, star of *The Devil In Miss Jones*, can be seen live onstage at 8, 10 and 12 midnight."

"Not if she's still in jail," I moan.

"Tickets are available at the..."

I hang up. Not too encouraging. But wait. Obviously, the managers are already on their way to bail me out. That's why the phone at the theater's on automatic pickup.

"Nobody home?" asks the matron as I return the handset to her care.

"Do they always bust the strippers on their opening night here?" I ask in a friendly attempt at conversation.

"Nope. You're the first one I know of. You must be special."

She wasn't being sarcastic. At least, it didn't sound like it. She waddled away, coiling the cord of the antique phone over her forearm in a practiced manner.

I was still liquored up just enough to cope. It was three hours later, around midnight, that I began to think I might never know freedom again. Nobody who loved me even knew where I was! I had no idea what had become of the folks I was supposed to be working for. I was cold and I was going into withdrawal. That's when the puking starts.

My sweet, grandmotherly matron had left for the night, I guess. For the next eight hours, not a single person materialized in the hall space beyond my four-by-six cell with its glaring overhead light and shiny aluminum crapper. Sleep was out of the question. I stretched. I jumped up and down to try and get warm. I did a ballet barre. I tried to meditate. I did another barre. I finally just curled into a fetal ball and shook and puked. Mostly I puked.

Finally, around ten the next morning, several folks, including the chubby manager who had been so nice the night before, appeared at my cell door. Richard (I finally remembered his name) handed me the lovely, warm velour jumpsuit I had worn to the theater. More importantly, he had my purse, which contained the elements of my survival: wallet, make-up, Swiss Army knife, brush, vitamins, FLASK. I didn't pull that out of the bag, but I surreptitiously jiggled it to see if the contents were still there. They were. Relief was only a private spot away.

From the pokey we went directly to the diner across the street from the theater. Fuck privacy. Several cups of vodka-laced coffee and a plate of scrambled eggs later, I began to feel like a human being again.

The guys explained their tardy rescue by telling me that the authorities lost me. That's right. They couldn't find the arrest report and nobody seemed to know what had been done with me. It took all night for two lawyers and a judge to find me. Once they did, everything seemed to be hunky-dory. Richard even managed to get my baton back in time for the first show. That's when I learned it had been designated a lethal weapon.

There were no other incidents for the rest of the week. Then, on closing night, a bunch of us from the theater strolled across the empty street to the diner as we had done every night all week.

Suddenly a squad car careened around the corner and skidded to a halt in front of us. Out jumped my two friends from the night of the bust. Yes, sir. The very same two fellas who tried to put the cuffs on me as I was stripping off my business suit and getting into my wet tee shirt, hat, toe shoes, et al. At that frantic moment, I hadn't been able to hear what they were saying. I thought they were asking for an autograph.

"Just wait right here," I had told them, firmly. "I'll be right back."

And onto the boards I bouréed, did my bows, then bouréed back into the waiting arms of the two guys in the wings. That's when they got the cuffs on me and perp-walked me out the stage door.

Now they amble toward us. We converge on the sidewalk.

"You all are aware that you just jay-walked across the street, aren't you?" asks the taller, more robust of the two.

"Oh, come on. You guys are in the only car within ten blocks..." Richard, unwisely, begins to argue.

"We're gonna have to write you up," states the smaller, more nattily dressed of the two.

They're in mufti – plainclothes – as they had been the night of my bust. I might have been more cooperative at the initial confrontation had they been in uniform. But then again, I might not.

Well, write us up they did.

I was really pissed. I bitched my way into a booth and looked at the summons. The arresting officers' names were carefully printed above their signatures. I stared in disbelief. I asked to see the others' summonses. We compared our paperwork and found that the officers' names were, indeed, Stansky and Haas. No shit.

"You're lucky that's the only night you ever spent in jail," observes Jay, the entrepreneur responsible for my short-lived career as a stripper. Just back from New Orleans where a couple of his girls were recently busted, he reacts to my telling of the Stansky and Haas tale, not with laughter, but with genuine anger.

"It's a crime the way they treat these girls, don't you think?" he asks Mom. She feels no need to reply to the obviously rhetorical question.

"So, Al (the owner) tells me you're a bit under the weather," he continues in a genuinely sympathetic tone.

"Yeah," I sniff, "bad cold."

Yeah sure. I know he knows exactly what's causing my "illness," But if he wants to be gallant that's fine with me.

He reaches into his inside coat pocket. Mom tenses ever so slightly. Does she think he was gonna pull a gun? He withdraws a huge stack of greenbacks and begins counting out hundred dollar bills onto the dressing table.

"...thirteen, fourteen, fifteen. There you go. Full week's salary but Al says it's OK if you split now since you're not feeling too good. He's switching features a couple of days early."

He doesn't look at me, just taps the stack of bills into a neat little pile.

"He says you were such a draw, his entire clientele was here the first few nights. He needs to draw them back with some new stuff."

He hands me the stack of bills.

I glance over at Mom. She is totally aware of what's going down. I was being fired in the nicest possible way. I throw my arms around Jay and almost break into tears. He gently squeezes back then pushes me away.

"Now, you go on down to Texas with Mama and get all better. When you feel up to it, give me a call and we'll set you up with a new tour. Here are your bus tickets back to New York."

I didn't see any point in telling him he wouldn't be hearing from me. He probably knew that.

"I've got to go check on a couple of my other girls now." He starts out the door. Turns back to say, "Oh, Roberta says to keep in touch. You can write her here at the theater or in care of the office. If she's touring, I'll get her mail to her."

"Thanks," I manage to say, "for everything."

"Thank you, George. It's been a terrific year. You're a class act. Don't ever forget it."

With that, he strode off toward the dressing rooms at the rear of the theater and I never spoke to him again.

I never wrote to Roberta, either. Now, there was a class act.

Time Out in Texas

"PETEY?" CALLS DAD through the door of the bathroom. "There's someone on the phone for you. Want me to get a number?"

"Please. Tell them I'll call them right back."

Petey has been my family nickname since I was a rug rat. The story goes that Dad came in from the nearby oil field one day to find his four-month-old daughter sooty black from crawling about the floor of the porous cabin we called home. A popular comic strip character of the time was a soot-covered little guy known as Smokey Pete. That became my moniker and was later "feminized" to Petey.

I'm soaking in my third baking-soda bath of the day. Grasping the spigot with my toes, I turn off the hot water cascading into the big square tub in Mother's bathroom. It's just something I've done as long as I can remember: turn off the faucets in the tub with my toes. That's why it ended up in the suicide scene in my great film triumph, *The Devil in Miss Jones*. It's also how Jimmy Nygren recognized me when he saw the movie.

This is day four of home rehab. I was actually able to take nourishment at breakfast without immediately returning it to nature.

The baking soda-laced baths are to get rid of the drunk stink that's still oozing from my pores (per Mom). An open box of soda in the refrigerator gets rid of "icebox odor." I hoped it would work on booze-soaked flesh. I'm not sure if it's had any effect or not, but soaking in the hot water is lovely.

I dry off and don the old, worn but comfy sweats Mom dug up for me. Running a brush through my damp hair, I look in the mirror over the sink. The puffiness around my eyes has gone down a lot. The eyes, however, still look like a couple of piss holes in the snow.

Who could be calling me here? No one here knows I'm in town. At least, I hope not. I told Dee, my trailer mate at The Swallows, that I would be spending a week with my folks, but were it she, Pops would have recognized her voice. They've spoken many times. So, who?

"The number's on the pad by the kitchen phone," says Dad from his chair before the TV.

He's watching reruns of *M*A*S*H* – his favorite show. Well, after *Gunsmoke*.

Watch TV is about all he does any more. Sometimes he watches it when it isn't even on.

He's now retired from the oil company where he worked for my entire life, and most of his.

About twenty years after being promoted to head of the maps department for the East Texas fields, Corporate decided to get computerized. They told Dad he must move to Houston and learn how to use the program. Dad had never even touched a typewriter, much less a computer keyboard. He decided to save the company the money it would cost them to train him at the age of sixty-four and take his retirement six months early. The company was delighted. That option cut his retirement benefit in half! He could not bring himself to risk life and limb trying to drive in Houston traffic, however, so he ate it. Then he sat down in front of the TV.

The note in Dad's spidery scrawl says "Teddy." It's a Los Angeles area code. I'm not sure I want to talk to anyone from Los Angeles in Dad's hearing. I fake a call.

"Busy. I'll try later."

"I'm gonna run to the market," I continue. "Need anything?"

"See if we have enough Cokes in the garage."

"OK," I agree as I lift the keys of his '67 Chevy Impala from their hook and fly out the back door. (Boy, was that a great car.)

I stack a bunch of quarters on the shelf under the pay phone, dial the number on the slip of paper, wait for the operator's instructions to "deposit one dollar and twenty-five cents for three minutes," and do so.

"Hello?" answers a female voice on about the fifth ring.

"This is Georgina returning a call from Ted."

"Georgie?" squeals the voice, enthusiastically. "This is Betty. Ted's out by the pool. Hang on, I'll tell him to pick up."

Ah. Now I know. It's Ted Paramor, producer of the best-paying porn-film jobs I've done to date.

"Georgie?" says the familiar sweet voice.

"Hey, Teddy. How ya doin?"

"Fine. You?"

"OK (pause) now. I'm sure you heard I've been having a little trouble keeping my head out of Moscow..."

(That's a cute way of referring to a vodka bottle. I picked it up in a strip joint in San Francisco. One of the Mitchell Brothers' aides-de-camp suggested I wasn't going to make it through my week's gig there if I "couldn't keep my head out of Moscow." The expression stuck with me even if the advice didn't.)

"Yeah, I heard. You sound pretty good, though. Are you up to doing a few days on a film in three weeks?"

"You bet. I'm flying back to San Diego next week. I'll call you from there."

"I'll get a script right out to you. What's your address in Texas?"

"NO," I almost shout. More calmly, "No, no that's OK. Just send it to The Swallows. You have that address, don't you?"

"Sure....Do you need an advance?"

"No. I'm OK. But thanks for asking. Don't worry. I'm sober and I'm going to stay that way. I'll know my lines."

"I know you will. Same deal on your daily rate – one dollar more than any other cast member?"

"Super. Do I know anyone else in it?"

"Everyone. Annette Haven will be one of your daughters. You'll be playing a widow trying to find rich husbands for her two gorgeous girls..."

"Please deposit one dollar and twenty-five cents for the next three minutes," intones a mechanical voice.

"Should I call you back?"

"No, it's OK. I'm covered," I reply as I pop five more quarters into the slot.

"I think you're gonna like this one," continues Ted. "You'll be working with Nuzzo..."

"John Leslie? Be still my heart."

"We'll be shooting in Marin County again."

"Will Ye Olde Howard Johnson's just over the bridge be home base?"

"You got it."

"Yippee. Fried clams, here I come. Call you as soon as I get home. Love to Betty."

"See you soon."

I was turning in the drive when I remembered the Cokes. Back to the market, jig-a-dee-jog.

Well, so much for any resolutions about finding another line of work.

My primary focus now was on getting into shape. I set up my tape recorder in the "California Room." This was a screened-in covered tin box stuck onto the back of the house. It had all the charm and stability of the white-trash trailer for which it was designed to be a prefab extension.

Here I could stretch and bend amidst the philodendron growing in soggy pots all over the place. Most ran for 20-to-30 feet around the periphery of the space with four or five leaves sprouting from the terminus of each struggling vine. Mother was far too busy with her civic duties to be much concerned about the upkeep of this area, so Dad simply watered hell out of the plants whenever it occurred to him to do so – which was way too often. Mushrooms were growing up out of the indoor-outdoor carpet in the corners.

I'm still at it when Mom gets home from work. She parks her handbag on the breakfast table by the kitchen phone, sets a bag of groceries on the counter, and sweeps past Dad's chair, planting a kiss on his upturned cheek as she strides to the open sliding glass doors of the sunken (and still sinking) add-on.

She leans into the dampness and addresses my prostrate form.

"How ya doin'?" she asks, meaning have I managed to avoid imbibing any alcohol that day.

"OK," I answer in a way that tells her I am still dry, as in, not having imbibed any alcohol that day.

"Shall I cook dinner tonight?" I offer. This signals that I'm past the constant nausea stage. Seventy-two hours. It may vary in others, but that's my constitution's required time to get through withdrawal. I know. I've tested it many times.

"There's some pork chops and frozen fries in the bag on the drain board. Have at it. I'm gonna take a bath."

Mom shares my enthusiasm for hot water.

"Do you still teach dancing?" asks Dad as I walk past him on my way to change.

"Sometimes," I lie. "I have a few private pupils."

This was almost true. The kids at The Swallows were forever getting me to teach them song-and-dance routines. They would present these at the frequent talent night shows that were a favorite feature of the place.

"Didn't I send you a picture of the kids doing 'Steam Heat?'" I ask.

"Oh, yes. The one where they were wearing the bowler hats. That was last year. I just wondered if you were still doing any of that."

"Oh, sure. It's just recreational, though. It's not really like a school or anything."

"Meaning, you don't get paid for it?"

"You got it."

Here it comes. He's going to ask me how I do make a living.

"Well, at least you're keeping in good shape," he says as he hits the volume button on his remote.

Swan Song

THE SWALLOWS' RESIDENTS welcomed me home with a barbecue and dance in the Rec Room. There was a barbecue and dance in the Rec Room every Friday night of course, but any special occasion was always a welcome excuse for decorations and fancy garb. Nobody likes to get dressed up more than nudists.

For the first time in a very, very long time, I had money in the bank and another job on the horizon. Dee had added many nice touches to the trailer and patio in my absence. You would think with things in such good order I would be able to keep my balance on the old water wagon at last.

You'd think.

And I did – for a while.

The film I did for Ted Paramor was called *Desires Within Young Girls*. As promised, I was still sober when I flew up to San Francisco. I knew almost everyone working the shoot. It was a second homecoming.

"Are you still living in that funky trailer park? Where is it?" asks Dale, my favorite makeup man, as he pats pancake on my upturned face.

"Harbison Canyon. Just outside San Diego," I reply. "Would you hand me my coffee?"

The adept artist parks his sponge in the fingers of his left hand, which also holds an assortment of pencils and brushes. He ferries the steaming container to my outstretched hand. I take a hurried sip and hand it back. He replaces it on the makeup table and takes a sip from his own no longer steaming cup.

"You wanna run lines?" chirps Debbie, a darling little PA who looks about twelve but is actually pushing thirty.

"Not 'til Dale turns me loose," I reply.

"Give me another fifteen, OK?"

"Right." She turns to me. "You need anything? Danish? Bagel?"

"No thanks. I'm fine," I assure her. She spins on her tennies and heads back toward the craft services area, pigtails bouncing.

"So when are you going to move to San Francisco?" continues Dale, working his magic to create the glamorous Georgina. "Almost all the films are done here now, you know."

"I know. And I love coming up here to work. But it's too damp and cold to live here. Hell, it's supposed to be summer. I'm fuckin' freezin'."

"You're anemic. You don't eat enough meat, Baby."

"Ha ha."

Dale finishes painting my face and starts brushing my baby-fine hair in a futile attempt to make a proper "do" of it.

"Don't spray it!" I protest.

"It's gonna droop and get all messy!" he squeals in protest.

"So, it'll look messy. People look messy when they fuck," I reply.

"Not in porn films, they don't."

"I do."

"OK, Kiddo. It's your closeup." With that, he kisses me lightly on the cheek and helps me down from the tall canvas chair.

"Do you want to put this on now?" asks the wardrobe person, holding out a marabou-trimmed bit of transparent organza. (Why is it always maribou?)

"Not 'til we're rolling. Wouldn't want the feathers to wilt," I reply.

"OK. I'll hang on to it."

"Thanks," I throw back over my shoulder as I pull my kimono around my carefully pancaked nakedness.

Script tucked under my arm and coffee cup in hand, I make my way to the set. We're filming in a magnificent mansion somewhere in Marin County. There is a real fire going in the huge elevated fireplace and a snow-white imitation bearskin rug is spread invitingly before it.

I move the canvas chair that has "Spelvin" stenciled on the back closer to the raging inferno and sit with script in lap. I mumble my next speech over and over. My partner in the scene has no lines other than any responsive noises he cares to make during the scene. I, on the other hand, have been handed a page and a half of free-association racecar jargon. Not my native tongue. I am to spout this whilst "driving" my spouse to his sexual climax – and simultaneously fatal heart attack per the script. Yeah, it's a comedy. Really.

John Leslie, known to his intimates as Nuzzo, is wrapped in a copious terry-cloth robe. He's been "aged" into a gorgeous gray fox. Dale, the makeup artist, hovers with brush and powder puff at the ready.

"Can we have the actors in place for a light check, please?" calls the cameraman.

Nuzzo tosses his robe aside and stretches out on the rug on his back. I park my kimono and script on the chair, take a quick sip of coffee and cross to the rug. One of the ever-present PAs takes my shoes as I step out of them and onto the rug. The wardrobe mistress holds the short marabou monstrosity so that I can get it around my sweaty torso.

"I need you sitting astride, facing the camera, please, Miss Spelvin," says the cameraman. (It's our first shoot together. He'll be calling me George before the day is done.)

"Good morning," I say cheerily to my fellow actor as I plop my naked butt down on his equally nude supine form. "Sleep well?"

"Umpf, yeah. Not long, but well. Where'd you light out to in the shank of the evening?" The ruggedly handsome leading man places his hands on my thighs and wiggles himself into a more comfortable position.

"You OK?" I ask, solicitously.

"Yeah, sure. You don't weigh much more 'n a wet mosquito," he graciously responds with his signature sexy smile.

"Can you cheat your head up a bit?" asks the cameraman.

"Enough?" I ask as I peer at a spot just below the camera's lens.

"Fine. Take the key down a couple of feet," he instructs one of the grips, who quickly adjusts the stand of one of the many lights surrounding the area.

"We're gonna try to get the whole scene in one master," explains the director, leaning into the space between our heads. He speaks in a low, almost conspiratorial tone. "If you go up, just make stuff up. We'll pick up anything we miss in the closeups. We'll do the hard stuff after lunch, so keep track of your positions. OK?"

I nod my understanding. Mr. Wonderful beneath my loins grunts an acknowledgment. Nuzzo has to be one of the hottest studs in the business. Just looking at him is a real turn-on. Sitting on top of his groin is more than a little tantalizing.

"All right. Quiet on the set, please. This is a take," calls out the AD.

"Quiet back there," shouts a PA toward the green room. "We're rolling."

"OK. Camera…"

"Rolling."

"Speed," announces the sound tech.

"And… action."

I begin my dialogue. "That's it, Papa. Lemme hear those pistons pound. Oh yeah. Let's rev it up. Open up all the cylinders. Let me hear that baby purr." I'm writhing and wailing. The good sweat worked up hovering by the fireplace is being whipped to a froth by the lights and my gyrations.

"How ya doin', Baby? Ready for me to throw 'er into gear?" I gasp.

"Humph hump ugh, ahhhh," responds my co-worker, eloquently.

What's this? Method acting? Did my fellow thespian not understand that this is supposed to be the simulated sex master shot?

Nuzzo knows the ropes. What's going on here? Are we gonna lose the money shot? Not if I can help it. I'm not about to blow a take with casual inquiry. I slide back enough that the now fully tumescent member is in view. It's important the director be aware of the situation. I keep up the dialogue, now inventing a few lines to suit the occasion.

"Ah, here's my joy stick. Lemme feel the power, Baby." I slide down and grip and maneuver the throbbing extremity like a gearshift.

Our director signals me to go for it. There's a flurry of activity when the cameraman signals his standby crew of hand-held steady-cam operators to move in.

I'm spouting nonsensical racecar jargon in between bouts of furious fellatio and firm fondling. The object of my affection arches his back and explodes verbally and seminally. I make sure the evidence of this very genuine passion is captured by both cameras before thrusting the still stiff and throbbing member into the sanctuary of my anatomy. I subconsciously switch from racecar to runaway stallion, which brings me to a tit-quivering climax.

(I inserted his still-rock-hard cock into my pussy because according to the script I'm supposed to be in this position for the next dialogue. That's the only reason. Really.)

Following the script, I register the fact that my husband is no longer moving. Which he isn't. At all.

"Charley? Charley? Honey? What's the matter?" I wiggle his face with my hand. "Charles. Talk to me, Baby." Gentle slap or two. "What is it?" I sit back on my haunches and stare down at the still figure before me. I lean down and put my ear against his chest. This guy is good. I'm beginning to be genuinely concerned, but, no, it's OK. There's a heartbeat. I sit back and look out beyond the camera that is now zooming into my face (yeah, I can tell when they do that).

Quietly, almost under my breath, I deliver my last line of the scene.

"Oh, shit."

Hold – hold – hold…

"Cut and fucking print!" finally cries the director.

The surrounding coterie of grips, technicians, and cast members applaud. Actors live for that.

"Sorry, man," says Nuzzo to the director. "There wasn't a damn thing I could do about it, you know?"

"I know. No problem. No problem at all. We got everything we need and picked up half a day thanks to you old pros. Georgie, you're terrific. (He actually gives me a noogie.) And you – you were just fucking amazing," he says to Nuzzo.

"Thanks. I had a great time. Always a pleasure pleasuring you Madam." he says kissing my hand gallantly. He is such a card.

"Georgie, I love you," my wonderful director continues to gush as he squeezes my shoulder.

"I think we should have a round of applause for the crew. They're the ones who got rolling and got in there. I was just enjoying myself." I applaud the blurs of activity around us. They hate when you do that – thank all the little people...

"Hey, that's why we get the big bucks," quips the boom operator as he carefully stashes the mike and begins to coil the cable festooning the set. We both know the rules.

"We can get the bathroom two shot with George and Annette before lunch," posits the AD.

"Good. Dale, can you get George ready for street wear in a half-hour?" asks the director.

"If she'll let me spray her hair," replies my bulwark petulantly.

"Well, that's it for me for today," says Nuzzo. "I'm headin' to the beach."

"Great scene," says our director. "Thanks."

"Thank you," says the actor, then turns to me. "And thank you. Being your husband for even just one scene was an honor."

"Well, I won't say the pleasure was ALL mine, but a lot of it was," I smile as we shake hands.

"Come on, Missy. We have scant time to restore you to fashionable matron status," declares Dale as he drags me away to the makeup room.

I grab my script and find the scene between my character – sort of a hard-core Mama Rose – and Annette Haven, who plays one of the two daughters I spend the bulk of the movie trying to marry off to rich husbands. I told you it was a comedy.

I loved living at The Swallows but I couldn't find a way to make a living between films. One of the members got me a job cleaning windows and bathrooms at a construction site but it was only a three-month gig. I tried packing avocados. I got fired. I couldn't keep up with the conveyor belt. I gutted and scaled fish. Nice outdoor work but seasonal. Finally, I sold my trailer and moved up to Los Angeles.

Stella, the sanest of the Pickle Factory denizens, now lived in Hollywood. She invited me to crash with her until I could find my own place.

Another bungalow in her complex became vacant and I pounced on it like a chicken on a June bug. A wonderful collection of folks filled those twelve tiny houses that crouched around a long narrow courtyard. Musicians, grips, writers, editors, actors: seemed like everyone was connected to The Industry (the non-porn one) in one way or another. Evenings usually found most of the tenants gathered in the courtyard, enjoying the California flora and each other's company. We had a lot of great barbeques.

Stella dubbed the place "Rancho Beyondo."

Yes, I was still drinking. I always sobered up to work a film when one came along, but my services were required less frequently as time went by. This was only natural. Fucking on film's a sport for the young. I'm amazed I was able to do as many films as I did, being somewhat long in the tooth to begin with. A blow-by-blow description of each and every film that kept my liquor store in business for the next year would bore us both to tears. All the gory details are on the Web, anyway.

It was time to get that day job. I did the old cold-turkey trot and on the predictable third day, I rose from my sweat-soaked bed of pain and hauled out the yellow pages. The first temp agency I called had me come in for the old typing, spelling, grammar, and punctuation tests the following day and placed me the day after that. Thank God Mom, in her wisdom, made me learn to type.

My first assignment was in the communications department of a physicians' professional association. My third day on the job, Jerry Damiano called from out of the blue. How many years had it been since I'd heard from him? He wanted me for one day, one scene, and it would be with old friend Milt Engly, one of the sweetest studs in the biz.

Thank God I had sobered up to look for a job.

I told him, "OK. But you know… we've got to stop meeting this way."

The next day my boss, a crusty old campaigner who had been a war correspondent in The Big One (WWII), called me into his office.

"You've been a breath of fresh air around here," he growls jovially. "How would you like to come aboard on a permanent basis?"

What? And give up Show Business?

*And what about Jerry and my promise
to be in his movie?*

"I'm glad you're happy with my work," I begin, "and I do think I would like to accept the offer. I have, however, already agreed to be in a movie that's shooting next week."

Mr. Z. doesn't seem the least bit fazed. Nor does he seem particularly impressed. He doesn't ask me what movie, for whom, who's going to be in it: none of the questions one would expect from a civilian. It occurs to me that he knows exactly what kind of movie I'm talking about and has no intention of demanding details. Good.

"How long is that going to take?" he says.

"Through Thursday, but it's shooting up in San Francisco. I couldn't get back to work until Monday."

"Have you any further commitments beyond this one?" he asks, quite sternly, peering intently into my eyes.

"No," I respond. Now I'm sure he knows the score. "This is the last film I plan to do – ever. And I wouldn't do this one, except I promised a good friend some time ago that I would," I lie.

"Fine then," he continues, "we'll get another temp for next week. Go on up to personnel and fill out the paperwork. Tell 'em you're going to start week after next," he orders in his brusque baritone.

He turns back to his 1945 Royal and resumes the three-fingered, blinding-fast pecking out of his column for the next edition.

The flight to San Francisco arrives on time. They did that back then.

A production assistant meets me and delivers me directly to the set somewhere in Marin County. I was the last one into makeup, and it was only eight in the morning.

"You look terrific," purrs Jerry as he plants a big smooch on top of my head where it won't smudge the makeup.

Dressed in a slinky cocktail dress with hair and makeup done to the nines, I'm actually feeling pretty good about myself. Did I hang up my G-string too soon?

"Did anyone give you a script?" continues the great Damiano.

"No," I reply. "Is there one?"

"Hell, yes. What do you think this is? A porn shoot?" replies the ever-agile wit. "Randy. Have you got sides for Georgie?" he calls into the swarming activity of the elaborate cocktail lounge set.

"Flyin' in," responds a techie scooping up a few pages from the production table and scooting across the room to where we stand.

"Now," says Jerry, "you're this high-class madam…"

Surprise, surprise.

I look over my few lines and get a brief rundown of the story.

The dialog scenes go like greased lightning and they're down to serious fucking before lunch. The hard-core action is finessed by an impressive coterie of gorgeous young folks in every conceivable combination.

While all that's going on, Milt and I linger over lunch and wax nostalgic over the films we've done together, laughing at the merry exploits of our youth. Milt is a very sweet person. As reliable as death and taxes. Yup. One of those Rolexes. I was delighted when Jerry told me he would by my partner if I chose to accept this assignment. He didn't tell me it would be a threesome until I got here.

When we're called to the set for our scene, I meet the third member of our little ensemble. His name is Paul Thomas and he is gorgeous. I don't know if he was new to the business, but he was new to me. We would meet again, but not for many years.

Aside from the body count, the scene was pretty pedestrian: just plain old fornication in all the stardard Kama Sutra poses. No chains, no whips, no whipped cream…and no bananas.

I couldn't have asked for a nicer swan song.

California to Texas – 1983

Dancing Lessons From God

WORKING FOR A LIVING WASN'T HALF BAD. After a year, I even got a vacation. First time anybody ever paid me to do nothing!

My chum and former trailer-mate Dee had taken a small apartment in San Diego when I had to give up the trailer and move to Los Angeles. The boyfriend of one of our pals at the park owned a 24-foot Chris Craft. He had often taken us girls fishing. Just such an excursion in celebration of my forty-fourth birthday was arranged. I hopped a train to San Diego after work on Friday. We spent most of Saturday bouncing around the bay. Late that afternoon Dee and I pulled into the driveway of her new home, one of those delightful old houses near downtown that had been broken up into small living spaces.

"Just throw the fish in the sink. I'll gut and scale 'em in a minute," yells Dee from the carport.

"Hey, I'm the guttin' 'n scalin' champ of Whitewater Fish Hatchery, remember?" I sing out with great bravado.

Up the wooden steps and through the screen door I plunge, then swivel and back through a colorful beaded curtain into the compact kitchen area. Swooping the foam cooler up onto the drain board, I dump the ice and shiny critters that nearly fill it into the sink.

"Oh, yeah," says Dee, carefully maneuvering the fishing poles through the beads, "that was your first job out here, wasn't it?"

This fancy, beaded curtain separates the kitchen nook from the living room. The bedroom is still folded up in the wall.

"Yup. Followed shortly by my one-day stint at the avocado packing shed across the road from The Swallows," I reply.

"I remember that day. You got fired, didn't you? Was it the language barrier?"

"Nope. I was getting along fine with my fractured Texican. It was because I couldn't get the little suckers into the right crates. I couldn't tell a small from a medium or a medium from a large."

"Ah," commiserates my pal, "it wasn't the work; it was the decisions?"

"Don't laugh," I admonish as I begin to disembowel our catch. "It's not easy to spot the right sized ball of green when it's zooming by on a belt ninety-to-nothing. I felt like Lucy on the candy line." I deftly slit open a slippery underbelly and flip the innards into the waiting bucket. These will get dug in under the rose bushes by the carport.

"That poor guy, the foreman, he kept moving me down the line 'til by the end of the day, I was the last lady in front of the belt. He paid me for the day and said, "Thees yob... she not for you, I don' tink."

Dee laughs with me at the memory of my day as an inept avocado packer.

I had called Mom the night before to wish her a happy birthday. Yeah. We're two days apart, three in leap years. She, Dad, and I said all the expected things. Then, as I heard what sounded like Dad hanging up, she whispered, "I don't want to upset your father..." there's a long pause. "A little while ago, I threw up some dark, icky stuff..."

"Did you call the doctor?" I ask in alarm.

"I have an appointment to see him in the morning, anyway. I don't think it's anything, really." She doesn't sound distressed. "You go on your fishing trip. Call me again tomorrow night, OK?"

"OK," I reply, hesitantly. "Maybe you should call Bud?"

My brother lived only about one hundred miles from them.

"If I think it's necessary, I will." She uses her don't-tell-me-what-to-do voice. "Now, don't get crazy. I just wanted to let you know what was going on. Catch a big one. I'll talk to you tomorrow night."

With the fish properly dressed and in the fridge, I plop on the couch and pick up the phone. Dad answers on the first ring.

"Pops? It's Petey. Mom there?"

"She's supposed to be in the hospital," he quavers, "but I can't find her."

"What? What do you mean, you can't find her?"

"The doctor called an hour or so ago and told me he was sending her to Medical Center for some tests and I shouldn't worry. Why do they say you shouldn't worry when they tell you something you should worry about? The minute they say it, you know it's something serious that you should worry about."

"True. I don't know. Waddaya mean, you can't find her?"

"Well, I called Bud and he called the hospital and they said she wasn't there."

"Let me call Bud. I'll call you right back."

Bud answers on the first ring.

"I called the Medical Center. They say she's not there." My brother is one of the straightest arrows you'll ever encounter. He also got most of the good sense genes. Not one to panic, he did now have a distinct note of alarm in his voice.

"Did you try Mother Francis?" I ask. That's the older hospital in town.

"Her doctor said he sent her in an ambulance to Medical Center."

"I'll call Mother Francis and get back to you."

Just as I suspected, Mom had insisted that the ambulance driver take her to the older hospital. She used to volunteer there and knows everybody. Nobody had any idea they should inform her doctor. Who countermands doctor's orders?

I called my best friend and neighbor, Stell. She said not to worry, she'd continue to feed my cat and to "…remember what Buddha says, 'strange travel plans are dancing lessons from God.'"

A change of skivvies, my toothbrush, and about fifteen bucks was all I had taken to San Diego with me. I was on the next plane to Texas in my fishing clothes. My brother purchased a ticket for me, as I was without credit cards at that point in my life. He met the plane and we drove through the rest of the night to the hospital.

Mom was not conscious. She had not been conscious since she had made quite certain her instructions regarding the hospital to which she should be taken were being followed.

I'll say this for her doctor, he tracked her down and found her just shortly before we did. We cornered him outside her room and demanded a prognosis.

"I've never seen anyone sicker and still alive," he states bluntly.

"How the hell could she get this sick without your getting in touch with either of us?" I shriek, sounding a lot like Shirley MacLaine in *Terms of Endearment*, I'm sure.

"She didn't let anybody know how sick she was," he counters defensively. "She was in good shape the last time I examined her."

"Which was?" asked Bud, in a born CPA's reasonable tone.

"About six months ago."

"What's the problem?" calmly asks my brother.

The doctor replied with a long spiel of medical jargon that had something to do with thinning blood – or clotting blood – or keeping blood from clotting. I have no idea to this day what was wrong with her. And, quite frankly, I'm not sure the doctor did either – the many drugs he had prescribed for her through the years notwithstanding. Her medicine cabinet looked like a Walgreen's warehouse.

Three days later, she wakes from her coma – if that's what it was. I hear the slightest movement and almost leap from the chair where I've been curled up reading. Bud and I have been taking turns watching for Mom to wake up and trying to keep Daddy from losing it.

"Mom?" I whisper. Her eyes blink and she turns her head about, her brow puckered in mild puzzlement.

"What are you doing here?" she asks, accusingly when she spots me.

"I might ask the same of you," I respond, defensively.

"I think I ate something I shouldn't have," she mumbles. "Why am I tied up?" She pulls at the restraints on her arms.

"They did that so you wouldn't pull out your IV in your sleep."

"Well, I'm awake, now. Get these damn things off me."

"I've already buzzed for the nurse. She'll be here in a minute. We'll see if we can't talk her into turnin' you loose."

"And see if you can find a bedpan. I'm about to pop."

This much I can do, but when I try to position it, I find that she is, of course, catheterized.

"It's OK," I tell her. "They got you piped to a bag. Just let her rip."

"Where am I?"

"Mother Francis Hospital."

"Oh, right. Good. Have you talked to Dr. Sam? What's wrong with me?"

"He'll have to tell you. I couldn't understand a word he said."

"What makes you think I'll be able to? Where's that nurse? I gotta scratch."

"Where?"

"Nose."

I scratch. Finally a nurse comes in. She removes the restraints and catheter; fiddles with the various machines beeping and flashing beside the bed; answers all questions with the expected cheery comments, and departs without enlightening either of us one iota.

"What did you eat?" I query.

No response. She's snoring away. I call home to let Bud and Daddy know that she is, more or less, back with us. Bud says they'll be right over.

She's still snoozing away, but responds to my touch.

"Daddy and Bud are on the way over," I tell her.

"Hum?" Still halfway under.

A bit louder, "Bud's here. He's bringing Daddy over to see you."

"Ohmygod! Where are my teeth? Find my teeth."

I do, in the drawer of her bedside table. I get her into something close to a sitting position.

"Your father's never seen me without my teeth," she explains, fixing the dentures securely in place.

I find a washcloth, brush and lipstick for her. She's looking almost normal by the time the boys arrive.

Daddy sits beside her, holding her hand. He refuses to leave her side when Bud and I suggest we all go to the cafeteria for a snack, as she is again snoring away.

When the doctor comes by later in the afternoon he has no better luck explaining her condition to my father than he did to us. He does say, though, that they will be moving her out of the ICU and into a private room the next day.

"Where are you taking me?" she asks the orderly as he wheels her bed out of the room.

"Down to the third floor." He checks the clipboard dangling before him. "Room 305."

"Oh good." She turns her face up toward me. "That's the garden side. The other side overlooks the parking lot," she explains as I walk beside the rolling bed. "When can I go home?" she asks the orderly. "Oh, you don't know," she surmises. "Do you?" she asks me.

"No."

"I feel fine, now. I really need to get home."

"What do you need from home? I'll bring it to you."

She doesn't answer. She's asleep.

A few hours later in her new room, she stirs. I lean over as she opens her eyes and looks up at me.

"My DAR notebook. The minutes of the last meeting are in shorthand and I have to transcribe them before I forget what they say." It takes me a minute to realize she's answering the question posed hours before.

"OK. I'll tell Bud to bring it with him when he comes over this afternoon. What does it look like?

She's out again.

My brother has to get back to his family and job. Mom is awake a little longer each day. Doctor Sam says she'll be able to leave the hospital in a few days. I'm doing bedpan duty, but except for the little bit of exercise getting positioned on it affords her, there's not much point to it.

Except for quick trips home to shower and change into another set of my mother's clothes, I sit by her bed and read or knit. I go home and fix dinner for Daddy and bring him back to the hospital to visit with Mom for a bit in the evening. Once I've gotten him back home and settled in bed for the night, I return to the hospital to sleep in the big padded chair beside her bed.

One would think this the perfect opportunity to get all the stuff that's been parked on my chest all these years, off? Yes? But how can you cause someone in pain more pain? Well, she wasn't actually in pain, she assured me, just uncomfortable. Still…

I really, really tried to keep my alcohol intake under control. I hadn't had a drop since arriving. Then I went to lunch with some of Mom's best buds one day and had a beer. Well, hell. It was a Mexican restaurant. Whoever heard of eating Mexican food without a beer?

Mom's nose wrinkles as I lean over to kiss her upon my return.

"You had a drink," she accuses.

"Just a beer with the girls," I defend.

"Well, either smuggle me in one or stay on the other side of the room," she says in a neutral tone.

"Sure. I'm sorry." I look at the untouched tray beside her bed. "You didn't eat a bite of your lunch."

"The smell of food makes me sick to my stomach. Makes me want to throw up and there's nothing in there to throw."

"I know the feeling," I wryly remind her.

I wonder if this has been reported to her doctor.

"I wish I had a drink," she confesses. "But even more, I wish I could have a good BM."

"Well, you're not going to until you start eating something," I observe.

There's no response. She's out again.

I slip out and go back to the house to fix dinner for Pops. He doesn't feel too good, and decides not to come back to the hospital with me.

Mom's still out like a light when I return, so I settle down with a trashy novel. Eventually I fall asleep in the big, almost comfortable chair.

Sometime in the middle of the night, her voice wakes me.

"Did you call Marge and tell her to notify the Rose Society I won't be at the meeting?"

"You told her when she was here yesterday," I remind her as I get up and lean over her, thinking she wants to talk. Looking at her, though, I realize she has either spoken in her sleep or fallen back there immediately. I go back to my chair, wiggle into a comfortable position, and join her.

Strange beeping sounds and shadowy figures fill the room. The bright overhead light comes on. There are several figures in scrubs around the bed.

"Clear!" says the one leaning over Mom.

I know what that means! I watch TV.

"What's wrong?" I ask in alarm. The blanket slips to the floor as I jump up.

A nurse grabs my arm and tries to drag me from the room.

"Would you please wait outside? You don't want to get in the way, do you?"

Well, no. Yes. I don't want to wait outside in the hall. I want to see what is happening to my mother. I shake off the nurse's hand and move behind the chair.

"CLEAR!" comes the dreadful cry again. And again. And again. I don't know how many times.

A doctor – not Mom's doctor, but a doctor – pulls me into the hall. He holds my shoulders in his hands and looks directly into my eyes. His are warm... and sad.

"We've done all we can, I'm afraid."

"What do you mean? She was fine when I went to sleep. She's been getting better every day. What did you guys do to her?"

I'm pretty sure I was screaming. Someone shoved a couple of pills in a cup at me. I downed them. They helped. I finally stopped shaking and went back into the room.

Mom looked about as she had when I fell asleep. The little scowl lines between her eyes, though, were as smooth as I'd ever seen them. That look of studying the next item on her always-packed agenda wasn't there. I touched her cheek and squeezed her hand. It wasn't warm, but it wasn't really cold. Not yet. I knew there would be no response so I didn't say anything. It was too late to say anything. But I had to stand there for a while. I couldn't move. The pain in my chest had paralyzed me.

A nurse finally draped my sweater over my shoulders and guided me out into the hall. There were papers to sign. The nurse – or maybe she was a volunteer – asked which funeral home to call. I couldn't think of the name of any. I hadn't lived here for twenty years. I think I asked her for a suggestion and one was named. The nice lady even offered to make the call and take care of the transfer. "Sign here," she said. "You can go by tomorrow, and you and your daddy can make all the arrangements then."

Dad!

What the hell was I going to tell Dad?

Higher Education

HE SIMPLY DIDN'T BELIEVE IT.

He didn't believe it when I sat on his bed that morning about 4:30 am, attempting to get what little I understood of the particulars out between sobs. He still didn't believe it when my brother arrived a little before noon. He didn't believe it when we went to the funeral home to pick out a coffin.

Throughout the services at the Episcopal Church, and later at the cemetery, he just stared blankly ahead and moved only if I took his arm and gently propelled him along. A few days later, when a Japanese Maple tree was planted ceremoniously in the town's showplace Rose Garden in Mother's honor, he responded in muted monosyllables to the condolences offered by just about the entire population of that moderate-sized burg.

After nearly a week had gone by, I went in to kiss him good night as usual. He looked up from the New Testament open in his lap. Tears streamed down his carefully shaved, furrowed cheeks. He swallowed with difficulty and spoke.

"She's really gone, isn't she? Oh Petey, what am I gonna do?"

Then the nightmares started. His. I would hear him thrash about, and sometimes a muffled cry of alarm would erupt. After the first time, I didn't run into his room to see what was wrong. It seemed to embarrass him.

I had moved into Mom's room. It was larger and (don't laugh) she told me to. Just like she told me to put her prayer book in her hands before they closed the coffin. No. I didn't – don't – hear her voice... exactly. It's just that a thought will pop into my head with her special mode of expression stamped all over it.

One night, I was startled awake by a bright light shining in my face. I could just see the barrel of a gun pointed at me from the darkness behind the flashlight.

"Daddy?"

I know it's him, but does he?

"Is that you, Petey? Where's Mom? Is the window open? I heard some-one breaking in. Are you alright?" His gruff voice is shaking.

I sit up and turn on the bedside lamp. Dad is in his pajamas. He holds the loaded forty-five he keeps in his bedside table clutched in his right hand, the powerful flashlight in the other. He raises the hand with the gun to shade his eyes from the table lamp. At least it's no longer pointed at me.

"It's OK, Daddy. It was probably the wind. The window's only open a little at the bottom, see?" It is, of course, a dark and stormy night.

He switches off the flashlight and sets it on the bed. Putting the safety on the gun, he sits down in the little boudoir chair Mom had lovingly re-upholstered. The gun still dangles from his hand.

"There've been a lot of dope smugglers coming through here lately," he explains. "I can hear 'em going through the backyard."

I don't doubt that he does... hear them. I do doubt that any dope smugglers with any sense at all would use this neighborhood as a regular route. It's all fenced, manicured, and patrolled to a fare-thee-well. I also rather imagine that he is not the only homeowner in the area who keeps a loaded forty-five in his nightstand and a shotgun (also loaded) under the bed – as did his daddy before him.

He's up. I'm up. We go into the kitchen and he begins his morning rit-ual. The coffee starts to perk; the bacon starts to broil. I go to the bathroom to throw up and sneak a hit of vodka from the stash in my laundry hamper.

Oh yes. I'm still "maintaining." When we make a run to the county line for the two cases of beer and bottle of Wild Turkey that are his week's ration, I turn around and head right back, alone, to get my own two quarts of Two Sisters vodka for my secret stash. I don't go back to the same liquor store, of course. I don't know why I bother with such subterfuge: everybody ends up knowing everything about everybody in these parts eventually anyway.

If Dad ever wondered why I always had to go shopping right after we came back from the county line, he never asked me about it. He never asked me about a lot of things.

One day, when I had passed out on the couch after my afternoon tryst with the Russian Sisters (my vodka brand of choice at the time), Dad became alarmed enough to call the family doctor. A trip to the emergency room landed me in a ward with "chronic alcoholism" stamped clearly on my chart.

Mid-morning, day three: I've stopped puking constantly, but I still feel like shit. One of Mom's closest buddies drops in for a visit.

"...so I just thought I'd see if you'd like to come along to a meeting with me."

"You're a member of AA?" I ask in astonishment.

"For the last seven years," replies the diminutive, smartly dressed pillar of the community.

Jean and Mom had been close friends for umpty-ump years. Her husband worked for the oil company where Dad had served his life sentence. They, too, were pals.

"I probably wouldn't be alive today without it," she assures me.

I cannot imagine this paragon of virtue in her cups, but she assures me that alcoholism is an equal opportunity disease.

"You know," she nods to the Amazonesque nurse's aide tidying up my bed sheets.

"Oh yes," smiles the large, cheerful woman who would become a good friend and another staunch ally in the booze battle. "You're just not gonna believe who all y'all are gonna run into at the meetings."

There seems to be no question about my attending these meetings.

Indeed, it did turn out to be the biggest secret lodge in town. There were chapter meetings in every neighborhood every evening, and a few here and there at lunchtime. As my recovery got underway, I was volunteered to cover the downtown chapter over the Christmas holidays. Downtown being the closest thing to skid row this mid-sized model town had to offer.

Mostly I tried to find things to do around the house. It was about the most heart-warming, if saddest, Christmas of my life.

For our Christmas dinner, I made a miniature meal of stuffed Cornish game hen, creamed pearl onions, those little bitty French green beans, teeny Parker House rolls – even one of those 7-Eleven baby pecan pies. I didn't want to have leftovers for the next two months.

We dined on the good china, using as many pieces of the silver as I could justify putting out on the linen-laden table. The crystal glasses reflected the colored lights of the miniature tree in twinkling splendor.

Friends who insisted we attend their holiday parties all seemed to know I was "in the program," though it was never discussed. They just put a ginger ale in my hand when they put a bourbon and branch in Daddy's.

We fell into a comfortable routine. Every other week, I played Bingo with Mom's posse. Wednesday night was choir practice. AA meetings took up the other evenings for a couple of hours after supper.

Then one Wednesday night at choir practice, I asked the director if he knew a piano teacher. If I was going to be home all day, I might as well fulfill a life-long dream and learn to play the piano.

"Why don't you enroll at the junior college?" suggested the maestro. "The greatest piano teacher in the county teaches there, and it will cost a fraction of what private lessons would run."

I wasn't even the oldest person in line! There were several adults in the queue that snaked across the manicured grounds of the best little junior college in Texas. Entering the mammoth gymnasium, the line split into little rivulets that flowed toward the card tables of the various departments. I oozed into the music line and was nearing the table when a stentorian voice cut through the ambient roar and called me by the name I hadn't used since high school.

"What are you doing in the music line? Get over here and sign up for drama. I need an Amanda for *The Glass Menagerie*," the amazing voice roared.

Everyone who knew her will recognize this reference to the head of the drama department at this junior college. She was one of the more remarkable women of our time. She left a legacy of devotion and discipline in a vast legion of thespians – some of whom have names that would ring a bell if I felt free to reveal them. I don't. The theater on campus that her influence brought into being is named for her.

Explanations of why I was in town weren't needed. Like I say, everybody knows everything about everybody in all small towns in Texas. And even though this town had long ago graduated from the small category in numbers, the rules of engagement had not changed.

I dutifully signed up for every class she suggested and still had some time left for the music theory courses I wanted to take, along with the piano lessons I came for in the first place. The next semester, I added a welcome dose of American history, English (comp. and lit.) and even some solid remedial math and algebra.

No, I never learned to play the piano, but not because I didn't try. The teacher, like all those I encountered there, was excellent. My enthusiasm, however, couldn't quite make up for a severe lack of dexterity.

Theater arts went a little better. Just as the formidable director of the Theater Department predetermined, I played Amanda in *The Glass Menagerie*. I had played Amanda's daughter Laura in the senior play edition of the classic at the local high school in 1953. There was a satisfying symmetry in this shear coincidence. (Or was it?)

Besides Amanda, I got to sink my teeth into the role of Tituba, the black slave in *The Crucible*. I took "black" lessons from one of the drama department's star students, Bernardo. He carefully schooled me on my pronunciation of the patois the character spoke, and the mannerisms that could so easily have been comedicly stereotypical.

The final touch came though when he said, "We've got to do something about your buttocks! They're just plain honky, you know?"

I knew. Hmmmm. I rolled up a large sweatshirt and stuffed it in the back of my drawers.

"How does that look?" I asked him as I waddled around in my developing "slave woman" gait.

"Pefect," he assured me.

I got excellent reviews.

Another production from that time must be mentioned. I was asked to choreograph the musical, *Scapino* – a Comedia del Arte pastiche. In the course of fulfilling this assignment, I met and fell madly in platonic love with David Greer, one of the students. His antics as the headwaiter were the hit of the show – perhaps of the season. We found each other again years later through email, a shared addiction. He and several others of like disposition that I've met through him are my daily companions on the great cyber sea. We refer to ourselves as a coven because we first got together around Halloween. But we do not claim to have "powers." Really we don't.

After the regulation four semesters, when most students move on to some institute of higher learning or other, I just signed up for other courses that caught my interest. I would have continued doing this until they took out an injunction against me, I suppose, if Dad's beloved bacon and grilled steak hadn't ganged up on him.

Admonish him as I might, he would have his bacon every morning and his pan-grilled rib eye at least once a week. I really think he decided to commit suicide by cholesterol. It took him a bit over two years to do it, but one morning while he was tending his beloved bacon, he just keeled over. The paramedics who arrived within minutes told me he was gone before he hit the floor. I knew better. When I rushed to him, his eyes were looking about wildly. I was making reassuring noises, I guess. The eyes focused on me and he smiled, then his face just sort of relaxed.

He always said he wanted to go like his dad.

"Papaw was walking toward the cabin with an armload of firewood when he just pitched forward." Dad had told us the story of his dad's passing on more than one occasion. "He hit the ground like a felled pine tree, never even twitched."

I remember Papaw's funeral. Family and friends gathered in the big room of the old plank structure that this pioneer – who had walked to East Texas from Ohio with his father – built with his own huge, gnarled hands.

A preacher said some very long prayers while everybody stood around the pinewood coffin. Then everyone filed past it to say a final goodbye. Mother lifted me up so that I could blow him a goodbye kiss.

"Where are his legs?" I asked in alarm. Only the top half of the double coffin lid was open. I was concerned that he might not be all there and would have trouble getting around Heaven. Mom assured me that he was complete, just unseen, and you didn't need your body in Heaven anyway.

Then they nailed the coffin shut and the larger males of the gathering hoisted it onto their shoulders. They walked it down to the family graveyard in the hollow and lowered it into the grave that had been dug that morning by those same stalwart men: Dad and his three brothers among them. The crude stones that marked the graves of Mamaw and their three children that had died in infancy of scarlet fever, were shifted awry in the soft sandy red earth. Papaw's stone would be added later when the men finished filling in the hole.

The group returned to the cabin and sat about in the rocking chairs on the front porch – all hand-carved by that industrious farmer who sired my sire. When the sun finally warned that it was done for the day, we piled back into cars and jostled back to town along the deeply rutted road.

Mom, a city employee, had long before picked out and purchased the best gravesites in the local cemetery for her and Dad's final address. The double stone of native pink granite had been beautifully carved by none other than the father of my high-school flameout, BD. There was only the date of Dad's departure to be added in the space provided. It took Mr. B., the stonemason, about two hours to complete the task.

Dad's service was held at the Episcopal Church. Raised in a fundamentalist Church of Christ home, he rarely attended services anywhere. He and Mom were married in her hometown Episcopal Church. I didn't think he'd mind if the "Pissalopians" officiated for his sendoff (even if they did dress like sissies). If asked, Dad would tell you he was a "Piscatorian." That is, he spent his Sunday's fishing whenever possible.

"The Bible says the days a man spends fishing are not counted against his allotted time," he would tell Mom if she complained about his long absences in pursuit of this beloved activity.

I sure wish he'd gone fishing more often.

The cause of death on Mom's certificate said pulmonary embolism. I know she finally died of embarrassment, even though she always swore no one ever did. Dad's "suicide" was, as any suicide is, his own business. Should I have tied him down and fed him gruel and kept him here for years when he clearly wanted to get to wherever it was Mom was so he could be with her in whatever way is provided? That some such provision exists, he never doubted. Nor do I.

Hollywood – 1983

A Hollywood Ending

THE ESTATE SALE WENT ON for a full week. One old codger offered us fifty bucks for the three mounted heads that had adorned my Dad's bedroom wall. When we said "Deal," he almost danced for joy. I'm sure the two huge multi-antlered bucks and the lovely little striped antelope that had been Dad's prized hunting trophies had cost him hundreds (if not thousands) to find, shoot and have stuffed, but I was happy to have someone who also prized them take them home. Dead animals have never been my first choice of décor.

My brother and I sorted and picked and packed and repacked, dividing the onus of preservation between us in a fever of activity. Bud needed to get home, and I couldn't get out of East Texas fast enough. We sold the house to the first realtor to answer the ad. I'm sure he did very well on the deal. That, too, was as it should be.

Fond as I had become of my parents' friends, and in spite of the close ties formed at the junior college and ubiquitous AA meetings, I could not see myself as a permanent resident of this community. Whatever it was I was still looking for, I was pretty sure I wasn't going to find it here. It was time to click my heels together three times and get my ass back home to Hollywood.

Stella greeted me and looked askance at the truckload of huge family antiques that I foolishly thought I could fit into my doll's house of a Hollywood hovel. They would be sent back to Texas within the year when an unexpected turn of events altered my life forever.

Meanwhile, I began to look for a house to buy. I thought my half of the proceeds from the sale of our parents' place would be enough for a down payment. I had no idea how I would come up with the monthly payments after that, but I knew I wanted a roof that nobody could raise the rent on.

Jonathan Lucas, the director of *Urban Cowgirls*, had become a good friend. When I confided my dream to him, he introduced me to a friend of his: a young actor (not in sex films – Jonathan also directed mainstream TV) named Mike who was also a real estate agent – as is often the case in Lalaland. It was a match made in heaven.

About the sixth or seventh house he showed me was a three-bedroom ranchette nestled in a bend of the Los Angeles River. There was only one thing wrong with it – it wasn't in Hollywood. My dream neighborhood turned out to be way out of my price range.

Mike, my new friend and realtor, sweeps through the open floor plan and out the door to a lovely rear patio.

"Man, if I had the money for a down, I'd snap this up, live in it while I fixed it up a bit, and turn it over for a LOT of money."

"Would you really like to live here?" I ask.

"You bet!" He spins to face me, arms sweeping the scene around us. "It's a perfect location. Near the freeways, but not in earshot. A great backard. Mature, low-maintenance landscaping. Room for a pool. The price is right. Even if you only lived here a year and did a few cosmetic repairs – there's not much needed, really – you could sell for a tidy profit, no matter what the market does. And if you catch an upswing, you could make a MINT."

It sounded good to me, but… it wasn't in Hollywood.

"My roommate's a carpenter," he continues. "He's good. Reliable and reasonable. I'll take you over to my folks' place. He just refinished their Craftsman living room…"

I'm not smart enough to do business with anyone unless I have complete confidence in their character. I have to trust my gut. (Me and Blanche Dubois, always "dependin' upon the kindness of strangers.") My instincts tell me I'm dealing with an honest man. I have an idea.

"I have an idea," I announce. "I'll buy the place. You and your roommate move in here and pay me just enough rent to cover the monthly PITI (principal, interest, taxes, and insurance – a sum that proved less than their current rent). You guys fix it up, and in a year or so, we'll sell. You'll get back whatever you put out for materials off the top and we'll split whatever's left of the profit fifty-fifty.

It takes awhile for him to realize I am quite serious.

"You're quite serious?" he finally asks in amazement.

I nod.

"Why would you do this?"

"If I don't put this money where I can't touch it, it will evaporate. Maybe when we sell this house, I'll be able to afford one in Hollywood."

And that's just how it worked out. But not for another year or so and not until after that thing that changed my life forever happened.

OK. O-Kay. Here's what happened.

I was receiving a monthly stipend from Dad's insurance that was just enough to cover my rent at Rancho Beyondo – that cunning circle of bungalows that Stell had discovered in the canyon that reaches south from the famed Hollywood sign. This income would continue for a whole year. Voila! I could give show biz one last shot.

Now that I was sober, surely I would be able to find an agent and get character roles on TV and maybe even in real movies. Hadn't I just wow'd 'em with my Amanda in *The Glass Menagerie* at the junior college?

Delusions do not dissipate immediately upon the cessation of alcohol consumption.

Deluded or not, instead of looking for a good day job, I was home reading the trades one morning when fate in the form of the handsome and talented CB called. Yes, the very CB to whom I was married for about fifteen minutes in an earlier life. We had remained close through the years.

"A friend of mine is directing a production of *The Hostage* in North Hollywood." (CB had played the young British soldier in the Broadway production in the '60s.) "He's talked me into playing the old Codger and wants me to come in and read with some folks auditioning today, but Morgause had my car impounded. Can you give me a lift, Luv?"

Always happy to hear my first husband's dulcet British tones, I am even happier to provide transportation.

Morgause wasn't really her name. It was the name of the witch who was good King Arthur's undoing. It was CB's pet name for his second wife. The mismatched pair had met when he was doing the role of Mordred, bastard son of Morgause and Arthur, in the road company of *Camelot*. It was to enable that marriage that I faced the triumverate of scowling Priests in the hallowed halls of St. Patrick's Cathedral. Two children and a bitter divorce later, they spoke only through lawyers. She had commandeered most of his earnings for the last ten years. He had, alas, fallen a month behind in his child support payments. Hence the hijacking of his most prized possession, a classic little MG roadster. A tragedy for CB, it was a fortuitous turn of events for me.

CB and I sit side by side in the semi-darkness of the tiny theater. We are watching the candidates for roles in the play do their thing. The director peers up from the stage area and asks, "What role are you reading for?"

CB nudges me. It was I being addressed! Before I can explain that I'm only the chauffeur, CB pushes his script into my hands and says, "I think she should read for Miss Gilchrist."

So I did. And got the part! Meanwhile, CB got another gig and wasn't even in the show after all.

A week later, the cast is sitting around a large table on the stage of the North Hollywood Theatre Exchange. A read-through of the script is the first order of business on this first day of rehearsals. Danny Goldberg (the director) is leafing through three or four different incarnations of the script. Bits and pieces of each of the scripts would be pasted together to form our version of the Brendan Behan classic, *The Hostage*.

"You probably don't remember me, but I was in an industrial show you choreographed in New York in the early '70s." The very attractive gent to my left leans toward me, hand outstretched, and introduces himself. "My name's John."

"Sorry," I reply as we shake hands. "I'm afraid I don't remember a lot of what happened around that time. I drank a bit, you see," I crinkle my eyes in merry self-deprecation.

I was about to add, "My sobriety date is November 11, 1980," but the director demanded our attention at that point.

Just as well. Reformed drunks are rarely invited to the really good parties, and a week or so into the run, John came up to me at the end of a performance and said, "My cousin Raf wants to know if you'd like to go to a Fourth of July party with him."

Raf was a frequent member of the audience and a great laugher.

The show got rather good reviews and the houses were almost always sold out. A rare thing for Equity Waiver theater in Los Angeles; sometimes equated to Off-Broadway in New York. But even with a full house, Raf's laugh was always discernable.

John played the role of Rio Rita, a screamin' queen. We discovered in our many friendly chats that we went to the same gym in Hollywood. I knew it to be a watering hole for the local gay community. I assumed John was of like mind, so his asking me to go out with his cousin seemed logical.

The day arrives and Raf and I drive to the snazzy gated community in the Pacific Palisades in my car. His couldn't be trusted in the mountains.

"What an amazing house and view and pool and I feel like a cockroach that needs to find a crevice to hide in," I mumble to my date as we wind our way up the elaborately landscaped entry path.

"What a crazy thing to say!" screams Raf in genuine rage. "What makes you say a crazy thing like that?"

"Just look at those women. They're all gorgeous. Especially the hostess. She's a movie star, right?"

"Well, she's done some movies and TV shows, but so has John and most of the rest of the bunch. So have I. Big deal. Come on. You're the best-looking woman here."

(He was being way too kind, but I was grateful.)

"These guys have all known each for years," he continues. "They work together as an improv group. Hell, they have their own language. Believe me, I'm as much of an outsider here as you. Come on. Let's go sit in the hot tub with Bunny and Norm. They're in the business, but they're not part of the Improv group. Bunny's going to give birth at any moment. They're a great couple. You'll love 'em."

They are and I do.

(Bunny gave birth to Casey, their son, about a week later. At his Bar Mitzvah a few years ago, I reminded him that I had known him since minus eight days. He wasn't particularly impressed.)

John arrives with a very attractive female on his arm! I spot them doing the chitchat thing with the group on the patio.

A bit taken aback, I lean over to Raf and whisper, "Who's that with your cousin John?"

"Some dame he's been seeing. I can't think of her name," he replies.

"Isn't he gay?" I ask nonchalantly, as though it matters to me not one wit.

Raf stopped laughing July 17th.

The show ran for another six weeks, a very long stint for this type of production. But all things come to an end, and when it did, we gathered at my house to bid farewell to each other and make our hollow promises to meet for lunch.

A goodly crowd strains the confines of my tiny bungalow. Raf threads his way through the throng and stops beside me.

"It was nice of you to include me tonight. I had a wonderful time," he says as he kisses my cheek.

"Hey, you came to so many performances you count as an honorary member of the cast," I assure him.

CB is also present. After all, he was responsible for my being part of this delightful group of actors. Of course he was invited.

Also in attendance is the stalwart Stell, my best pal through all the tumultuous years from 1968 to the present. Roommates off and on throughout those years, we now each have our own bungalow – side by side, of course.

Stell and CB have not yet seen each other through any but friendly eyes. It would be several years before they become man and wife number five. At present, she's married to a volatile photographer turned Rock 'n' Roll Roadie. (A marriage that lasted a few months longer than it should have.) An adorable pair of Baby Rockers – friends of theirs – are currently renting my extra bedroom. They needed a place to crash. I needed the money.

Some thirty or so people had been squeezed into the tiny two rooms and kitchen that make up the ground floor of my toy-sized, two-story house. Most had now taken their leave. The stragglers were seeing to it that there weren't too many leftovers for me to deal with, which was appreciated.

John (the charming actor who had so skillfully played the raging queen, Rio Rita, that I was convinced he was gay) had become an even closer friend through the run. We found we had numerous mutual acquaintances from the New York theatrical scene. I had joined him, Raf, and other friends of theirs who caught the show, for drinks after the performance on several occasions.

Now, as the last of the guests headed out the door, he began picking up glasses and dishes and ferrying them to the kitchen sink. I followed with ashtrays as soon as I had bid the stragglers farewell. We chatted and tidied, cheek to cheek, at sink and cupboards.

He was intelligent, talented, handsome, and funny. He was also one hell of an actor, and talent has always been my major turn-on.

Truth to tell, I was totally smitten, and had been since about the second day of rehearsal – even when I thought he was gay. I just knew from the first moment we met that I wanted to be friends forever.

Dishes put away, I pour him a fresh glass of wine and refill my glass of cranberry juice and soda. (Yes, AA had finally kicked in. I'd been dry since November 11, 1980 – as I mentioned. I mention it a lot.)

We sit, side by side, on the couch. After a bit of inane banter, he leans toward me and begins to kiss me softly on the lips. I do not pull away. He moves closer and reaches his arm around me to pull me even closer to him. I feel like a freakin' teenager! My vulva is on fire and throbbing like a Nelson Riddle baseline.

I want to fling him to the cushions and absorb him, but I suddenly remember that my Baby Rockers could come barreling through the front door at any minute. When they were at a recording session, as they had been since early morning, there's no telling when they'll zero into their nest to crash.

He feels me tense, and pulls back.

"What's wrong?" he asks softly.

My God, he has the most beautiful blue eyes. They look right into you and hide nothing.

"My roommates may come in," I gasp in as normal a tone as I can manage.

"What? You're afraid a couple of teenage rockers are gonna come in and catch us making out on the couch?"

He is simply incredulous. It cracks me up.

It *is* a bit ridiculous to worry about the sensitivities of a pair of rock musicians who are shacking up in my spare bedroom. Particularly as making out is mostly what they do when in residence, anyway.

One issue resolved. Now the perverse persona who seems determined to fuck up my life butts in.

"Doesn't the fact that I've been in porno films bother you?"

"Evidently not," he replies.

The evidence is, indeed, compelling.

This, too, strikes me as hilarious.

In spite of our mutual amusement, we manage to get out of most of our clothes in a trice.

I'd been celibate since my last film. I had rarely had sex offscreen the whole time I was doing porn anyway – except for Claire, who'd been out of my picture for quite some time. The horny lady of my dancing days had not been around for ages.

Now I found I was wetter than I could ever remember being before in my life. Miss Puss was aching to fold her lips around that jaunty cock. However, this charming half-Italian Mick wasn't about to let me rush into anything. He had a few passages he wanted to play first.

Eventually, we had our way with the boy, though, and after an appreciable time I noticed that John's hipbones fit perfectly inside my own. As I briefly pondered this comfortable phenomenon, a more amazing thing happened.

I came.

I'm not talking about one of those delightful clitoral firecrackers. Those had been going off since we started wrestling. This was the big one: the no-kidding heart-thumping breath-catching eye-bulging cervix-dipping full-throttle vaginal climax that had, to this point, eluded me except during secluded solo flights.

I'll be damned. It's all in the FIT!

We haven't spent many nights apart since that evening: none, willingly.

The antique furniture went back to Texas. I sublet the bungalow and we moved into an even smaller cottage, which we shared for a year or so.

When it was finally apparent to him that we were going to spend the rest of our lives together – as it had been to me since the gitgo – we decided to take the Big Step.

We went house shopping.

Remember my real estate partner, Mike? As planned, we sold the now fixed-up fixer for the anticipated tidy profit, and I was able to cover my half of a down payment for a house, not only in Hollywood, thank you very much, but smack under the Hollywood Sign!

John and I moved in April 1, 1986.

We were married January 16, 2000.

OK. So we had a fourteen-year engagement. Like I said, we're not the sort to rush into things.

Hollywood – 2004

An Offer I Couldn't Refuse

"IS THIS GEORGINA?"

It's a familiar voice, but I can't quite place it. I'm a tad circumspect when anyone asks for Georgina. I signal John to pick up the extension.

"Who's calling, please?" I inquire politely.

"This is Paul Thomas."

"PT!" I gush with genuine warmth.

Paul and I had worked together only that one time: the Damiano film that was my swan song. He always made it a point to stop and say hello at the award shows, though – when I still attended them. He grew up to be a director.

This was not the first time we'd spoken since those glory days. He had called from out of the blue a few months earlier asking me to do a cameo role in his planned remake of *The Devil in Miss Jones*: the film that rocketed me from oblivion to poverty. I turned him down because I could see no reason whatsoever to ever again wear mascara.

"How ya doin'?" I continue.

"Fine. Look, George, I know you've told me at least a dozen times that you don't want to be in my picture, but just hear me out."

"You know it's not you or your script…" I begin the explanation for my reluctance that was by now familiar to him.

"I only need you for two scenes, three or four lines. I'm not sure how many. I haven't written it yet. Two days, back to back, and I'll pay you…" (A dollar amount that must remain confidential was mentioned.)

John almost broke his neck nodding yes.

A few days later, PT arrives at our door with a contract.

John sits perched on the edge of his recliner. Paul sits beside me on the couch. They discuss the terms.

I glance out the picture window that backs the couch and take stock of the garden that has been my joy and despair for the last twenty-odd years. Visions of retaining walls and paths that might be dug into the steep slope we affectionately refer to as the backyard distract me. They don't need my input anyway.

But that John had been there to look after my interests back then…

A brief flash of la dolce vita grips my imagination. However, I realize that had John been there to "handle my interests" in those days of yore, there would have been no interests to handle, so it's moot. Having him to speak on my behalf now though, and settle all the niggling little particulars of a business agreement, is a delicious luxury.

My life is filled with delicious luxuries: food, indoor plumbing, a gym close enough to walk to, and wheels (albeit a beat-up pickup) so I don't have to walk anywhere I don't want to. It's so much more than most folks have on this old globe that I feel guilty, embarrassed, and totally unwilling to part with any of it.

Once the guys have finished ironing everything into place, I accept the pen PT extends and happily sign on the dotted line.

Paul tells us about the locations he has lined up. Impressive. He goes through the script and picks out lines he wants me to deliver. The fact that these are currently assigned to other characters doesn't seem to perturb

him. I see no reason why it should perturb me. A few adjustments in word-
ings are made and that's about it as far as a script to study is concerned.

In the course of closing amenities – "what's new with you," and all
that, PT says, "This publisher gave me a hundred thousand dollars for my
biography, and I don't even have to write it."

(He was referring to Judith Regan, the lady who put Jenna Jameson's
book out and later got into all manner of hot water with the O.J. Simpson
thing, *If I Did It*. I was sorry to hear PT later had to return the advance.)

After a few more parting remarks, we see him out our front door and
return to our accustomed nests. John reclines in his recliner and I wiggle
into a comfortable position on my Rube Goldberg construction of pillows
and lumbar supports on the couch.

I open my ever-ready laptop and John picks up his crossword puzzle.
After a moment or two he turns to me and says, "So when are you going to
write your book? It's not like you have all that much else to do."

He has a point. After working some twenty years as a desktop publisher, I was now retired. Filming on the new improved *Devil* would not start
for several weeks, and it wasn't going to take much time to learn six lines.

But, the truth is, I'm still waiting to see some of that spare time everyone assured me I would wonder what to do with when I retired. I can't tell
you what all I do all day, but it takes me all day to do it.

Still, the prospect of actually making some money out of all those
years of irresponsible debauchery did have its appeal.

I pictured John at the rail of a cruise ship, silk scarf streaming in the
breeze.

We took a cruise to Alaska in August of 2000 – sort of a honeymoon
after we "eloped" to Las Vegas. There was a heated swimming pool on
deck. (You may have noticed that I love getting in hot water.) We're tooling
through Glacier Bay and I'm doing the backstroke up and down the pool,
peering up through the steam. Great green ice walls loom into view on both
sides of the damn ship! Towering into the sky, they look close enough to
touch. It was cosmic. Yeah, I could get into more of that.

"OK. I'll do it. And this time, I mean it."

From under the bed I retrieve the box of myriad notes and numerous
Chapter Ones I've penned and/or typed up through the years. The box is

covered with so much dust I have to vacuum it before I can find the tape that seals it. Out tumble the dozen or so little stained spiral notebooks and a blizzard of old envelopes, napkins and sundry scraps of paper.

The handwritten notes are barely legible, and are every bit as rambling and incoherent as their author had been at the time they were committed to paper. Committed is what I should have been by the look of the notes. Well, in a way, I was. Remember the two bizarre weeks I spent as the guest of the rehab ward at County Hospital in Manhattan for which I have Marc Stevens to thank? And I do mean thank.

I saw Marc one last time in the early eighties. He called me at my office one day. I have no idea how he got the number. We met for lunch at the Howard Johnson's that then occupied the hallowed corner of Hollywood and Vine – once home to the original Brown Derby. He did not look well, but assured me he was fine, did not need nor want any help, and was looking forward to a lovely evening with his young companion whom he introduced as... "this lovely little piece of street trash I just picked up." Marc always told it like it was. I'm glad I got to thank him again for saving my butt even if he wasn't about to let me do anything about saving his.

The computer files of my thirty-odd Chapter Ones are much easier to read. They were written after I stopped drinking and had a job – and access to a computer.

I do my homework. After studying dozens of memoirs at my favorite used bookstore, I determine that they average about three hundred pages with approximately 300 words to the page. Armed with this literary insight, I set to work.

Before I get very far, it's time to shoot my two big scenes in Paul's remake.

A driver arrived at our door at 8:33 a.m.

No, it wasn't a limo. It was a small coupe with a bad cough. It made its way into the bowels of downtown Los Angeles by a fairly direct route of ever decreasing width.

"We're here," announced our guide, swiveling skillfully into a small space between two other vehicles in front of what looked like a warehouse, not unlike those surrounding it.

Inside, it looked like a warehouse full of porno sets: a labyrinth of fornacatoriums, complete with swings, shackles, mirrors, and the like; several unisex bathrooms and showers; and even a well-equipped kitchen completed the assemblage. All were spotlessly clean, and, though a bit garish, richly appointed in assorted periods and styles. The decor ranged from Executive Office Hi-tech to Marquis de Sade Baroque.

This emporium was called the Entertainium. It was rented out for private parties, porn shoots, and combinations thereof. The green room (a space reserved for makeup, wardrobe, snacking and schmoozing) had couches, chairs and tables – all the comforts of home. John spent most of the day there. Considering the constant flow of bare-breasted beauties through the makeup area, and the sounds of screaming orgasms blasting forth at regular internals, it's amazing the number of crossword puzzles he was able to complete. He's an actor. He knows how to concentrate.

A pixie of a woman, in a hat just like the type I wear constantly to keep wisps of hair out of my face and the sun out of my eyes, approached with a warm smile and a polyester maid's uniform held before her on a hanger.

"Hi, Georgina. I'm Penny. I guessed on your size, but I've seen all your movies, so I bet I got it right."

She did.

Have you ever met someone whom you are convinced was your twin, separated from you at birth? That's Penny Antine and me. We bonded immediately and have been pals since. Penny writes under the nom de porn Raven Touchstone. She co-wrote the current *Devil* script with PT, as well as managed wardrobe and who knows what all for the shoot.

The makeup artist was no beginner. Five minutes in the chair and I was done – except for lipstick and mascara. He knew full well the scenes I was to do wouldn't be shot until all the wildlife footage was in the can. That didn't happen until a full eight hours later. Par for the course.

A PA roused me from my knitting and comfy couch when they were ready to block my scenes. Mr. Makeup Man quickly touched up my kisser. I swished on some mascara and applied some neutral lipstick.

PT, script in hand, stood before the camera in a long narrow hallway constructed for the occasion. Plain white walls stretched to a door through which could be seen an old-fashioned, claw-foot tub. No furniture, no swings, no toys.

No, wait. There was a Boy Toy in the tub. All I could see of him was one leg hanging over the side. I saw the rest of him later in the makeup room. Very attractive young man.

Savanna Samson, the new Miss Jones, is as young and lovely as any starlet in the trade. She was doing her best to look as old and dowdy as the original Miss Jones had been. Our two short scenes together were heavy lifting, and we shared the load equally. The young man did his part by holding absolutely still in the tub.

The three of us met again on the second set. He had some dialogue in that scene. Good actor. "Not just another pretty butt," I said to myself. Turned out he was Dick Smothers, Jr. – son of one of my all-time favorite comedians! (He told us about having recently been outed in a tabloid, so I'm not betraying a confidence here.)

I was wrapped at 8:30 p.m. The same PA who had picked us up that morning drove us home. He was young, in a hurry, and seemed bent on becoming a stunt-driver. My husband is a white-knuckle passenger under the best of conditions. At our door, John told him he needn't bother to pick us up for the second day's shoot.

"Just give me the directions and I'll get her there," he said between clenched teeth.

My call was for 2 p.m. We arrived at one. The drive through the hills above Malibu was delightful. It is some of the most spectacular scenery in southern California. At the very top of the range, we found the production sign marking the approach to the location where the bulk of the film would be shot. At the end of a serpentine drive, a steel and glass mansion of palatial proportions glittered in the early-morning sun. From an expansive patio at one end of the building, a huge sculpture rose thirty feet or more in an abstract twist of agony silhouetted against the cloudless sky. An equally huge water tank teetered on an elevated outcrop where the drive made a convenient loop before the looming entrance. A darling little PA appeared and offered to park our car down the hill in the staging area for us so we wouldn't have to make the climb back to the set. Star treatment. I loved it.

We entered the outrageously expensive retreat in awe. A neatly framed sign hung in a conspicuous spot just inside the front door. Printed in an elegant font was the information that if the toilets were to be used, there would be an additional charge of two hundred fifty dollars per day. Good thing this was a big-budget production.

I have been on some pretty amazing locations in my checkered career, but this one topped them all: even the Rolls Royce scene in *Desires Within Young Girls*, the Ted Paramour extravaganza.

That scene called for Annette Haven (one of my daughters in the film) to make out with the chauffeur on the hood of a Rolls Royce Silver Ghost parked on a grassy expanse overlooking a panorama that included The Golden Gate Bridge. When I heard where they were shooting, I went along to kibitz. Right in the middle of some heavy action, a troupe of girl scouts came marching along the perimeter of the field!

There was a mad shifting of reflectors and flags and equipment boxes.

I don't know if they ever finished the scene or not. I was laughing so hard, I wet my pants and had to go back to the motel.

There seemed to be fewer folks at the Malibu set than there had been at the Entertainium. The expanse of the place may have just made it seem that way. Through the course of the day, about a dozen adult entertainment reporters (each complete with tape crew) arrived to do interviews with all us movie stars. Still, the numerous vast galleries never seemed crowded.

Unfortunately, nobody told the crafts people that there were going to be dozens of extra people on the set, and nobody told the reporters that they weren't invited to lunch. No running to the nearest McDonald's from up here. I had brought my usual lunch of pears and cheese with me so I was covered. John and the crew, however, were righteously pissed when the food ran out. Armies are not the only things that run on their stomachs.

A half a football field's span of emerald turf surrounded a pool of rather modest proportions behind the mansion. A small tent had been set up to provide the only shade in the area. Beneath it sat the cast and crew members not involved in the shot. The view of the majestic Malibu Mountains shouldering their way to the sea below this precipitous bluff was breathtaking. It was not the only breathtaking view.

At the end of the pool a strapping stripped Adonis was poised for a plunge. The sun danced over rippling pecs and sculpted buns as he dove into the water and swam the length of the pool. Savanna teetered in impossibly high heels at the pool's edge. She was clad in a gorgeous shimmering cocktail dress. The heels sank to her instep in the lush turf. The Adonis surfaced and spoke to her. I guess he told her to take off her dress because she did. This action was repeated many, many times and caught from every possible angle. They were shooting like they owned stock in Kodak.

Just as the action was heating up, a PA summoned me for the first of my many interviews that day. I dutifully followed her back into the vaulted arches of the mansion and spilled my guts to the elite of smut media.

John remained by the pool and later reported that he had never seen sex performed in so many ways by just two people. And yes, the high heels stayed on. His major amazement was at the new vogue of shaved pubes. I had to agree with him that it looked more like a medical anatomy book than a cozy tryst. But what do we know about porn?

Eventually, I'm summoned to get into wardrobe and makeup. I find the new Miss Jones, Savanna, sitting in the tall makeup chair in the pool-side changing room.

"Can I ask you a question?" She speaks carefully between motionless lips so as not to interfere with the makeup artist's ministrations.

"Sure," I reply.

"How did you get the snake into your pussy? PT said to get this role I'd have to do a snake."

The idea of doing so does not seem to perturb her as much as the logistics of how to go about it. I'm flabbergasted. I hastily assure her that my relationship with Herman the boa had been strictly platonic.

The very nice makeup lady asks what she's supposed to do about me. Did the guy from the first day's shoot leave no notes? He might not have been told I had a second day on the film. It doesn't take much to get me ready, though. It's so nice not to have to get gorgeous.

Ready for our closeups, Savanna and I proceed to the set.

The mansion's main bathroom almost gives me vertigo. Marble, mirrors, and glass forever: a lighting designer's nightmare. In the middle of blocking the scene, the Director of Photography points out that if they wanna get the sunset they must do so NOW.

Director and crew, heavy with camera, weave their way out the door. More reporters materialize and take advantage of the hiatus to tape more interviews. Dick Smothers, so like his dad, keeps us all amused with banter and anecdotes. I ask him if he was a Master of Yo like his uncle. (For you youngsters: Tom Smothers can make a yo-yo do anything, hence the title.) The younger Mr. Smothers says he does not Yo.

By the time we resume the washroom scene, it is dark out. This turns the wall of floor-to-ceiling windows into a wall of floor-to-ceiling mirrors. These, of course, face the wall of actual floor-to-ceiling mirrors. Oh, did I mention the floor itself is a shiny black pool of marble? The shiny gold-plated fixtures send off blinding kicks against the also black marble basins. We actors have no latitude of movement whatsoever. One inch out of range and the shot's blown

They got it in three takes. Yeah, that's bragging.

I got to see some of the footage at Vivid Video when I was called in to record comments and stuff for the DVD. Savanna's snake scene is to mine as Mt. Shasta is to an ant hill. They must have piled twenty giant pythons on top of that poor child. The mirrored bathroom was indeed spectacular.

All in all, it was a pleasant enough experience. I'm just sorry I didn't get to do more than exchange "how-ja-dos" with the rest of the cast. Especially the Big Star of the film, Jenna Jameson. Now there's a success story!

Vacation over, I dedicate my time and energy to entering the salient (and salacious) details of my life in porn into neatly organized files on my handy dandy new laptop, purchased for the occasion.

Three hundred pages later, I give copies to the folks nearest and dearest to me: the cast of characters in my book. I ask them to correct any inaccuracies they find and to tell me if they're OK with the phony names I picked for those not in the porn trade. (For them I use the phony names they've already picked for themselves.)

I didn't ask for their opinions, but fortunately they were good enough friends to offer them anyway.

"It's too bad you don't have grandchildren; they would love this," says my new friend, Penny Antine.

I'm having a luscious lunch with her at her lovely art-bedecked home. I boggle at her amazing photographic work. Oh yes, she's also an accomplished photographer – right up there with the legendary Annie Sprinkle, whom I've adored since we met during filming of the first *Devil*. Hung among Penny's photo prints are the numerous awards she has won for her scripts. One is from AVN (Adult Video News) for co-writing the script of the *Devil* remake – the film that brought us together.

Penny is also writing a book. Well, who the hell isn't? She gets paid for writing, however, so I pay attention to what she has to say.

"You have a great story to tell, but you haven't told it here." She pats the three-ring folder bulging with the fruits of my labor.

"It's the story of my life," I whine.

"Sweetie, nobody cares if you liked to go fishing with your daddy." She leans toward me and pats my hand sympathetically.

"They want to know how big Harry Reams' cock is."

Oh.

"I haven't read very much of it yet," says Mims, my bosom buddy, and partner of John's cousin Raf, the great laugher, "but my feeling is, it starts off too slow. You should start with your most exciting material."

Mims has won many awards for documentary films she has written and directed; and in some instances, produced. She probably knows what she is talking about.

"My boss used to tell me," she continues, "'Start with the volcano.'"

We're standing out on the patio with a few dozen of our more intimate friends. It's our annual Fourth of July cookout. John (excellent actor that he is) saunters over, extending a bottle of wine, and emotes.

"Bang. Bang. Bang. Bang. Four shots ripped into my groin and I was off on the greatest adventure of my life."

"But, first," I chime in, "let me tell you a little about myself." I finish the familiar quote, which is the opening paragraph of a very funny book by Max Shulman. It's about the tobacco industry and is titled *Sleep 'Till Noon*.

"Well, something like that, I suppose," laughs Mims, accepting a refill. John returns to the barbecue pit to turn his blackening bratwurst.

"It's a page turner," offers my oldest and dearest pal, Stella. "That may be because I know you, of course. You're a little skimpy on details, though."

"I can't remember most of the details," I state, truthfully.

"Yeah, well, booze will do that," she says with remarkably good humor considering the number of times she had to pour me into rehab during the course of our thirty-plus-year friendship.

She and CB began keeping company about the same time John and I did. They beat us to the alter, though.

The Big C got him in his 65th year. The four of us were very close through those last years of his life. His ashes are in both their garden and ours. Most of the plants in ours came from theirs as well.

"How could I have any objections to what you wrote? You were downright flattering and exceedingly kind to me. I'm sure there must have been times when you didn't feel that magnanimous toward me." Ian is having lunch with us on the terrace, having returned my manuscript in person.

"Only that time you hired what's-er-name to do the role of Irma in *Irma La Duce* instead of me," I reply.

"Well, I *was* trying to get in her pants, you know," he admits with a wry grin.

Somehow that made it better.

Though we hadn't really kept in touch, John and I met Ian for lunch one day when we were in New York. Then a few years later, on my fiftieth birthday, Ian knocked on the door of the cottage John and I were sharing and joined the small party in progress. He had been at a meeting and suddenly realized the address was across the street from ours, so he just popped in. That was the last time we heard from him until I contacted him about this book.

Having spent the last several years as a valued staff writer with one of the major studios, he was well-equipped to offer me many helpful pointers on my subsequent rewrite.

Our email friendship blossomed right up to his untimely demise two years later. His lovely wife invited us to attend the celebration of his life held at their magnificent home in Sherman Oaks. Class act, all the way. I got to say hello to two of his three sons who insisted they remembered their "wicked stepmom" with affection. They grew up to be great guys. Big, too.

That was some swell party. Big surprise: present was Martin Gage, a top-notch agent who had been my dance partner in the Vegas review back in 1960 when he was but a darling chorus boy. I had no idea the two, Ian and

Martin, even knew each other. Ah, how the threads of life do twine back upon themselves.

In an article that appeared in *Politics Today*, Kurt Vonnegut wrote:

"Writing allows even a stupid person to seem halfway intelligent, if only that person will write the same thought over and over again, improving it just a little bit each time. It is a lot like inflating a blimp with a bicycle pump. Anybody can do it. All it takes is time."

With that assurance and Ian's guidance, I start from scratch and take my time. After all, if for thirty years I shunned every offer to publish a book about my experiences as a porn actress (as long as I would let someone else write it the way the publisher wanted), what was the rush now?

Life in the Fast Lane

"HELLO, AGAIN," SAYS DR. THOM breezing into the exam room and perching upon a small swivel stool. He leans over the bulging file he has placed on the gleaming white table and flips back and forth through the top pages.

It's a very large file because I've been his patient a very long time. We met when I was working at the physicians' association. I staffed several committees he was on.

"Why are you here?" He continues flipping through the pages sure an answer must be in there somewhere.

"I need to renew the Protonix prescription," I respond, helpfully.

"Well, let's see if you're still alive." He whips out his handy dandy stethoscope and listens to my heart and lungs.

"Clear as a bell." He looks at the chart. "Your BP and cholesterol levels are the envy of the block." He smiles as he makes mysterious notations in the sheaf of papers.

It's true. I've been blessed with the constitution of an iron skillet. Not one to brag, however, I murmur coyly, "I bet you say that to all the girls."

"We've never done a bone density test on you, have we?" A seemingly futile search through the stack of papers ensues.

"You're gonna be... what?" He consults the chart. "Seventy in March? I think we ought to get a reading – just as a benchmark."

"Why? So I can monitor my disintegration?" I quip.

"No. So you can brag about your remarkable preservation, Smartass."

"What does it involve? I assume they don't saw through a bone and measure it?" I am notoriously leery of medical procedures.

"Dexa Scan. You won't feel a thing," my good doctor assures me. "They do it right here in the building."

"I have to come in and get my oil checked in April, anyway. Can we do it then?"

"Oh, right. Have to get a Pap smear if you want me to renew the Evista. Do you?"

"You bet," I reply emphatically.

Evista is a hormone replacement pill. Some years ago during my annual checkup, Dr. Thom had asked, "So, how's everything?

"Well, my ears are ringing, but my love-life ain't," I'd flippantly replied.

"Sorry. Nothing we can do about the tinnitus. There's a pill for the other problem, though."

He gave me a crash course on hormone replacement. He wanted to be very sure I understood all the possible side effects. He reeled off more statistics than a baseball commentator.

"Wanna give it a try?"

I did and have been a happier camper since. John, too, of course. Been using it for over ten years now and the only side effect I've noticed, other than a reawakened libido, is improved skin tone.

I know conventional wisdom has it that John and I will have to stop this childish behavior at some point in our lives, but neither of us have ever paid much attention to conventional wisdom. The truth is, like with most activity, practice makes, if not perfect, certainly constant improvement.

Besides, I have this fantasy...

When I worked for the aforementioned physicians' association, I was sent to USC Medical School to stir up interest in membership among the undergrads. The meeting I was to address was scheduled for one of the lecture halls. My student escorts thought it would be a hoot to route me through the anatomy lab. As we strolled along the rows of cadavers, I surprised them by neither fainting nor barfing.

Not entirely because of that experience, John and I have willed our remains to the school's anatomy program for the education of these fine young men and women.

In my fantasy, it takes 'em two weeks to untangle us.

The doctor quickly reads through a litany of possible complaints. No changes, no problems, no reason not to continue the acid reflux pills.

"How's the back? Still going to the gym every day?"

"John goes to the gym. I go to the spa."

"Whatever. Keep it up. Between your scoliosis and your bulging discs, I'm surprised you don't need a walker by now. Still no arthritis?"

"Nope. I don't give it chance to stick. I rub hell out of anything that even starts to act like it might ache. Also, I down a lot of cod liver oil, just like my Granny taught me."

"OK, then," he smiles and hands me the new prescription, "you're good to go for another thousand miles, I guess."

"Oh, I almost forgot." He fishes in the pocket of his lab coat. "I had lunch with Sharon Mitchell and another one of your old buddies last week. A guy named Bill Margold? He asked me to give you his number. He wants you to call him." He hands me a scrap of paper with a number scrawled on it. I consider it for a moment, then put it in my pocket.

Dr. Sharon Mitchell (PhD in Human Sexuality from the Institute for the Advanced Study of Human Sexuality in San Francisco, California) got in touch with Dr. Thom several years ago. His work with the AIDS community – and civic health problems in general – had come to her attention. She asked for his help in establishing AIM (Adult Industry Medical) healthcare foundation and clinic. Bill Margold has also been an activist in addressing the health concerns of the sex-film industry. That's why the three were meeting at lunch. Both Sharon and Bill were surprised to learn that I was Dr. Thom's patient. Not as surprised as I was to find out he knew them.

Should I call Margold? Bill has become the self-proclaimed Papa Bear of the porn industry. He works tirelessly with several organizations he has founded for the benefit of porn performers.

I know what he wants. He has contacted me numerous times through the years asking that I accept induction into something called the Legends of Erotica – a wall of concrete plaques with impressions of various anatomical parts belonging to the better-known fornicators and fornicatrixes of the industry. It's in Las Vegas.

I have declined in the past. Not because I object to being immortalized in concrete. I did, after all, willingly place my feet and the paws of my kitten (right, pussy prints) in the damp sidewalk in front of the Pussycat Theater in Hollywood once upon a time many, many years ago. No. It's just that I can't stand Las Vegas.

Yes, John and I were married there in the Candlelight Chapel on January 16, 2000. Monsieur Jean Claude Something-or-other officiated. During his charming recitation of the traditional vows, he waggled his finger under each of our noses in turn as he warned that we would be "forzaking all uzzers" by taking this step. That was fine with me. I'd had no eyes for "uzzers" since meeting my love, and knew it would always be that way.

John later asked, "What's an uzzer?"

Vegas was way too Disneyfied and crowded even then. It sure as hell was no longer the crazy cow town I dearly loved when I worked there at the old Rancho Vegas for six months or so in 1960.

Yeah, Baby. Ring-a-ding-ding. The Rat Pack reigned, and there was not only room to swing a cat, it was mandatory behavior. Because of my serendipitous meeting with Sammy Davis, Jr. in the early '50s, I got to be part of a benefit they did at the long-gone Silver Slipper Saloon.

The Pack parodied the burlesque sketches that were the main attraction of that old-style Western Casino. Old Blue Eyes sang "A Pretty Girl is Like a Melody" while the rest of the bunch paraded in showgirl drag. Then they took the traditional roles usually done by Hank Henry (as Top Banana) and his sidekick, Shorty. You know the sketches: the doctor ("Oh Nur-urhs"), the butcher ("How's your salami, Shultzie?"), the street corner pickup ("Meetcha round the corner…"), all those routines and more.

The major headliners in town paid big bucks for tickets and squeezed into the tiny grade-school auditorium seats in the little theater. Everyone from our show loved it – well, except for Anita Bryant who dubbed it "crass." Yeah, she had a major bug up her ass even then.

No. I really did not want to go to Las Vegas again. I shared my misgivings with John.

"You at least owe Margold the courtesy of a call."

John has a high regard for courtesy. He is, of course, right. He almost always is. Not easy to live with, but comforting overall.

"…I know it isn't so, but a lot of the old guard think you look down on the industry (he means porn) and them because you won't accept this honor." Mr. Margold sounds like he is close to tears.

I look at John who is listening on the extension. He shrugs eloquently.

"Well, since you put it that way, how can I refuse? When is it?"

"Next January, during the AVN convention."

(The AFA once gave annual awards called Eroticas – kinda like Oscars, but a great deal more fragile. All those I received broke at the base or lost their little spears within a month or two. The AVN gives awards on plaques, suitable for hanging. The one I received for Lifetime Achievement hangs just outside our bathroom.)

"I won't have to sit and sign pictures and be nice to people for hours and hours?" I've been to a couple of porn/horror conventions.

"No. You'll just field a few questions from the audience."

OK. I've done a lot of that.

"Then we'll press your little feet – or whatever you like – into a block of wet cement. All expenses paid, of course."

"For John, too?" I ask. It's not that I can't function without him. It's just not as much fun, and why should I have to?

"Of course."

"I'll get back to you," I promise.

Shortly after that, PT called and told me a Jackie Markham, the press representative for his remake of *Devil*, would be calling me to set up some on-air radio interviews.

Speaking with Jackie was like hearing the ghost of the beloved Selma Diamond. Remember her? The gravel-voiced clerk on *Night Court?* If not, watch the Peter O'Toole flick, *My Favorite Year.* She played the wardrobe mistress who confronts O'Toole's character, Swann, when he enters the wrong restroom.

"Hey," she growls, "this is for ladies!"

"Well, so is this," replies Mr. O'Toole seriously as he glances down, "but sometimes I have to run a little water through it."

She also glances down and rewards Mr. O'Toole with a congratulatory smile and nod.

"It," of course, remains off camera. This is not a porn movie. More's the pity. I, for one, would have loved to get a glimpse of the renowned O'Toole tool. But, I digress. Oh, if you watch the film, pay close attention to the "Three Musketeers" sketch. John plays Arrogant, the cute one in the midddle of the three-shot with O'Toole and Joe Bologna.

David Wren is an alumnus of the junior college I attended while I was living with my Dad after Mother died. He is one of the treasured e-pals I met through my dancing partner, David Greer. Mr. Wren has been responsible for raising scads of money for the AIDS charity, "Broadway Cares," among other worthy causes. To honor his contributions, Sardi's had his caricature drawn. Then they threw him a party to celebrate his birthday and the addition of his likeness to those of the Broadway nobility that grace those hallowed walls. He invited us to the hanging.

Just the year before, Mr. Wren had treated me and a former roommate, my oldeast and dearest friend, Kay, to lunch there for her eighty-third birthday.

Kay had just lost her husband, who had already lost their book business due to his prolonged illness. Left with nothing but her $800 a month Social Security check and a mountain of debt, she was advised by their lawyer to "get out of Dodge." I flew to New York to help her pack out of the apartment they had called home for over fifty years. It required some tunneling.

She really needed a treat. When Dave heard I was in New York, and why, he trained up from Philadelphia just to take us to lunch at Sardi's. We then took in a matinee of *Wonderful Town*, starring Brooke Shields. It was the show Kay and I did scenes from for Bill Hickey's acting workshop a hundred years or so ago. We had a grand time.

At that luncheon, the grandson of the original Mr. Sardi insisted we go upstairs and see my name in teeny print at the bottom of their *The Pajama Game* poster. I was still in the chorus when it was printed. By the time I was doing the dance lead, they weren't printing any more posters. But, who cares? There I was, immortalized on Sardi's wall – right next to the ladies' room. Well, the former me, I mean. Not Georgina. Her "immortalization" came later in Vegas.

A Living Legend of Erotica

AFTER THE EXCITEMENT OF PAUL'S SHOOT, we were glad to be home in our nice comfy rut.

Then the damn phone rang.

"It's Bill Margold." John hands me the infernal instrument.

"Hi, Bill. Sorry I haven't gotten back to you."

"No problem, lovely lady." Bill gets a little flowery at times.

"I need to get moving on the induction, though. We can count on you, can't we? I mean, you are THE Living Legend of Erotica. You gotta be there."

It sounds like a political call to arms. In a way it is. I feel compelled to appear when invited to things like this, if only to defend porn's right to exist – like something that's been around since Homo sapiens learned to scratch images on a cave wall will ever be seriously threatened.

But, truth be told, I am not comfortable in its midst. There's just some-thing about floor-to-ceiling reproductions of genitalia that gives me the creeps. Am I as big a hypocrite as the Blue Noses I so disdain?

What should I do?

John is no help at all.

I mouth, "Should I say yes?"

"It's up to you, Hon. Do what you feel is right."

Deep breath. "OK." I resist a groan. "We'll be there."

It took fifteen minutes of shouting into our cell phones for Patti to find us.

Patti Montes works for Ray Pistol, owner of the Showgirl Video em-porium where the Legends of Erotica Wall of Fame resides. She and I be-came e-pals as she coordinated the details of our trip to Vegas for the great induction ceremony.

Her last message had been, "I'll pick you guys up at the airport."

As many times as I'd flown in and out of Vegas, it never occurred to me that I might need a map to the front door.

The Vegas airport is like pond scum. It doubles in size every 24 hours.

"I'm wearing a red sweater. Mrs. Pistol is with me. She has a puppy in her arms," crackles the voice on my antique instrument.

We spot them across the busy parking lot and wave. Patti and I laugh-ingly conclude our conversation as we meet. The puppy is adorable.

The ladies fill us in on the Who's, When's, Where's, and Whatever's as we tear along the Vegas thoroughfares at speeds up to fifteen miles an hour.

When John and I were there to get hitched, we took the bus to our Chapel of choice. The pedestrians were making better time than the bus. We had to get off and run the last mile to make it on time.

Vegas traffic is also subject to the pond scum principle.

Patti drops us at the hotel and says she'll pick us up at 7:30 for the show, which is scheduled for 8 p.m. John and I find our way through the cacoph-ony of the casinos to the quiet of a standard hotel room: the kind with a wall-to-wall bed that could accommodate the Lakers, pillows like trampo-lines, and a thermostat designed to force patrons out of their rooms and into the frantic stream that courses through the blinking buzzing ringing flashing sea of slots.

The water in the compact bathroom is hot. I'm content.

Patti is right on time, and the video store is a scant ten-minute drive from our hotel. The place looks like a bunker: a good place to be in the event of an aerial (or vice squad?) attack. There is a lit marquee in front, however, that shows it to be a place of business. The names of the stellar cast expected to appear that evening are listed, including that of Larry Flynt, who didn't show though he was in town for the convention and subsequent awards show. I question that he even knew the place existed.

Cara Lott stands in the parking lot in front of the place posing for a photographer. She wears a slinky silver dress slit up to her left nostril. I smile and nod, and continue my beeline to the front door.

John calls to me. I look back at him. He snaps a picture of me wearing a grimace that must pass for a smile.

We start to go in the front entrance and a very large man stops us and asks for money.

"This is Georgina," shouts Patti over the roar of the crowd.

"Who?" The large man shouts back.

"Georgina SPELVIN," sings out Patti at the top of her lungs. "She's being inducted tonight."

"Oh, OK. Go on in." Mr. Big nods to me. Then a ham fist shoots out to stop John who is right behind me.

"He's with me," I shout.

"Oh, OK."

Whew. A far cry from the red-carpet premiere in Toronto a jillion years ago. I look at John to see if the "he's with me" rankled. If it did, it doesn't show.

We're the first participants to arrive. I guess everyone else knew the thing doesn't start on time. The house is about half full. Bill Margold's up on the platform with others of seeming relevance to the proceedings, trying to get the sound system to work. (It never did. At least not well. No reflection on their skills. You couldn't hear a damn thing in that concrete box. At least I couldn't. Wrong. I could hear the noise. I just couldn't understand a fucking word anyone said.)

Bill motions me up onto the stage and hands me the mike. Cara's right behind me. As soon as she hits the stage, she flashes her headlights. They are as firm and round as the day she bought 'em.

I say hello to the audience and hand the mike to Cara. She starts asking me questions about people I don't know or can't remember. Fortunately, more of the honorees arrive and the house begins to fill up. I flounder along trying to think of something to say. Finally the cavalry arrives!

Bill spots Veronica Harte in the back row and calls her up to the stage. She strides through the resounding wave of applause. Those impossibly long legs, svelte torso, and inherent grace make her tailored pantssuit look like silky haute couture lounging pajamas as she mounts the steps to the stage.

Veronica and I have been friends since we did a steamy lesbian scene together for a film back in the late '70s. Gary Graver, the director and cameraman, was thrilled with our ability to duplicate our positions and action as needed for various camera angles. She and I, we learned, both knew from jump cuts. One of many things we found we had in common. Another was our taste in men. She married the longhaired hunk of a soundman that lured me into the world of rock 'n' roll 'n' underground film in the first place: the ineffable Iron Mike.

When I ran into her at one of the company picnics (the Adult Film Association Awards) and she told me that she and Mike were together, I nearly dropped my dentures. I didn't even know they knew each other.

They have two wonderful, grown sons now. She stayed in the business and grew up to be a director/producer. He continues to ply his trade as a sound technician and lighting designer.

I've treasured her friendship through the years. Now I cling to her for dear life.

"Oh, GOD! I am so glad you're here," I whisper into her ear as we hug.

"Are you OK? Bill didn't even tell me you were going to be here. He just said I had to show for this thing tonight. I'd have been here on time if I'd known you were here. Have they stoned you yet?"

"What?" I ask and lean my ear close to her lips. We are whispering so as not to distract from the inductees who are taking turns with the mike.

"Have they put your tits in concrete yet?"

"Not that I noticed." Bill had announced her arrival by pointing out her concrete tribute ensconced above his head on the Wall of Fame. "What am I supposed to do now?"

I thought she would know.

"I have no idea," she whispers into my ear. No matter. I'm just glad she's here.

We take seats beside each other as the next inductee begins her chat with the audience.

Jody Maxwell is another of the old guard whom I'd never met. She was understandably involved, chatting up her pals, so we did little more than exchange hellos when she mounted the stage. She is a broad-based gal with a voice to match.

Veronica whispers into my ear, "Mike was back in the hospital last week."

"What?" In my shocked dismay, I almost shout.

Ms. Maxwell glances at us but never misses a beat as she tells the now-more-attentive audience how much she loves to come, and how in all her years and many films, she never, ever, EVER faked it. (John insists he believes her.)

She also went on and on about what a great lover Joaquin was. Yes, the very same sexy Brazilian cinematographer who drove me bananas during the fruit scene in the original *Devil*. I guess she wasn't as reticent about getting into his pants as I was. It IS a small world.

I whisper back to Veronica, "Why? What happened? Why didn't you call me?"

"He made me promise not to. He's OK now."

Mike had undergone a double transplant the previous year: liver and one kidney. Stella and I were part of his recovery team. Seems transplant patients can't depend upon hired help. Not wanting to forfeit the money, paid attendants have a bad record of bringing colds to work. A cold can be lethal to a transplant patient because the immune system is deliberately destroyed so the body won't reject the new organs. It does make for a rarified existence. It also requires a team of volunteers who really care about the patient to monitor them through the first three months of recovery.

You see, Mike, Stell, and I are water brothers. You'll have to read Robert A. Heinlein's *Stranger in a Strange Land* to grok that, but it was part of the Pickle Factory construct. We volunteered for the recovery-care team.

Mike's brother, Charley, also a water brother, flew in from the East Coast for the "opening." Dear Charley, he of the restored antique pickup that transported Dr. Yakalot's Traveling Space Circus on its rounds. I hadn't seen him since he rebuilt the carburetor on the Dorabelladona (the thirty-foot-long school bus with a smokestack sticking out the back), thus enabling it to chug its way to Cal-i-forn-eye-ay. It was so good to see his sweet, always-smiling face again.

Poor Mike practically became a Bubble Boy. Not his style. But he is a very spiritual guy. I was sure he had the inner resources to deal with it. What could have gone wrong?

"I'll tell you all about it when we get back to L.A.," hisses Veronica. We dutifully turn our attention back to the proceedings.

Mr. Margold has been extolling, in an unending stream of superlatives, the virtues of each player as they arrive. He keeps prodding us to tell funny stories about ourselves and each other, and solicit questions from the audience who are quiet, attentive, and infuriatingly uncurious.

Paul Thomas arrives and makes his way to the stage through a worshipping throng. I knew that he was now considered the top director in the biz, but I am amazed that the men in the audience applaud him with even more enthusiasm than they showed for Cara Lott's tits.

PT sweeps up the steps and is mobbed by those onstage. He is adored. I'm not surprised. He is still cute as a button. When the tide subsides, he sits down on the other side of me. He and Veronica lean toward each other in front of me and kiss-kiss. I hug them both. I'm feeling a lot better.

"How're you doin'?" whispers Paul into my ear. There's a lot of whispering going on – all around us.

"So far, so good. I have no idea what I'm supposed to do, though."

"I saw John in the audience. That's great that he came with you. You guys aren't into porn, are you?"

"Don't even own a pornagraph," I quip.

I can tell he is fully aware of how like a fish-out-of-water I feel.

It's not so much that porn has gotten any more – well – pornographic. I just wasn't exposed to it when I was making the movies.

A film set has an intimacy about it that is difficult to describe. It's really a very private space. In the pornatoriums, there is not only little intimacy, there's no privacy whatsoever.

Paul is known as something of a wild man, but he has always been as deferential to my Victorian sensitivities as an antebellum beau.

"You handling it OK?" he inquires solicitously.

"Oh sure." And I am. Now.

"You know, I'm a lot like Groucho Marx myself," he confides. "I don't really want to belong to any club that would have me as a member."

The familiar reference, so damn apt, cracks me up.

"Yeah. Me too," I chortle as quietly as possible.

Jody Maxwell has been holding the audience in the palms of her hands, figuratively. John says she was a hoot. I wish I could have heard what was going on.

Down the aisle bounced an aging imp in a football jersey. "Fred Lincoln" is stenciled on the back. He's the only one present who predates me in the trade, but we had never met. Listening to him greet his old friends and banter with Bill, I could see why he is so beloved. His humor is exceeded only by his exuberance.

I guess he was the headliner Bill had been waiting for. As soon as Fred finished hugging everyone he could reach and sat down, our emcee called to owner Ray Pistol to bring out the first box of wet cement.

The stoning begins. The featured and favorite parts of each star in turn are pressed into the frames of damp concrete.

"OK, George. It's your turn. Ladies and gentlemen," intones the indefatigable Mr. Margold, "Gloria Leonard regretted she could not be here in person to induct Georgina, but asked me to read this message from her."

He then proceeds to read a tribute to the talents of La Spelvin so glowing I could only stand there and blush. I was embarrassed to death. When, and if, I get to see that great lady again, I'm gonna noogie her good for it.

As if that weren't bad enough, the house erupts in a standing ovation. I do a deep and humble bow, sincerely overcome by it all. Then Bill motions me over to the side of the stage where my tray awaits.

I reach in my pocket and withdraw the single edged razor blade it was unbelievably hard to find. You have to go to a hardware store for them these days. I press my left forearm into the mush and then embed the unsheathed blade in the wrist area of the imprint.

To complete the montage that possibly four people in the world will understand, I rip off my shoe and sock and place the toes of my right foot beside the arm image. Yes, the very toes that turned off the faucets in that suicide scene so long ago – the toes that were recognized by fellow Gypsy Jimmy Nygren, thus blowing my cover in the New York theater scene – the toes my podiatrist wanted to straighten out surgically! How could he know they were an icon of erotica?

Lest the audience feel cheated, I flash my boobs.

(John ran out of film just before I did, thank heavens. Pissed him off. Running out of film. Not my flashing. His acceptance of my past constantly astounds me.)

"You have to sign and date it," demands Bill. I had noticed that all the plaques had messages of some sort or other. I hadn't thought about this beforehand. I sign "Georgina Spelvin," put in the date, and then for reasons known only to my subconscious, write, "Don't do it!"

Tiffany Mynx bares her beautiful butt to a round of cheers and plants it in the soon-to-be-rock. With all parts properly pressed into their respective squares of goo, Bill passes out gold-plated roses ("real roses" it says on the box) and gold swords to the participants. The boys get the swords, of course. Boys always get the best toys.

John is waiting for me at the foot of the stage steps and holds out his hand to guide me down. Veronica is right behind me.

As we reach the audience level she leans toward me and shouts, "Are you going to the awards show tomorrow night? You're nominated for best non-sex performance for the *Devil* remake, you know."

"I know," I respond. "Are you going?"

"No, I'm going home as soon as the floor closes tomorrow afternoon. I've got a mix Monday I've got to get ready for. But you're going, aren't you?"

"No."

"Why not?"

"I wasn't invited – thank goodness!"

She must not have heard the "thank goodness." The fans pushing past us to get down front for a better view of the strippers now filling the stage probably drowned me out. She must have called PT because there was a frantic message from him on the answering machine when we got home, apologizing for the oversight and insisting I run right over and join the Vivid crowd at their table. I guess he thought he got my cell phone. Boy, am I glad he didn't or I might have buckled and attended, which would have been miserably uncomfortable, especially as I didn't win. Mr. Margold did. As he should have.

John said I should let Paul stew, but I couldn't do that. He's too nice a guy. I emailed him that all was forgiven. I didn't let on he'd done me a favor. Let him think he owes me, right?

Truth is I owe him. Were it not for his insistence that I do that cameo role in his remake of *The Devil in Miss Jones*, I would not have reconnected with so many old friends, nor made so many new ones. Nor would I have gotten my backyard terraced. For sure, I would never have finished writing this book. Now I have.

The End

Apologia

There are no photos in this book except for those of the three kind souls who volunteered to read it and give me their comments as quoted on the pitch page. By self-publishing I am limited to non-glossy paper and photos look like shit, as you may have noticed. Any pictures of me that I've been able to find (and many thanks to all of you who helped me round them up) are on my website: GeorginasWorld.com. The captions identify them and you can figure out where they belong in the book yourself.

There are also links to video clips from my films and to the Web homes of some of those you've met in these pages. It's a fast shrinking world, isn't it? I'm totally boggled by it all. Still, I'm glad my life fell across this great digital divide in the human experiment.

Apologies, too, to everyone I failed to mention who might have wanted to be mentioned. Ron Jeremy comes to mind. Cindi Loftus (staff writer at Xcitment Magazine, and publicist for this book) said I had to mention Ron so he would tell everybody he knows to buy my book, and he does seem to know everybody. So, even though we never got to work together, here's to you, Hedgehog.

Also, David Nahmod, who writes for several gay magazines and has produced many films for that market, must be thanked for casting me as the bereaved and repentant mom in his film, *Red Ribbons*. Meeting fellow cast member Quentin Crisp was a real high point in my life.

Speaking of high points: thanks to Paul Maslansky for casting me in the two *Police Academy* romps. May his tribe increase.

Lord knows there are many others I should and would love to mention, but I have to save something for a sequel.

Thank you for buying, or borrowing, or just browsing my book.

Georgina

from STOP REQUESTED

At Fairfax and Beverly, a very tiny old woman was waiting alone at the bus stop. She was on her way to a local senior rec center where she spent most days.

"You knew I was coming, so you baked a cake," she said to the driver as she slowly climbed the stairs into the bus. The driver laughed.

Soon, another elderly woman boarded and sat facing her across the aisle. The second woman's clothes were covered in loud, abstract upholstery patterns and cut in the loose-fitting, elastic waistband style preferred by older ladies, while her hair was dyed a familiar shade of fried amber. Her fashion sense was in dramatic contrast to the other woman's; her friend wore her white hair short and opted for casual but conservative dress. But they knew each other from the center and were friendly.

"Oh!" The flashier woman said, brightening suddenly. "It was your birthday, wasn't it? How did that go?"

"It was fine," her friend shrugged. "There were some problems."

"There were problems?"

"Well, some of the people drank five cups of coffee! And when I wouldn't give them more, they said" - she leaned forward and stage-whispered - "I was *prejudiced!"*

"They said that?"

She shook her head solemnly. "One cup of coffee is fine, maybe two."

"Or three," her friend added quickly, covering her own occasional indulgence.

"But if I had to serve *everyone* five cups of coffee, I'd be dead." She eased back into her seat. *"...And* there wouldn't be any more coffee!"

STOP REQUESTED

WYATT DOYLE

ILLUSTRATIONS BY STANLEY J. ZAPPA

If you ever rode the bus, these are your stories.

www.newtexture.com

Who ARE These People ?

Self Portrait

The Drawings of Irv Bramberg

Compiled by Joyce Bramberg
Captioned by his family and friends

Printed in July 2019
by Rotomail Italia S.p.A., Vignate (MI) - Italy